A TIME TO RISK ALL

The incredible untold story of Mary Elmes,
the Irish woman who saved children from
Nazi concentration camps

CLODAGH FINN ∼

Gill Books

Gill Books
Hume Avenue
Park West
Dublin 12
www.gillbooks.ie

Gill Books is an imprint of M.H. Gill & Co.

97807171 7561 1

Print origination by Carole Lynch
Edited by Ruairí Ó Brógáin
Printed by TJ International, Cornwall

Pictures courtesy of Caroline and Patrick Danjou
unless otherwise stated.

Map adapted from iStock illustration.

This book is typeset in Linotype Minion and
Neue Helvetica.

The paper used in this book comes from the wood
pulp of managed forests. For every tree felled,
at least one tree is planted, thereby renewing
natural resources.

A CIP catalogue record for this book is
available from the British Library.

5 4 3 2

For Bernard and Janet Wilson, who have done so much to bring Mary Elmes out of the shadows of history.

ACKNOWLEDGEMENTS

The word that Caroline and Patrick Danjou use to describe their mother, again and again, is *discreet*. Yet they were willing to answer question after question and open up a family archive that was full of unexpected treasures. Patrick spent several hours, on more than one occasion, poring over the archive with me, and later brought me on a tour of all the places significant to his mother. *'Je vous parfume le livre'* (I'm flavouring the book for you), he'd say, as he recounted an evocative detail, adding another note of scent to the narrative.

There were many e-mails from Caroline, who replied to questions with incredible speed and always with a big 'thank you' at the end. The 'thank you', of course, should go in the other direction. I am very grateful.

I had two guiding lights on either side of the Atlantic: Professor Ronald Friend, who was saved by Mary Elmes, and Bernard Wilson, both of whom have spent years trawling the archives and piecing together a story that needed to be told. They were both tremendously generous with their time, research and encouragement. This book builds on a substantial body of work that was already done by them. They offered invaluable comments on the manuscript and many extra insights. It would have been impossible to write this account without them. Many thanks also to Bernard's wife, Janet, who enthusiastically shared the many insights she had gleaned about Mary Elmes from her study of the archives.

It was a rare privilege to hear the testimony of Michael Freund, Ronald Friend, Gilbert Susagna, Brigitte Twomey, Charlotte Berger-Greneche, Georges Koltein and Paul Niedermann, who shared their experiences of the Spanish Civil War and the Second World War. They spoke freely so that we might never forget.

Mary Elmes's relatives Mark Elmes and Pauline and Mack Morum could not have been more helpful. Mark opened the family archive and patiently explained the family tree. From New Zealand the Morums sent stories, details and clarifications. There's at least another volume in the history of the Elmes family.

A huge thank you to Jacinta Ryan of Ballintemple. Jacinta was born in the same room as Mary Elmes. We sat in it together, wondering about the woman who had risked her life in two wars yet didn't dare to revisit her former home. Jacinta is also the most generous host. She opened her door to this stranger, and together we tried to tease little bits of history from 'Culgreine'.

Dr Sandra McAvoy was the first to suggest that I write a biography of Mary Elmes and alerted me to her mother's involvement in the Munster Women's Franchise League. A big thank you too to Dr Alicia St Leger: I owe much to her and her meticulously researched book, *A History of Ashton School*.

Other historians and authors offered their comments, time and expertise. Their contribution was invaluable. Many thanks to Dr John Borgonovo of UCC; Michael Kennedy of the Royal Irish Academy; Mark Derby, author of *Petals and Bullets,* who generously sent me Dorothy Morris's letters and took the time to read the section on the Spanish Civil War; Dr Susan Parkes, fellow emeritus of Trinity College, Dublin, and editor of *A Danger to the Men? A History of Women in Trinity College, Dublin,* who shared many insights; Dr Xavier García i Ferrandis in Valencia; Rosemary Bailey, author of *Love and War in the Pyrenees*; and the historian Marc J. Masurovsky.

A special thank you to John Baskin, author of *A Fierce Light: An Improbable Story of the Good War,* who shared the notes of an interview he had with Mary Elmes in 1996.

An enormous thank you for the patience, expertise and kindness of those at a number of archives: Don Davis at the American Friends Service Committee; Brian McGee, Steven Skeldon and Michael Higgins at Cork City and County Archives; Aisling Lockhart at the Manuscript Library of Trinity College Library, Dublin; Sue Donnelly at the London School of Economics; Jennifer Milligan and Lisa McQuillan at Friends House, London, and Gregory O'Connor at the National Archives in Dublin. Many thanks too to those who shared their personal archives: the present Sir George Young and

Lady Aurelia Young, Charles Young, and Mary Jane Gunden. Thank you to Adi Trudler, who did research at Yad Vashem in Israel, and to Guy Brunet, who did research in Marssac-sur-Tarn.

Not only did Deirdre Waldron and Mary Moynihan do much to herald Mary Elmes's work, but they also helped me along the way. Thank you to John O'Mahony and Jayson Carcione at the *Irish Examiner*, who first published the story, and to everybody at Gill Books, who did so much to take it to the next stage. The team at Gill are true professionals.

I can't say enough for my family's unstinting support. Thank you, Mum, Nuala, Brendan, Ciaran, Claire, Ciara, Darragh (and the Finnolans, Emma, Arthur, Matilda and Charlie), Uncle Eoin and Auntie Marie, Aideen and Cliona, Conor, Grainne and Seán. Lots of thanks to my northern family too: Bob, Dorothy, Inga, Rob and Sorley. Then there are my wonderful friends who provided everything from moral support to superb editing. I'd need another book to tell you all the ways in which I'm grateful. A very special *merci* to Síofra Pierse and Paul Elbourne. Thank you very, very much, Margaret Jennings, Anne O'Connell, Emer O'Beirne, Anne Sheridan, Colleen McFadyen, Joyce Fegan, Sophie Gorman, Rowena Walsh, Karine Bigand, Marguerite Moran, Mary Kemple, Angela Kelly, Stephen Daly, Vickie Maye, Irene Feighan, Aílín Quinlan, Vic Connerty, Nikki Kroon, Margaret E. Ward, Bryan MacMahon, Jane Ellis and Kate O'Leary. And to my husband, Douglas Smith, *Merci infiniment.*

CONTENTS

INTRODUCTION
An extraordinary coincidence

On a clear, bright morning in late June 2014, Professor Ronald Friend set out along the Rue du Nord to find the school where he and his brother had been hidden in plain sight, along with other Jewish children, in the latter years of the Second World War. He was looking for landmarks on the quiet road that goes down to the Tarn, the river that gives Marssac-sur-Tarn in south-west France its name, but he had no real memories to speak of.

Yet, despite the passage of time, he had flown from his home in Portland, Oregon, specifically to recall those dark years. A few days earlier he had attended a ceremony to honour Mary Elmes, the Irishwoman who had extricated him and his older brother from a notorious detention camp in 1942, saving their lives. She played a vital role in rescuing hundreds of Jewish children from the cattle wagons that were destined for the Nazi death camps that year. Later the Gestapo arrested and imprisoned her for six months, but she continued to work to help refugees of all nationalities. Her work went unheralded for decades, but, thanks to Ronald Friend's nomination, she had just been awarded Israel's highest honour for risking her life to save Jews during the Holocaust. Now Ronald, his son Sean and a French friend were revisiting the community that had protected them as children while the occupying Germans held their parents.

He wasn't sure where the old school was, so when he saw a couple approach he asked them for directions.

The man looked at him and asked: 'Are you Mario Freund?'

'No,' replied Ronald, completely taken aback. 'I'm his brother.'[1] (*Freund* is the German for *Friend*.)

The man introduced himself as Guy Brunet and said that he and Ronald had been schoolmates – in 1943![2] The two men could not believe the chance encounter some seventy-one years later; and together they went to see the old school. The front of the building was utterly changed, but the back yard was just as Ronald Friend remembered it when he played there in the 1940s. The former classmates walked down to the Tarn to the spot where Ronald's brother Mario, then six, used to swim.

They went back to Guy Brunet's house and, over a *pastis* on the patio, recalled the school, their peers, and the Germans who had been stationed there during the Second World War. Guy Brunet, an engineer, had recently moved back into the original family home in Marssac. Ronald told him that he had gone to England after the war, then on to teach at a university in New York and was now a professor emeritus of psychology in Portland, Oregon.

Guy was able to tell Ronald that people in Marssac still remembered the Freund/Friend family. One neighbour even recalled the particular Sunday after Mass in July 1942 when some of the townspeople were worried that the family had been arrested. They hadn't been seen for a few days and people feared the worst. In fact they had all left town, in the greatest secrecy, to attempt an escape over the Swiss border. It almost succeeded. Ronald's father and brother made it over the border but they turned back when they saw that Ronald and his mother had been stopped by the police. They were all arrested and taken to Rivesaltes, an internment camp in south-west France near the Spanish border. The children would eventually make it back to Marssac, followed months later by their mother, who was freed from a second camp, Gurs. However, Hans Freund would never see his family again: he perished in Majdanek camp in Poland in 1943.

In the years that followed, Guy Brunet had often recalled the two brothers.

I often spoke to my family about the Jewish children who were with us in school. At that time, there was a lot of mistrust between people and we were told to keep quiet and say nothing, as there were collaborators about. Every time I spoke of the Freunds, I would add, 'I don't know whatever became of them,' and I worried for their welfare. Because of those conversations, my wife wondered if the person asking for directions to the old school that day [in

June] was Jewish. I immediately thought of the Freunds. I was very happy to see Ronald again.[3]

Ronald felt the same way, and after the astonishing reunion he continued his tour of the town. He passed the town square and went into the church, where he took photographs of a plaque honouring Resistance fighters. It was signed by Fr Louis Bézard, a name familiar to him. The local priest had played a big part in his escape. When Ronald first revisited France, in 1956, Fr Bézard had been able to recount, in great detail, what had happened. He had described how, in November 1942, Ronald (then three years old) and his brother (aged six) were smuggled to a safe house in Toulouse and taken to Marssac.

In a six-page written account, the priest described how he and his colleague André Violier hid the children on that perilous journey. He wrote: 'The return [to Marssac] was difficult . . . in particular going across Toulouse and at the train station, which was under heavy Gestapo surveillance. We had to hide the children in our luggage and under a big overcoat.'[4] By the time they got to Marssac the little boys were 'upset, frightened and starving'.[5]

They were not the only Jewish children taking refuge there: five others had found refuge at the presbytery too. After a few days, when they had regained their strength, the Freund brothers were placed with foster families and they were soon absorbed into daily life in the town. They were baptised as Catholics and mixed in with local children at the school that Ronald had just rediscovered seven decades later.

The tour complete, Ronald returned to his hosts, the family who had once fostered him, in Albi, a town about seven miles away. As they were having dinner the doorbell rang. His former classmate Guy Brunet was at the door. He had a class photo from 1943 that showed a group of twenty-six rather serious-looking boys and their teacher outside a building with peeling plaster and decaying wooden shutters. Guy pointed himself out: first on the left in the second row, near Ronald (third from the left in the same row). Behind them, Mario (now Michael) had a protective hand on his younger brother's shoulder.

It is one of few pictures that Ronald has of that time, although over the years he has gathered a number of documents that have helped him piece together what happened after his parents were forced to flee an increasingly anti-Jewish Berlin in 1933. His father, Dr Hans Freund, was German and worked as a consulting engineer at Dresdner Bank (which was, ironically, Hitler's bank). His mother, Eva, a physician, worked at a Jewish hospital before they were forced to move to Milan. The couple's first son was born there in 1936. They called him Mario, in the hope that he might get Italian papers.

But with the rise of fascism the family was forced to move again, this time to Paris, where Ronald was born on 28 October 1939. He was given a French name, René, and again his father tried, unsuccessfully, to get him French papers. There was a step-daughter too, Suzanna (Sanne). Her mother, Hans's first wife, had died. Sanne had been sent to relatives in England before the war but was very unhappy to be separated from the rest of the family, and sent postcards saying so, although in a letter written in June 1942, five months before her father was deported, she sounded rather cheerful, describing life at an English school, hiking with the Girl Guides, and a ballet performance in Oxford by the Sadler's Wells Ballet. 'I think ballet is like acting, only everything is arranged symmetrically,' she wrote, before adding that she hoped the family would all be able to go to America soon.[6]

They would never make that journey, although Dr Freund did receive a job appointment from the Stevens Institute in New Jersey. However, his attempt to get an exit visa for the United States failed. He tried Mexico too, and a number of countries in South America, all without success; yet he continued to explore every possible avenue while interned at Rivesaltes.

Ronald Friend had always known of his father's efforts, but for decades he wondered why his mother was eventually freed but not him. He also wondered who had taken him and his brother from the camp to safety in September 1942. The answer to that question would eventually come in an e-mail many years later when, in January 2011, Katy Hazan, historian and archivist at the Jewish aid organisation Œuvre de Secours aux Enfants provided a name. The woman who rescued the Freund boys was a Miss Elms.

In fact this was Mary Elmes, who, Ronald Friend would discover, had saved many lives but had quietly turned down any recognition for it when the war was over. He went on to uncover several references to this forgotten aid worker. In 1942 she risked her life several times by hiding Jewish children in her car and driving them to safe houses in the Pyrénées-Orientales region. In a two-month period in the autumn of that year, some 2,289 Jewish adults and 174 children, some as young as two, were herded onto cattle wagons at Rivesaltes and taken to Drancy transit camp outside Paris and then on to Auschwitz. An estimated 427 children were saved from the convoys, thanks to the work of Mary Elmes and other women working at the camp.[7]

It is impossible to calculate precisely the number of lives Mary Elmes saved, but she 'spirited away nine children' from the first convoy on 11 August 1942, according to one surviving document. After that she made several trips to and from the camp, loading her car with the Jewish children most at risk of deportation. Many years later she would tell her son, Patrick Danjou, that on one occasion she managed to hide six children in her car.

After the war she also mentioned in passing that she had hidden a family in her flat in Perpignan. However, she never made much of the work she had done as head of the Quaker delegation in Perpignan, when she helped hundreds of people to secure exit visas from France. She also made sure that hundreds more, mostly children, got out of the camps to take refuge in one of a number of Quaker convalescent homes she helped to establish all over the south-west of France. Some of the children she placed there were saved from deportation and death.

By the time Ronald Friend found out who had saved his life it was too late to thank her in person. Mary Elmes died in 2002, aged ninety-three, in Perpignan, where she had lived the rest of her life after the war.

To honour her memory, Ronald nominated her for inclusion in the 'Righteous Among the Nations' at Yad Vashem, an award conferred by Israel on non-Jews who risked their lives to save Jews during the Holocaust. Oskar Schindler and his wife, Emilie, are among its more famous recipients, recognised in 1993 for saving the lives of an estimated 1,100 Jews.

Ronald Friend was determined that Mary Elmes would also be honoured for what she had done. 'Mary Elmes was clearly a figure who had not been given the recognition that she deserved. She was head of the Quaker delegation in Perpignan with up to thirty people working directly under her. She had been given a prominent role and she showed the way. She was obviously a woman of great intelligence, strength and character.'[8]

If Ronald Friend had been in any doubt about that, the remarkable character of the woman who saved his life began to emerge when he started the long, taxing process of nominating her for the award at Yad Vashem. He enlisted the help of two British Quakers, Bernard and Janet Wilson, who had an interest in the work done by the Quaker delegation in the south of France during the war. Together they uncovered details of the life of an extraordinary woman who left a brilliant academic career behind to volunteer to work with children during the Spanish Civil War.

When more than half a million refugees fleeing Franco's forces poured over the border into France in 1939, Mary Elmes followed them. From her base in Perpignan she helped set up schools, canteens, workshops, travelling libraries and convalescent homes for children. When the Second World War broke out she helped refugees from that war too – displaced Belgians, Germans and, increasingly, Jews who had been rounded up and interned.

In 1943 her work in the camps brought her to the attention of the Nazi authorities. She was arrested and jailed, first in Toulouse, then in the infamous Gestapo-run Fresnes prison outside Paris. The Quakers, and her mother in Cork, mounted a hard-fought campaign to get her out. Her neutral Irish nationality worked in her favour, and when she was finally released she made little of the experience. When a Quaker official, Howard Wriggins, asked her about it after the war, she remarked: 'Well, we all experienced inconveniences in those days, didn't we?'[9]

Even though Mary Elmes spoke little of her work, the Quakers had archived hundreds of thousands of documents that allowed Ronald Friend and the Wilsons to collect enough hard evidence to prove that she had saved the lives of the Freund brothers. On 27 June 2014, she was posthumously honoured at an award ceremony in Canet-en-Roussillon in the south of France. Ronald Friend was proud to be there to see her become the first, and only, Irish person to be named Righteous Among the Nations.

This is her story.

Chapter 1

WAR CASTS A LONG SHADOW

*'We . . . therefore take this opportunity of asking you
to vote for the deletion of the word "male" . . . and thereby
establish once and for all the principle of woman suffrage.'*
— Elisabeth Elmes, Munster Women's
Franchise League

There were heart-rending scenes on the quayside in Queenstown (Cobh), Co. Cork, in the late afternoon of 7 May 1915. A few hours earlier, at 2.10 p.m., a German submarine torpedoed the pride of the Cunard line, the *Lusitania*, eight miles off the Cork coast. It sank within eighteen minutes, killing 1,198 people and leaving the 761 survivors struggling to stay afloat while trawlers and tugs in the vicinity came to their aid. Ashore, people rushed to the water's edge to see how they might help. Every minute more 'sightseers filled with pity and profound sympathy' arrived on the scene.[1]

The harrowing descriptions of the procession of barefoot, bewildered men, women and children who struggled ashore would provoke worldwide outrage, and increase the pressure on then-neutral America to join Britain and the Allies in the Great War. But on that afternoon in May the focus was on the human tragedy that was just unfolding. Eye-witnesses described the 'fearful explosion' that hit the starboard side of the luxury ocean liner with 'terrible suddenness' while many of the passengers were still having lunch. The vessel, which had been en route from New York to Liverpool, listed to one side, making it almost impossible to launch lifeboats in time to save lives.

By early evening, partially clothed men, women and children, their 'strained features stamped with the fear of death', were being helped onto the quayside in Queenstown in what contemporary accounts described as 'poignant scenes that bled the heart'.[2]

An *Irish Times* reporter was struck by the efforts of local people, who rushed to help survivors from the fishing boats that had come to their assistance.

> Willing helpers with their arms around their [the survivors'] bodies, assisted them to walk to the hotels, hatless and shoeless, scarcely able to toddle through injuries to their [l]egs, arms and bodies. They were in their sea-soaked apparel and in a sad plight. Many of them were unable to walk, and had to be removed on stretchers to their resting places in boarding houses and hotels, where they were comfortably housed and humanely treated, and given hot drinks to resuscitate their fatigued and shocked frames.[3]

Others told reporters of the outpouring of 'great help, practical comfort and kindly sympathy' extended to the victims. 'Police, naval men, the military, and civilians all vied with each other to render succour to the distressed survivors, and to care for the many injured cases. All the hotels are converted into hospitals, and every other house is a home of mercy.'[4] Local people came with hot drinks and food, and, between 'great draughts of tea and mouthfuls of meat', people enquired about their missing relatives. In the street there were women crying for their husbands or children, fathers hoping against hope that their loved ones had been saved, and orphans weeping disconsolately. Queues formed outside the makeshift morgues in the town market as survivors faced the horrifying prospect that their relatives might be among the dead.[5]

When news of the disaster spread to Cork, eighteen miles away, the lord mayor, Henry O'Shea, and the city coroner, John Horgan, went to visit the American consul at Queenstown, Wesley Frost, to reassure him that the citizens of Cork would render every service they could. Dr Winder, a solicitor and secretary of the Cork Branch of the Irish Automobile Association, telephoned all the car owners of Cork and organised a fleet of cars to transport the injured to hospitals in the city if necessary.

———

Two days earlier, Marie Elisabeth Jean Elmes turned seven at her home in Ballintemple in the suburbs of Cork. Although she had just started at Rochelle School on the Blackrock Road, the memory of what happened off the coast that year would stay with her for the rest of her life. The house had neither a telephone nor a motor car in 1915,[6] but Mary's father, Edward Elmes, a pharmacist, may have felt compelled to join others of his profession who were administering restoratives to the injured. In any event, the Elmes family travelled to Queenstown to join the thousands who had gathered there to pay their respects to the dead. What Mary Elmes saw that day made a lasting impression on her. She would later tell her children, Caroline and Patrick, that she met some of the survivors and that people in the streets were crying openly.[7] Even 'the most stoical could not look on the mournful happenings of the day unmoved,' the *Cork Examiner* commented.

At 3 p.m. on Monday 10 May 1915 a solemn procession of hearses, private mourners, mounted police, clergy, corporation officials and military and naval officers filed through the town to bury more than 150 people in mass graves that had been dug by members of the Royal Irish Regiment at the Old Church graveyard on the outskirts of town. Some forty-five of those bodies were never identified, their coffins marked only with a number.

The following day, the *Cork Examiner* captured the sombre mood and grief felt by the thousands of ordinary people who lined the route to the cemetery.

It was an exceedingly sad procession, but an event which attracted the sympathetic interest of thousands of people from the City of Cork. Queenstown was in general mourning. All the shops were closed, and from one o'clock out people took every point of vantage to witness the dismal sight of the funeral proper of the victims. Only at the cemetery could one get an even approximate idea of the full meaning of the terrible tragedy . . . Three graves remained open . . . In these were all the horrors of the calamity mirrored. One of them contained 65 coffins and a total of 67 bodies – two babies had been interred with their mothers. The next yawned its full length, breadth and depth, and so also with the third grave of the Catholics . . . It was all too ghastly to comprehend and too sickly to dwell on.[8]

For weeks afterwards, the press reported on the disaster, chronicling the political repercussions (later, there were reports of a second explosion) and the growing list of casualties. It was clear by now that the Irish art collector Hugh Lane had gone down with the ship, as had the wealthy American magnate Alfred G. Vanderbilt. He was one of many prominent passengers who had received a telegram advising them not to travel on the *Lusitania* before it left New York. The Imperial German embassy had also taken out advertisements in the American press to warn passengers that ships bearing the British flag were in danger of coming under attack in British waters. Vanderbilt was not alone in ignoring the warnings. When the torpedo struck, he is said to have been calm and unperturbed. 'In my eyes he cut the figure of a gentleman waiting unconcernedly for a train,' resident artist at Covent Garden, Oliver P. Bernard, told the *Cork Examiner*. 'The last that was seen of him, he was giving a lady passenger his lifebelt.'[9]

Germany stood firm. While it apologised for any American deaths, it claimed the ship was a legitimate target, as it had on board arms and ammunition destined for British soldiers. Controversy would rage over that point for a century afterwards. At the time, though, Britain and its allies felt entirely justified in condemning the attack. On 10 May 1915 the *Irish Independent* said in its editorial: 'The whole civilised world shudders at the black deed and a cry for vengeance has gone up.' It went on to say that the 'foul and ghoulish crime' was exactly the same in character as if 'a band of assassins had suddenly swooped down upon the town of Cavan and in a few minutes murdered every single one of its inhabitants'.[10]

In the immediate aftermath, there were daily reminders of what had happened. For months, bodies were washed up along the coast of

Co. Cork, keeping the disaster in the forefront of public consciousness and bringing the war closer to home. The people of Cork were already accustomed to seeing wounded soldiers being brought into the city, where they were treated in military and civilian hospitals. In December 1915 Mary Elmes made her own personal contribution to the war effort: she knitted pairs of socks and sent them to the soldiers fighting on the front. She included a pair for a senior British officer, Field-Marshal John French, apparently a birthday present. It's possible that he was a family acquaintance. Months later, in August 1916, he wrote her a personal note of thanks. It read: 'My dear Miss Marie, many, many thanks for your kind thoughts . . . on my birthday. I shall always keep and prize your present, Your . . . grateful friend, French.' The framed letter, a treasured possession, is still in the family archives.[11]

The suffering Mary Elmes witnessed after the sinking of the *Lusitania* may have partly influenced her decision two decades later to join the Spanish Civil War relief effort. Even if it did not, when she sailed from London for Gibraltar in 1937 she had some inkling of what awaited her, because she had already seen the effect of war at first hand.

———

Marie Elisabeth Jean Elmes was born on Tuesday 5 May 1908 on the first floor of the family home, Culgreine, 120 Blackrock Road, Ballintemple, Cork. She came into the world in an airy upstairs bedroom that had one large window overlooking the tree-lined front garden and a second giving onto the back garden, with its greenhouse, pond, rockery and well-planted flower and vegetable beds.[12] It was a wet day in late spring and there was some mist, but the temperature was moderate for May.[13]

The newspapers were already looking towards summer: in the Munster Arcade, in the city centre, 'the latest ideas in summer millinery were particularly charming'. Charles Frohman's *Leah Kleschna* was running at the Opera House, a five-act drama about a master jewel thief who raised his daughter to follow in his footsteps. In the council chamber of City Hall, the Cork Branch of the Women's

National Health Association was hosting a late-afternoon lecture on the home treatment of consumption (TB). A ticket on the ferry from Cork to Fishguard cost 15 shillings (one way, with cabin) and a night at the Clarence Hotel in Dublin (including breakfast) cost 4 shillings. If money was tight, several moneylenders were advertising their services on the front page of the *Cork Examiner*. On the news pages inside, the paper published an encouraging report about an 'astounding decrease' in emigration.[14] The previous year nearly 40,000 Irish emigrants had left for America, but the figure in 1908 was not expected to exceed 15,000.

That was good news for Cork, a busy port city with a population of some 75,000 people. Marie's father, Edward Elmes, was a pharmacist in the commercial heart of the city, working in the business founded by his wife's family. J. Waters and Sons was a large dispensing chemist's shop in Winthrop Street, but it also manufactured picture frames and supplied glass. Plate, sheet or mirror glass 'could be supplied at the shortest notice', customers were promised in a contemporary advertisement.[15] Edward Elmes, who was originally from Waterford, had been in the city from at least 1901. The census of that year lists him as lodging at Pope's Quay in the city centre. Pharmacy, like dentistry and veterinary medicine, was an occupation that had recently gained a new respectability: these were no longer apprenticeships but certified professions.[16]

This can only have been in Edward Elmes's favour, because on 11 September 1906 he married his employer's fourth and youngest daughter, Elisabeth Octavia Waters, at St Luke's Church in a service conducted by the bride's older brother, Rev. Richard Waters. At the time, 8½ per cent of the city's residents belonged to the Church of Ireland and many of them retained significant commercial and political power.[17] The newly married couple were among the well-to-do, and their first child, Marie (later generally called Mary), was born into a prosperous home. The 1911 census offers us some hints of that prosperity. On census night, which fell on 2 April, Mary and her brother, John, were visiting their uncle, Rev. Waters, and his wife, Jane, at Springfield House, a grand house in Gardiner's Hill, Cork. John had been born a year after his sister, on 18 May. The children's nurse, 41-year-old Mary Morgan, was with them.

Elsewhere in the city, Elisabeth Elmes was visiting her sisters, Marion and Juliet, at 17 Belgrave Square, Monkstown, while Edward Elmes was the only family member at home. The household had a second live-in maid, a nineteen-year-old Catholic, Julia Spence. That night she had a visitor, Mary Spence (aged fifteen), perhaps a sister. The fact that the family had two servants says something about their status: they were comfortable members of the professional middle class.[18] The children's nurse and servant lived at the top of the house in relatively spacious communicating rooms with windows overlooking the garden. The house itself was plumbed throughout and the bedrooms were fitted with porcelain wash-hand basins. It had a bath and an indoor toilet.[19]

There were more luxurious houses in the city at the time, Springfield House among them, but there was extreme poverty too. A sociological survey by Fr A. M. MacSweeney, conducted a few years later in 1915, found that 35 per cent of the city residents were 'in a chronic state of want', suffering from hunger, possessing a single set of clothes and often residing in tenements. Another 14 per cent were unskilled labourers living a 'hand-to-mouth existence'.[20] Like many privileged families, and in particular Church of Ireland families, the Elmeses had a strong tradition of giving to charity. Edward Elmes was a committee member of the Protestant Orphans Society, and the family regularly went to fund-raising events in the city.[21]

Culgreine was not only an affluent and charitable household but also a progressive one. Elisabeth Elmes was an active member of the Munster Women's Franchise League and campaigned for the vote for women. In October 1910 the leader of the British suffrage movement, Emmeline Pankhurst, visited Cork and spoke at City Hall; her speech 'put a match to the unlit beacon of suffrage opinion in the South'.[22] It is not recorded whether Elisabeth Elmes was there, but she certainly heard about it, because she joined the Cork branch of the league that was founded in its wake. In 1911 the Cork women broke away from the main organisation to form their own non-militant branch, and Elisabeth went on to become the league's honorary treasurer.

In 1913, she was one of four committee members who wrote to all Munster MPs calling on them to vote to delete the word 'male' in the Franchise Bill due before the House of Commons later that year.

The letter read:

> We feel . . . that we can rely on you for whole-hearted support,
> and therefore take this opportunity of asking you to vote for the
> deletion of the word 'male' . . . and thereby establish once and for
> all the principle of woman suffrage.

The letter's signatories argued that this was a unique opportunity to
vindicate the 'Irish love of liberty' and one that would not affect the
campaign for Irish self-government. 'We cannot believe that by
doing so you will in any way injure the cause of Home Rule, the
success of which must always be your first care, but rather further its
interests by winning the confidence of Irish and English women in
your love of justice and devotion to the principles of liberty.'[23]

Home Rule was granted the following year, but Irish and English
women would have to wait until 1928 to get full voting rights. From
1918 women over thirty could vote, but that was a few years off.

In 1913 the subject of women's rights was still a controversial one.
In May that year the *Weekly Irish Times* reported that a 'throng' of
two thousand people (and a few policemen on duty) packed the
City Hall in Cork to hear the Welsh suffragette Alice Abadam speak.
She had been invited by the Munster Women's Franchise League,
but the event was heated, to say the least. Before their guest said a
word, someone in the public gallery fired a revolver. She was quick
to react, retorting: 'I thank you for receiving me like Royalty – that
is, with the explosion of a gun.' She tried to continue but she was
shouted down with a sustained chorus of 'hostile cries' from the
audience. When she invited one particularly vocal female heckler to
come onto the stage and argue her point, she was told: 'No. I refuse
to stand on a platform with an Orangeman.' Miss Abadam insisted
that she was not associated with Orangemen, but the meeting ended
in disarray. The heckler was ejected by the police, five more revolver
shots were fired, and the speaker left by a back door. 'A large hostile
crowd hung around the front entrance awaiting her appearance,' the
paper reported.[24]

It is very likely that Elisabeth Elmes was at that event. She must
have spoken of it at home but probably not to her daughter, who

was only five at the time. The household, however, would have been accustomed to talk of conflict.

Several of Edward Elmes's siblings had been involved in war overseas. His brother, John Henry, and sister, Kathrina Elizabeth, had both served as medical personnel in the second Boer War. John, a surgeon, had survived the siege of Mafeking in South Africa, while his sister often talked of her time as a nurse in the same war. She moved back to the family home in Waterford, and visitors to the house, including Mark Elmes, a cousin of Mary's, recalled her exotic collection of ostrich eggs, snakeskin and feathers. Mary would have heard the story behind the snakeskin: it had belonged to a venomous black mamba that Kathrina found in her bedroom one evening. She ran out, saying there was a snake in her bedroom, and one of the men where she was working came in and shot it. She brought the skin home as a souvenir. She also had tortoises, and painted their shells in bright colours so that they wouldn't get lost in the garden.

There would have been talk of another uncle, William Morris Elmes, who fought and was decorated in the Second Boer War and the First World War but had gone missing in 1924. It took several inquiries from Mary's grandfather, Robert Samuel, before the family discovered he had been shot and killed in Angola four months previously. His effects – a small gold tie pin, 6,120 escudos and some war medals – were deposited in a police station but were later stolen. They did turn up at auction later, but never returned to Cork.[25]

Another story of war was also familiar to the Elmes family: one written by Susanne Rouvier Day about her experiences as a Quaker volunteer during the Great War between 1915 and 1917.[26] Susanne Day and Elisabeth Elmes had served together on the committee of the Munster Women's Franchise League, and it is highly likely that Elisabeth bought a copy of *Round About Bar-le-Duc* when it was published in 1918. The title referred to the town in northern France where Susanne Day worked with refugees and saw the harrowing effect of war on civilians. However, she never pretended to be part of some sort of heroic adventure. She wrote: 'Twenty months in the warzone ought, one would imagine, to have provided me hair-breadth escapes, thrills, and perhaps even shockers with which to regale you, but the adventures are all those of other people, an occasional flight to a cellar being all we could claim of danger.'[27]

She was light-hearted about her own experience, but her vivid prose paints an almost photographic image of the 'senseless cruelty' of war. As fighting began around Verdun in February 1916, she wrote of the 'little groups of bewildered creatures, muddy, travel-stained, dog-weary, yet wonderfully patient and resigned', who took refuge in the 'brown-coloured' air of a covered market. 'Perhaps you think this is an absurd thing to say, but it was so,' she wrote. '[The air] hung like a pale brown veil over the room, and as weeks went by the colour deepened, and in breathing it one had the sensation of drawing something solid into one's lungs.' She went on to describe the barracks, which had been divided into two narrow lanes with straw – 'thick, tossed-up straw' – on which human beings were lying in the last stages of physical and mental exhaustion. 'There are no sanitary arrangements of any kind in the building, there is not a basin, nor a towel, nor a cake of soap of which the refugees can make use.'[28]

She might well have been describing the conditions that Mary Elmes would encounter in the early years of the Second World War, when a similar procession of bewildered people swept south to escape Hitler, joining the hundreds of thousands of displaced Spanish refugees who had recently fled Franco.

Chapter 2 ∿

AROUND THE MULBERRY TREE

*'Between the acts we "promenaded" in the foyer and on the
"grand escalier". There were crowds of people and some
lovely frocks but my green and silver was as pretty as any.'*
— Mary Elmes, Paris, 1926

The colours of Mary Elmes's school uniform told a story in themselves. The green of the serge tunic, blouse and smart blazer and the red hints in her school tie and hat-band evoked an intriguing legend that purportedly explained the origins of Rochelle School.[1] The principal had deliberately chosen green and red to mirror the colours of the leaves and fruit of a mulberry tree in the school's grounds. And that tree, so the story went, was 'proof' of an adventurous past. Huguenots, persecuted Protestants fleeing from seventeenth-century France, came to Cork, where they established themselves as silk merchants. According to school tradition, they had come to this spot in Blackrock and planted mulberry trees to feed the silkworms associated with their trade. The school's very name, Rochelle, was reminiscent of the French city of La Rochelle, which was once a Huguenot centre.[2]

The tale had been embellished and embroidered by generations of schoolgirls, who told of a secret passage and smugglers. One pupil, Mabel Lethbridge, had even allegedly found the hidden tunnel, but in Mary Elmes's time there were still regular searches for it.[3]

The story about the tree and its origins may well have been the start of a lifelong interest in the Huguenots. Mary believed that a branch of the Elmes family, the Vickers, had a Huguenot connection, and she read extensively about them in her later years.[4]

In her school days the tree and its associated myths must have provided a welcome distraction, because outside the school gates the city was in social and political turmoil. Mary's school years, from 1915 to 1925, encompassed a world war, the Easter Rising, the War of Independence and the Civil War that followed it. Any one of those events might explain the fact that on occasion she was absent from school. Cork was a relatively dangerous city in 1921 and 1922; a strict curfew was in operation and a number of civilians were shot dead, randomly, on the street. Yet it is difficult to explain the dates and the extent of her school absences. The roll books for 1919, 1924 and 1925 survive, and in each of those years she had lengthy absences.[5] Given that she would go on to achieve exceptional results at Trinity College, Dublin, and later at the London School of Economics, her absence would not seem to be due to any lack of interest in education. Her mother, who actively pursued better opportunities for women, was likely to have encouraged her daughter from her early days. The school, too, urged girls to go on to further education.

Shortly before Mary and her younger brother, John, started school on the same day, 24 September 1915, a new headmistress was appointed. Christine Bewley, a progressive and committed principal, transformed Rochelle from a seminary that trained governesses into a school for the modern age. The girls who went there could expect to receive 'a thorough education on modern lines in preparation for professional or home life'.[6] Boys attended Rochelle too, but only in kindergarten, up to the age of eight. When she took over, Miss Bewley 'must have seemed as modern as a man from Mars', Dorothy Rudd commented in a history of the school written many years later.[7] Yet the school governors unanimously accepted her appointment and at regular intervals approved her suggestions to modernise the school, including the introduction of the green and red uniform.[8]

When the Elmes children first walked through the grand school gates they would have seen a stately Georgian building on its own extensive grounds, complete with two tennis lawns and a large fruit and vegetable garden. Inside, it was kitted out with modern equipment, a gymnasium, laboratory, cookery room and music rooms, according to an illustrated school prospectus of the time.[9] The syllabus was wide-ranging: in 1915 the subjects taught included English language and literature, history, geography, French, German, Latin, mathematics, science, housecraft, nature study, PE and singing.[10] During her tenure Miss Bewley expanded the curriculum. Quite soon after her appointment, for instance, she organised French conversation classes, which suggests that Mary already had a good foundation in the language before she studied it, years later, at Trinity College.[11]

The school had a tradition of giving to charity, and one of the first entries featuring the Elmes children is in the register of the League of Pity, a fund established to help needy children. On 3 March 1918 both Mary and John donated a sum of five shillings.[12] Later the school's pupils voted, unanimously, to donate the money that would have been spent on school prizes to the Red Cross Society.[13]

Rochelle had already attained a certain prestige. It published regular advertisements in the *Irish Times*, drawing attention to the school's 'Large and Fully-qualified Staff of Graduates and Specialists'.[14] One of them, a Miss Kyle, was a Trinity graduate and gold-medallist. Not only would Mary Elmes herself graduate from the same college but she too would be awarded a gold medal in 1932. As a young schoolgirl she may not have been aware of the significance of her teacher's achievement, but the school prided itself on preparing its girls for further education. Its prospectus affirmed: 'Pupils are prepared for University Entrance and Scholarship Examinations, and for the Examinations of the Intermediate Board and the Department of Technical Instruction.'[15]

The school's religious ethos was firmly Anglican. The school governors made that clear in 1914 when they advertised for a new principal: 'Candidates, preferably over 30 and under 40, should be members of the Church of Ireland or England.'[16]

When Miss Bewley was appointed there were 103 pupils on the roll, 39 of whom were boarders. The principal was paid an annual minimum salary of £150 (approximately €18,300 in 2017), with board, residence, coal, light and laundry. She lived in the school but had furnished apartments of her own and a housekeeper.[17] Under Miss Bewley's stewardship, the school thrived. The number of pupils rose, and the fees paid by boarders and day pupils helped to keep the school in the black. Mary's parents would have paid an annual fee of £3 15s (about €385 in 2017) for her kindergarten years and up to £9 9s (about €1,206 in 2017) for her senior years.

Miss Bewley succeeded in establishing a flourishing modern school, despite the political tumult that was unfolding outside its gates. In an attempt to safeguard her pupils from what was happening in the world around them, she imposed 'a rigid curtain of censorship'.[18] Newspapers were banned, along with any discussion of politics or modern history. However, it was impossible to ignore what was going on. There would have been days and weeks when pupils were unable to get to the school because bridges had been blown up or trains had been cancelled.

There were other risks too. Between 1918 and 1919 some 23,000 Irish people died of the so-called 'Spanish flu', a pandemic that spread globally and killed up to 100 million people. This might explain Mary's first documented absence from school, between February and October 1919. She missed 45 days of school, while John (incorrectly called Don in the roll book) was absent for 18 days.[19] It is tempting to imagine her convalescing in Culgreine, where the sun streamed into her bedroom in the late afternoon. She would later tell her children that her cat used to climb, on velvet paws, up the back porch and land on the windowsill of her bedroom, demanding to be let in.[20] Were girl and cat installed in that room during her absences from school? Perhaps she spent periods of convalescence there, expanding her horizons with books from the house's well-stocked library, which included everything from Hans Andersen's fairytales to books on cookery, history and politics.

When another wave of flu hit the city in January 1922, the Public Health Committee requested that the managers of all schools in the city and in the immediate vicinity close their schools 'for the present'.[21] Rochelle closed its doors for two full months, opening again on 1 March.[22]

If Mary was ill during her school days, she never mentioned it afterwards. There was no mention of a childhood illness either. She obviously enjoyed robust health; not only did she survive the considerable challenges of being an aid worker in two wars but she went on to lead a long, healthy life until her death at the age of ninety-three.

———

Mary did speak, however, about the political violence in Cork during the 1920s. The memory of the assassination of the city's first Republican mayor, Tomás Mac Curtain, on 20 March 1920 stayed with her for life. She told her children of the grief felt by people on all sides of the political divide and the widespread condemnation. The family business, along with all traders in the city, closed its doors as a mark of respect as 'vast throngs' accompanied the remains of the deceased from his home to City Hall, where the body lay in state.[23]

A few months later, in October, the city was in mourning again when the lord mayor's successor, Terence MacSwiney, died after seventy-four days on hunger strike in Brixton Prison in London. His death attracted international attention and criticism, but for Mary and her family, it had a personal significance. The late mayor's sister, Mary MacSwiney, and Mary Elmes's mother, Elisabeth Elmes, were friends; they had both been committee members of the Munster Women's Franchise League.

The Elmes family was to experience a further personal blow. On the night of 11/12 December 1920 British forces set fire to several buildings in Patrick Street in the city centre. The following day the *Cork Examiner* reported that Cork had never experienced such a 'night of horror'.

The residents in every part of the city were terrified by the rifle and revolver firing, bomb explosions, extensive outbreaks of fire, the breaking and smashing of windows and business premises and crashing of walls of buildings. These alarming incidents were in progress until the break of dawn, and it was then found that portions of the city were masses of smouldering ruins. Valuable business premises had been razed to the ground while many other establishments were brought to a state of ruination.[24]

Carnegie Library and City Hall, both in Anglesea Street, were completely destroyed. More than forty shops were gone and five acres lay in ruins following the 'orgy of destruction'.[25] The *Cork Examiner* published a long list of the damage, mentioning the fate of each trader in the city centre. Under a list entitled 'Premises badly burned' there were four entries for Winthrop Street, among them 'J. Waters & Sons, Ltd. oil and colour warehouse'.[26] It must have been the subject of much discussion and worry at home in Ballintemple. Some of those reading the paper that day may have felt irked by the too-late front-page advertisement for 'riot and civil commotion insurance', which included 'military and police damage'.[27]

However, the resilience of the city's traders was striking. In the days that followed, several businesses took out advertisements to say that it was business as usual. William Egan and Sons Ltd, jewellers and silversmiths, published a notice to say they had moved temporarily to the Victoria Hotel. Burton's tailoring firm, 'late of 23, Patrick Street, Cork', told customers that they were now operating out of number 2. Many others published notices to thank customers for their expressions of sympathy and to assure them that all orders taken before the attack in Patrick Street would be attended to as quickly as possible.[28]

J. Waters and Sons not only recovered from the attack but expanded; the following year it had added new services to the business. It now supplied lead, used for backing the mirrors that would become a big part of its business in later years. Eventually the glass side of the business took over from the pharmacy and it became Waters Munster Glass.[29]

Mary also kept a reminder of the dramatic battle for Cork that took place over three days in the city and its environs in August 1922. In her papers there is a travel permit, dated 7 October 1922, that allows the bearers – Mary and her mother – to leave the city and proceed to Passage West by boat. It is signed by General Emmet Dalton, the man who, with 450 Free State troops, landed in Passage

West and led the surprise attacks that forced the anti-Treaty forces into retreat.

According to Dr John Borgonovo, historian and author of *The Battle for Cork*, 'these permits would have been typical for people leaving the city limits; roads were guarded by troops, and docking boats would have been searched. Passage West would have been cut off by rail at the time.'

Back at Rochelle School on the Blackrock Road there must have been talk of what was going on, but Miss Bewley did all she could to make sure that school life went on as normal. While a plan to extend the school was postponed because of the 'disturbed state of the country',[30] Miss Bewley succeeded in steering the school into the emerging new Ireland. 'Rochelle was certainly not one of the Protestant schools that turned its back on the Irish language and all things Irish, and this must have been due, in no small measure, to Miss Bewley. Many people spoke of her courage, calmness and tolerance during those very difficult years,' Dorothy Rudd wrote.[31]

She introduced a more extensive sports programme, and the school held a series of ambitious theatrical performances on the lawn when the weather permitted. There are wonderful pictures from the 1920s showing the girls dressed in pale-green tunics performing Greek dancing and another of them kicking up their legs in a chorus line, with elaborate feathered headdresses and short chequered skirts. Miss Bewley was a great administrator, an excellent English teacher, and, to the delight of some of her pupils, she owned her own car. One former pupil, Gladys Gregg, commented: 'Wasn't she modern to drive her own car!?' after Miss Bewley brought them on a picnic to celebrate winning the local schools cup in hockey.[32]

Of course, as with all school reminiscences, there were dissenting voices too. Lily Fitzpatrick, a contemporary of Mary's, recalled the stern headmistress's 'iron rule': 'She was the coldest person I have ever met, with eyes like steel and no sign of affection for anyone.'[33] But if she found Miss Bewley severe, Lily had fond memories of the other teachers at Rochelle who would also have taught Mary. There was

Miss Edwards, dear Ted, whom we all loved . . . Miss Blair, who taught maths but never succeeded in getting them into my head.

We had a Domestic Economy teacher called Miss Smith. We nick-named her 'Big Smut' because we were all fond of her. She was particularly good at sewing, and was always encouraging us to put 'plates in our bosoms', which was her funny way of pronouncing pleats; and of course it became a cant [catchphrase] with us.[34]

Although Mary wasn't a boarder she must have heard them complain of 'breakfasts of porridge, stale bread and little butter, with perhaps a sausage on Sunday as a "treat"',[35] and tales of their late-night antics. Phyllis Hannaford (née Botterill) recalled:

The highly illegal amusement of bedtime was having eider-down rides, i.e. sitting on one end of an eider-down while the other end was pulled at top speed along the well-polished linoleum by two volunteers. Sometimes the more ancient eider-downs couldn't stand the pace and then the feathers would fly and a mad rush would follow to clear up the mess before the mistress on duty came to turn off the lights.[36]

———

In July 1925, after Mary finished school, her friend Maida Clarke sent her a swastika for good luck. At that time the ancient Indian symbol and its Sanskrit name were still considered tokens of good will, and Maida meant it as a happy remembrance of the friends' 'little pleasant trips together' and a wish for the future.[37] The letter – though not the swastika itself – is still in the family collection. Later on, Mary must have been struck by how such a universally positive emblem would come to symbolise the atrocities committed under Hitler and the Third Reich. She would see the effects of that regime in the internment camps in the south of France a decade and a half later, but in 1925 her friend's letter and enclosure were meant as a farewell message to send Mary on her way. She was leaving Cork to spend a year studying French in Meudon, on the outskirts of Paris.

She left Cork on 28 December 1925 and recorded her thoughts and impressions faithfully in a diary for the year 1926.[38] The entries are those of a young woman deeply interested in culture, art, architecture and nature. She was endlessly curious about the world around her and the people she met: well-seasoned travellers, veterans of the Great War, and the friends of friends who had a private gondola at their disposal one hot and mosquito-y summer in Venice.

In Meudon she was joined by a young Englishwoman, Lulu Agar, and later two others. They all lodged with Mme Pécontal and learned French while visiting the sights of Paris – Notre Dame, the Arc de Triomphe, the Champs-Élysées, the Louvre – and the cathedrals and castles in the towns and cities of northern France. Mary was particularly taken with Versailles and wrote about it with the eye of a painter. 'The sky was beautiful; soft grey windswept clouds with rose and *eau de nil* showing through, and it formed a perfect background for the blue black trees and the old brick of the Chateau. Hampton Court is a cottage compared to Versailles.' Although she had a keen visual sense, she didn't draw. 'I wish I could sketch; it would be lovely to draw the quaint foreign people, especially the men who are so different,' she wrote in early February.

She wrote too about what she saw: the horseflesh on show in the market ('absolutely revolting'); the women who loved to dress in black, 'this sad colour'; First Communion, French style: 'The girls' costume is really ridiculous, long muslin dresses and veils which can be of no earthly use after.' She wrote home to tell her parents when she saw an escalator for the first time. 'At this shop [the Grands Magasins du Louvre in the Rue de Rivoli] there are curious ascenders like moving staircases without steps; it is amusing to notice the expressions on the faces of those who used this method of getting to the upper floors.'

She took classes in embroidery and sewing, and her command of French, already good, improved dramatically. Three volumes of her homework describe, in perfect French, the places she visited, what she saw and the history of the area. There is little of herself in these neat, beautifully scripted pages. Her inner thoughts were reserved for her English journal, where she felt free to say exactly what she thought, which was often humorous and openly critical of any kind of affectation.

Mrs B – and her daughter came to tea; she wants to send her other girls here but I hope she doesn't as they seem very 'nouveau riche' people. They introduced at every turn the people they knew, the winter sports, Italy, Milan, the Opera! Somehow I don't think she will come; they are not exactly our kind.

Not that Mary Elmes had anything against the opera. She saw *Samson and Delilah* at the Opera House in November. It was 'splendid, voices, music and scenery. Between the acts we "promenaded" in the foyer and on the *"grand escalier"* [big staircase]. There were crowds of people and some lovely frocks but my green and silver was as pretty as any.'

There were trips to the theatre, tours of castles, cathedrals and galleries, a holiday on the French coast and a trip to Montreux on Lake Geneva. She didn't go back to Cork at all in 1926, though she kept in regular contact. There were several letters from home, including one with a sprig of shamrock from the rockery in Culgreine for St Patrick's Day, which, more than ninety years later, is still in the pages of her diary, dried and pressed in a bright-green ribbon.

There were visits from two of her aunts. One of them, Aunt Fanny (Frances), had studied French in France and perhaps inspired her niece to follow in her footsteps. There was also a much-anticipated visit from Mary's mother, Elisabeth. When she left, after three weeks, Mary wrote: 'Mummie's train went at 8.14. A most horribly blank feeling when she was gone; too miserable to even think.' But she quickly got back into the swing of her studies and her travels, recording the many books she read, the politics of the day, the plays she saw and the tips gleaned from Aimée, the cook, on days off: 'She told me a special secret – a few teaspoonfuls of caster sugar always improves the flavour [of a ragout]'. Her hostess, Mme Pécontal, remained a lifelong friend.

When she got back to Cork in 1927 Mary applied to study modern languages at Trinity College, Dublin, although she kept in touch with her former school too. When Rochelle established a past pupils' organisation that March she joined the committee.[39] Two years later she was still involved and wrote to the secretary of the Cork Child Welfare League to say that Rochelle Old Girls' Association would donate the proceeds of its annual dance to the Babies' Milk Fund in Cork.[40] The following year the *Cork Examiner* hailed the association's dance as an unqualified success. Mary and her brother were listed among those who attended.[41] Again the proceeds went to the Babies' Milk Fund.

Less than a decade later Mary Elmes would herself be providing milk to babies and children at a feeding station in Almería in the south-east of Spain, a country torn apart by civil war.

Chapter 3 ~

AN EXCEPTIONAL SCHOLAR

'*Miss Marie Elmes is a young lady of the highest character
and of unusual intelligence … She has a well-balanced
mind and excellent judgement.*'
— Professor T. B. Rudmose-Brown,
Trinity College Dublin

Shortly before 11 a.m. on 1 June 1931 crowds of excited
undergraduates, their parents and friends gathered around the
steps of the Examination Hall in Front Square, Trinity College,
to hear the provost, Professor E. J. Gwynn, announce that year's
scholars and fellows. According to 'ancient custom', the annual
scholarship elections took place every year on Trinity Monday.[1] It
had been the highlight of the college year since the early seventeenth
century, and there was an echo of the pageantry of bygone days in
the flowing scarlet gowns worn by the academic staff assembled on
the steps beside the college's ceremonial mace.

It was the end of a long and nervous wait for students, who
greeted the announcements with 'gasps of elation and of disappoint-
ment'.[2] We can only surmise what Mary Elmes felt when the provost
called her name.

That year there were seventeen foundation scholars and nine
non-foundation scholars. There was little difference between the
categories: foundation scholars were part of the body corporate of
the university, with certain voting rights; a new category, non-
foundation scholars, had been established when women were
admitted to the college. Women were not members of the body
corporate and could not vote, but they were entitled to similar
privileges.

The scholarship recognised exceptional academic achievement and was awarded to those who took an optional series of examinations in March. Typically, students took the exam in their second year, but it was clear from her first year that Mary Elmes was going to excel at her degree studies in modern languages (French and Spanish). The *Irish Times* described her academic performance in a short summary published the next day.

> Marie Elisabeth Jean Elmes, the third Scholar (Non-Foundation) in Modern Languages, was educated at Rochelle school, Cork, and matriculated in Trinity College in June, 1928. She has subsequently gained first class honours in French, Spanish, Modern Literature, and a Term Composition Prize in French.[3]

Trinity Monday was a day to celebrate, although women were not admitted to the 'Scholars and Fellows of the Decade' dinner that took place later that evening; instead they were taken to Jammet's, the famous French restaurant in Nassau Street, which the fashion magazine *Vogue* had described as 'one of Europe's best restaurants . . . crowded with gourmets and wits'.[4] Women were eventually admitted to the Scholars of the Decade dinners, and many years later Mary returned to Ireland from her home in France to attend them. It was an honour, she told her children, and one that was made all the more memorable in 1976 when she was seated beside the provost, the well-known historian Prof. F. S. L. Lyons. She even kept the menu (trout mousse, clear soup, roast duck, pears in red wine and angels on horseback).[5]

As well as the prestige, 'schol' (as it is known) also brought with it a number of practical benefits. All scholars' fees were paid. There was an annual stipend, and Mary Elmes would also have been offered a room in Trinity Hall, the official students' residence that had opened on a ten-acre site at Dartry Road, a tram ride from the college. It had hockey fields and tennis courts and became known also as a great debating arena, where women could discuss subjects that were normally the preserve of men.[6] Its warden, Miss Cunningham, was remembered as a woman who 'spared herself no pains, unobtrusively and tactfully, to lick her charges into shape, to train their minds, to develop their aesthetic sense, to help them to an appreciation of true values and fit them to think independently for themselves'.[7]

However, women students were still subject to a number of stringent regulations. Rooms in the college, for instance, were strictly off limits, except on special occasions and then only with 'explicit sanction' and if accompanied by parents or guardians.[8] There was also a curfew: women were asked to leave the college grounds by 6 p.m.; and when they were in the college squares and parks they had to wear their 'academicals' – formal cap and gown – unless accompanied by a chaperone.

By the time Mary started at TCD in October 1929 women made up a quarter of all students. In her junior freshman year (first year) there were 206 men and 62 women. Yet the admission of women to the country's oldest university was still relatively recent. In 1904 they had finally been admitted to 'this bastion of male exclusiveness' after long and fevered arguments that emphasised moral and social decorum.[9] The debate had been thrashed out between women's rights champions and their opponents, who warned of the potential disruption to male students. A man might unwittingly become 'entangled in an imprudent marriage', or might fall victim to fortune-hunters. There were concerns for women too: the experience of mixed third-level education might prove too much for the limited female mind, and there was a risk that it would affect women's 'grace and femininity'.[10]

The first women graduates, however, showed no such limitations. They were high-performing intellectuals, 'torchbearers on trial under a searching public scrutiny', whose academic achievement was out of proportion to their numbers.[11] Of the 160 women admitted, more than half won honours in 1908.[12] At the time, such subjects as modern languages and history were considered 'female' subjects, and the male establishment was rocked when women began to win gold medals in other disciplines, such as philosophy (1913) and experimental science (1916). The college's first female chemistry graduate (1908), Sydney Elizabeth Auchinleck from Dublin, wrote a poem gently chiding the college for not allowing her to study engineering. After she graduated, she continued to write poetry – and worked as a part-time mechanic.[13] Her poem expressed the hope that TCD would one day allow women into its 'haughty Engineering School', although she was 'very doubtful'.

Oh Trinity, dear Trinity, how proud I am to be
E'en the least of the alumni in the University
Full long you have rejected us, but fate has cleared the way
We come to you 'on trial', but we come to you to stay . . .
And now I study Chemistry, and hope that one fine day
Your haughty Engineering School will let me in to stay
(I know it's very doubtful) but what e'er my fate may be
I hope I never give you cause to be ashamed of me.[14]

In 1931, the year Mary was a scholar, her contemporaries were becoming more vocal about the restrictions on women, particularly the six o'clock curfew and the separation of men's and women's dining facilities.[15] That year five women stormed the men's lunch buffet in the dining-hall in protest. The incident is recalled in *A Danger to Men?*, a history published to commemorate the centenary of the first women students. 'The five girls gained entry by dressing up as men but were given short shrift by the housekeeper, Miss Jean Montgomery. The "Forward Five" – Barbara, Maureen, Joy, "Pic" and Maura – had considerable male support.'[16] While their courage and their objective were admired, an editorial in the college magazine said that 'a less militant protest would have been more dignified'.[17]

In some quarters, female undergraduates were dismissed as 'irritating impediments to work' as they attended 'lectures in chattering battalions',[18] but there was support too. The Trinity College Association argued in favour of giving women wider access to the college's facilities and was rather tongue-in-cheek in its report in the columns of the *Irish Times* on 2 June 1931: 'While there may be a difference of opinion on the desirability of the presence of women in the debating halls of the association, everyone is agreed that their presence at the annual dance in the Metropole next Monday is a necessity.'[19]

Mary never talked about those restrictions, but later in life she was vocal about anything she saw as unjust. Her surviving letters reveal an uncompromising humanitarian who went out of her way to make sure that the refugees in the camps in wartime France got what was due to them. She campaigned for her staff to get wage increases and wasn't afraid to stand up to her superiors if she thought something was unfair.

During her college years, however, there is no record of her being involved in the fight for greater rights for women. She may well have joined the college societies open to women. The Modern Languages Society would certainly have had an appeal. Founded in 1924, it was the most active in the college and its members took part in regular play readings. Outside the gates of the college, Dublin had much to offer in terms of cafés, cinemas and entertainment. Trinity students made popular haunts of the cafés in Switzer's department store and Mitchell's in Grafton Street and Johnston, Mooney and O'Brien's in Leinster Street, near the college's back gate.[20] Whatever about her extracurricular activity, it is clear from her consistent results – in the 'first rank' from her first year – that Mary Elmes was a diligent and committed student.

During her four years at Trinity her courses in French covered all aspects of the language, its grammar and theory. There were courses on modern French history and an extensive literature syllabus that included Corneille, Molière, La Fontaine and Balzac. It is very likely that she attended lectures given by the Nobel laureate Samuel Beckett, a fellow scholar and graduate, who had a short-lived career as a lecturer in Trinity from 1930 to 1931. In Michaelmas term, 1931, he gave a course on Racine, which made a deep impression on one contemporary of Mary's, Rachel Burrows:

> I was aware that here was a brilliant mind giving us exciting material which could not be found in a book . . . I remember his assessment of the Racine situation, A loves B and B loves C but there is no mutual desire. He called it 'the great pagan tiger of sexuality, chasing its tail in outer darkness'.[21]

Many modern languages students of that era also had fond memories of Dr Walter Starkie, a lecturer in Spanish who wrote *Raggle-Taggle* (1933), an account of his travels among the Roma of Spain.[22]

He later became the first professor of Spanish and was a colourful, influential character who made an impression on students. Many of them also recalled the ordeal women faced during oral examinations. 'Sir Robert Tate [of the Modern Languages Department] used to snap at the women, "Speak up, I can't hear you," then, when the student tried to oblige he would shout, "No need to shout, I'm not deaf."'[23]

However, oral exams were unlikely to have posed a particular challenge to Mary Elmes. Her French was near-fluent, and in 1930 she went on a year-long study trip to Madrid, which was to be the beginning of a lifelong love of Spain's language, its culture and, in particular, its people. She stayed in the same lodgings as the queen's chambermaid when she was there and told her own children years later that she saw King Alfonso wash the feet of twelve 'disciplines' during a religious ceremony at Easter. Afterwards an admirer, José de Gardoqui, wrote to her and sent her a book he had written on Spanish military history. She thanked him, apologising for her rusty Spanish. The letters and the book are still in the family archive.

During those years at Trinity there were regular trips home. The *Cork Examiner* offers a fragmentary insight into how some of that time was spent. In a snippet dated 20 December 1930 it reported that Mary Elmes and her brother, John, were among those attending a dance in the Imperial Hotel to raise funds for the Cork Coal Fund. A few months earlier the same paper had reported that John Elmes won the Palmer Challenge Trophy at the Cork and District Motor Club's motorcycling scramble in Coachford, Co. Cork. There must have been talk at home about his victorious ride on his 409 cc Rudge and his earlier performance in the trial when the judges singled out his 'fine display of motor-cycling'.[24] John Elmes followed in his father's footsteps and studied pharmacy; he passed his pharmaceutical examination on 5 August 1932 and went on to join the family business.[25]

In the same year, Mary graduated with a first-class degree in modern languages. She was awarded a gold medal and left with glowing references, which would help to secure a scholarship to study international relations at the London School of Economics.

In a letter to the LSE dated 8 November 1932, her former professor of Romance languages at Trinity, T. B. Rudmose-Brown, wrote:

Miss Marie Elmes is a young lady of the highest character and of unusual intelligence. I have taught her for four years and have found her work exceptionally careful, exact and thoughtful. She has a well-balanced mind and excellent judgement. She distinguished herself very highly in the recent final examination for the Degree of B.A. with Honours in French and Spanish. She speaks and writes French with complete fluency and accuracy, is unusually well-read, and has profited more than most students by her reading. Her mark in French (over 70%) was second only to that of the Large Gold Medallist of the year, and higher than that of many Large Gold Medallists of other years.[26]

Her former tutor F. La Touche Godfrey also recommended her without hesitation:

She has had an exceptionally brilliant Academic Career . . . As Miss Elmes' College Tutor I know her well, and cannot speak too highly of her personal character and Academic attainments.[27]

In mid-December the LSE wrote to Mary Elmes to say that, in view of her good record, it would be glad to accept her as a student. She started at the school on 9 January 1933 with a Trinity scholarship of £30 a year – just about enough to cover the basics.[28] Unlike Trinity, the LSE made no distinction between male and female students. From the time it opened its doors in 1895 it was seen as a pioneering institution. Courses were open to women and men, and qualifications were awarded without any discrimination. By 1933 'women had a considerable presence as both teachers and students', and the school even had a female professor: Eileen Power was appointed professor of economic history in 1931.[29] One of the joint founders of the LSE, Beatrice Webb, noted in her diary that it was a diverse place, with some '3,000 students of all races and professions – undergraduates and post-graduates, youths and maidens, and men and women in the prime of life – under the direction of a large miscellaneous staff of professors and assistant professors'.[30] Such a mixture, she said, was bound to lead to heated debate, and during Mary's time there some of those debates made the national press.

One of them, in 1934, led to the expulsion of the president of the Students' Union, Frank Meyer, by the director, Sir William Beveridge, after he refused to withdraw allegations printed in a left-wing newsletter that colonial students were being spied on. A furious debate about freedom of expression versus the good reputation of the school ensued. The discussion broadened out to include freedom of academic expression when a member of the staff, Professor Harold Laski, gave a lecture in Moscow, prompting charges that the LSE was 'a hotbed of Communist teaching'. But there was good publicity too. Academics exiled from Hitler's Germany were invited to teach on the school's postgraduate courses. Lecturers, readers and professors all contributed a proportion of their salaries to raise the money to pay them. The director would later warn that what was happening in Germany was a challenge for Britain: 'It is a challenge not to be taken up by protests. Protests butter no parsnips. It is a challenge given by deeds, not words – and must be met not by words, but by deeds. It is a challenge given by deeds of hate; it should be met by deeds of charity.'[31]

Perhaps those events, and what was said about them, influenced Mary Elmes, but, as Betty Scharf, a 1930s undergraduate and later school governor, put it, 'the institution was such that what went on high up was not known to humble folk like us'.[32] Those humble folk were more likely to attend the famous lunchtime dances or to complain about refectory prices, or the noise. The principal memory of one evening student, Roland Bird, was of 'sounds of every unharmonious kind – the mechanical screams from St Clements Press, the concrete mixer never long absent from Houghton Street even in the depths of the depression, the six-piece jazz band that used to entertain the queues outside the Stoll [Theatre], the rehearsals for The Pirates of Penzance that went on in the theatre one vacation.'[33]

Whatever the external distractions, Mary again proved to be a diligent student. Now that she spoke two languages fluently she hoped to explore the field of international diplomacy. Her core subjects included diplomatic history, general international relations, international institutions, international law and general economics and the economic factor in international affairs. She 'made a promising start', Professor Manning told the Scholarships Committee in 1933.[34] The following year he wrote of his student: 'Inclined, almost, to take her work <u>too</u> seriously. Seems to be getting on well.'

What made him remark that this student was taking her work too seriously, and to go to the trouble of underlining the word 'too'? Would he have said it of a male student? Was he surprised by this Irishwoman's dedication? Her proven academic ability? Or, perhaps, the clear-headed resolve that would help her to function in two war zones a few years later? He didn't elaborate and, rather disappointingly, simply said of her in final year: 'Has made good use of her time.'[35]

––––––

That year, 1935, Mary applied for a scholarship to the Geneva School of International Studies – but a day late. She wrote: 'My application is unfortunately a day later than the final date laid down in the Calendar, but I hope that you will accept my apologies for this and allow my name to be put forward with the rest.'[36] It says something about the quality of her candidature that her late entry did not stop her securing the only place offered that year.

In 1936 she was on her way to Geneva to further her studies in international affairs, but what was unfolding around her in Europe must have proved far more instructive than anything in the books on her course. In Germany, Hitler was planning a dazzling Olympic Games, a propaganda coup designed to portray a united Germany, obscuring its racist, expansionist core. In Italy, Mussolini had invaded Abyssinia (Ethiopia), flouting any half-hearted attempts by the League of Nations to stop him. Then, in July, a group of powerful right-wing generals attempted to overthrow the newly elected leftist Republican government in Spain. The coup failed but the fighting continued, erupting into a civil war that was characterised by atrocities on both sides and deliberate attacks on urban centres and civilians.

Given her love of Spanish culture and her interest in international affairs, Mary Elmes would have followed events closely as the civil war rent Spain apart. On one side, the pro-government Republicans took control of parts of eastern and central Spain, while General

Franco's Nationalists, with the support of the army generals and the Catholic Church, held large parts of the north and west. Germany and Italy sided with the Nationalists, sending abundant supplies of equipment and weaponry. The Soviet Union came to the Republicans' aid, as well as thousands of volunteers from more than fifty countries who formed the International Brigades.

There was a co-ordinated international effort to send humanitarian aid too. Despite Britain's non-intervention policy, millions of ordinary British people sent food, money and supplies to Spain. Sir George Young, a British diplomat and Mary's future employer, was also assessing the bitter war of attrition and its devastating effect on civilians. He had worked as a diplomat in Spain, spoke Spanish fluently and had a connection with the country stretching back decades. He was a journalist and author too and in 1933 had written *The New Spain*, a book that had called for international support for the Republic that he could see emerging. He had also warned of the chaos that might ensue if it was not forthcoming.[37]

When Málaga in the south of Spain fell to the rebels on 3 February 1937, Sir George was already over sixty years old. He foresaw a humanitarian catastrophe that would bring famine, reprisals and the flight of the local population 'on a scale that would leave widows and orphans in thousands'.[38] It was the spur that prompted him to make hurried arrangements to help his beloved Spain. He announced a plan to send an ambulance unit to the country on 6 February. He established the University Ambulance Unit, a name that acknowledged the representatives of the British universities that had sponsored it. For his part, he was planning to convert his house in Torremolinos into a hospital.

Mary Elmes may well have responded to Young's newspaper appeal for volunteers. It seems that she went to the Save the Children office in Geneva to say that she wanted to work as a volunteer. It is possible too that she was already acquainted with Lady Young, as the two women would later travel to Spain together. In either event, Mary never made much of her decision to venture into the centre of a conflict that had seen exceptional brutality on both sides. She had decided to go to Spain, and many years later she simply said: 'I [went] because I wished to know the Spaniards.'[39]

On 11 February 1937, Elisabeth Elmes arrived in London from Cork to spend some time with her daughter before she embarked on the first phase of a journey that would shape the rest of her life.[40] Two days later, Mary and Lady Young boarded the *Otranto* in the Port of London, bound for Gibraltar. Lady Young's 22-year-old son, Courtenay Trevelyan Young, was with them, along with a fellow volunteer, Mrs G. M. Petter, from Save the Children.[41] The departure had been so rushed that Mary had no time to put her affairs in order. Her Trinity gold medal was still in a vault at Lloyd's Bank; her fur coat was in storage. Almost a decade would elapse before she would be in a position to return to London to retrieve them.[42]

Chapter 4

INTO THE WORLD OF NIGHTMARE

*'To make them run more quickly, we sent our aviation to
bomb them.'*
— General Queipo de Llano, Nationalist leader

The talk on board the *Otranto* must have been of war, but
nothing could have prepared Mary Elmes and her fellow
passengers for the scenes of human suffering they would
encounter in Spain. They arrived in Gibraltar days after Franco's
fascist allies pounded the once-defiant Republican city of Málaga
into submission. It was bombarded from the air by Italian aircraft
and attacked from the coast by Francoist warships.

As Sir George Young had predicted, the population fled eastwards,
towards Almería, 120 miles away. Nowhere was the road visible.
Norman Bethune, a Canadian doctor who had just arrived in Spain
with a mobile blood-transfusion unit, wrote: 'Where the road should
have been, there wriggled . . . miles of human beings, like a giant
caterpillar, its many limbs raising a cloud of dust, moving slowly,
ponderously stretching beyond the horizon across the arid flat
country and up into the foothills.' He passed among the plodding
masses on the road to Almería and loaded as many children as would
fit on his vehicle. But there were still 'thousands upon thousands of
them, pressed together, falling against each other, like bees swarming
in a hive, and like bees filling the plain with the hum of voices, cries,
wailings, the grotesque noises of the animals'.[1]

Some 120,000 people – defeated militiamen, women, children,
the old – fled from the victorious fascists with whatever they could

carry. The sun was merciless, and there was no water or food. Some were on donkeys, most were on foot. They were exhausted and defenceless, yet they were picked out by searchlight and bombed from the air, shelled from the sea, and fired at by armoured cars patrolling the road. As the leader of the victorious Nationalists, General Queipo de Llano, had callously explained, 'to make them run more quickly, we sent our aviation to bomb them.' In the preceding weeks, the same general had instilled terror with his nightly radio broadcasts warning the local population to 'start digging graves', because his much-feared Moorish troops were ready to kill opponents 'like a dog'.[2]

Later, those distraught refugees would recount to Mary and her colleagues that 'they were pursued by cars with machine-guns which went up and down the road shooting any who couldn't take cover in time'.[3] They would testify that, when the planes droned nearer, they pressed themselves down on the ground on the sides of the road, the rocks and the shore, trying to burrow into holes. Dr Bethune's colleague T. C. Worsley, an English ambulance-driver, told how 'children lay flat, with one frightened eye turned upwards towards the sky, with their hands pressed tight over their ears or folded backwards to protect their vulnerable necks. Huddled groups crouched everywhere, mothers already on the brink of exhaustion, held down their children pushing them into every cranny and hollow, flattening themselves into the hard earth . . . They had been bombed before and knew only too well what to do.'[4] He went on to say that the refugees had no food and few belongings and in many cases were barefoot. 'A few of them were wearing rubber shoes, but most feet were bound round with rags, many were bare, nearly all were bleeding. There were seventy miles of people desperate with hunger and exhaustion and still the streams showed no signs of diminishing.'[5]

As Mary and her party landed in Gibraltar, word was coming through from Almería of 'the utmost confusion' as an estimated 80,000 people streamed into the city.[6] Several thousands more had turned back, and there were heavy casualties: 5,000 people died along the roadside in an exodus that became known as the 'caravan of death'.

An English nurse, Violetta Thurstan, was the first member of the University Ambulance Unit to reach the overwhelmed Republican-held city. She had been asked to go on ahead when Sir George Young and his convoy were delayed at Dieppe. She set out on her own, making a perilous, uncertain journey across France and war-ravaged Spain.

Mary would certainly have heard of that eventful trip.[7] Violetta's willingness to travel alone through France and Spain was just one example of the indomitable courage demanded of the women, and men, who had joined the University Ambulance Unit as well as the many others who volunteered with other organisations, such as the Quakers, to ease the plight of the Spanish people. 'It was rather a responsibility for me to take but I said I would do the best I could,' Violetta said rather matter-of-factly before taking a train out of Paris and heading south, alone.[8]

She got over the frontier into Spain, but just as she was approaching the suburbs of Barcelona the train stopped and all the lights were put out. 'Barcelona,' she explained, 'was being shelled from the sea. We sat in the dark for about forty minutes, a coach full of soldiers, sailors, militia, women, dogs, hens and rabbits, one of which got loose in the confusion and was found at last behind my suitcase.'[9] She finally made it to Valencia eighteen hours later, arriving at 4 a.m. She went to the British embassy and later tracked down the Basque minister, who gave her a letter of introduction to the governor of Almería and permission to use petrol, which was very scarce. She left the same night for Almería, though the authorities didn't think she would get through.

She arrived at Lorca to find there was no transport whatsoever. However, someone suggested that a car might stop for her if she went to a control station up ahead.

I put my belongings on a mule and walked along behind the mule till I got to the control station and got my guide to explain to the soldiers guarding the road what I wanted . . . After a couple of hours, a Ministry car came along and agreed, rather unwillingly, to take me. It took me about six hours to do this bit. The two men were rather haughty and disapproving at first, but presently we got into an air raid, though not very near, and a little after that we found a very badly wou[n]ded boy lying in the middle of the road. The car stopped, of course, and I got out and ministered to him, then we lifted him into the car and took him to the nearest hospital, and they were much more matey after that.[10]

Forty hours after leaving Valencia, Violetta arrived in Almería, where news of the ambulance unit, its stores and drivers was greeted as 'heaven-sent'. Violetta wrote of the 'nervy, ill-fed, panicky' population in dire need of medical help in a letter that would have reached Lady Young just as she and Mary arrived in Gibraltar. A veteran of the front lines of the First World War, she described what was happening in detail so vivid that Mary and her fellow volunteer Mrs Petter would have been left in no doubt about what was awaiting them. In a letter dated 'Feb. I think about 20th,' she wrote:

Everyone seems very anxious tonight and there is talk of a big attack pending. I *hope* it is only talk. A bomb has just gone off and the streets are so crowded that everyone gets into a panic. I have been told to sleep with a torch ready to my hand, and my dressing gown on the other arm so to speak, and make a dash downstairs if anything happens, as all the glass on one side of the house was shattered the other night and the Red Cross man was blown, chair and all, from one side of the room to the other.[11]

The city, she told them, was shelled from the sea every morning and there were air raids most nights.

A great deal of damage has been done . . . and a great many killed and wounded including the refugees.

Food is terribly short, there are long queues of people waiting for bread and yesterday the doors were shut because there was no more . . . Women with little babies had to go away crying. They [the British Consul and the Red Cross] say there is scarcely any more food in Almeria, and begged me to send you a telegram in case it was possible for you to send a few supplies by sea, so I have just done so, at this very urgent request, though I don't know if it is the least possible.

From Gibraltar, Lady Young, with the help of her son and the two newly arrived volunteers, Mary Elmes and Mrs Petter, were able to buy a consignment of food and send it by sea to Almería, where it saved many lives.[12] However, they had less success getting food through to the people still trapped in Málaga, hundreds of whom were summarily executed in the weeks following occupation. The University Ambulance Unit had hoped at first to help both sides in the conflict, but the authorities in Seville would not allow a British organisation associated with the Republican side to offer aid. The Nationalists took over the distribution, but not before it was 'depleted by the soldiery', as Sir George Young later noted. 'The Italians got the chocolate,' he said, and all further efforts to relieve Málaga were abandoned, despite the destitution and 'famine conditions in the surrounding countryside'.[13]

Mary had a permit to stay in Spain for five days, but she had always intended to stay longer. An urgent appeal had been put out for doctors and nurses, yet she was neither. She could speak Spanish – she must have made that point strongly – and she was eager to volunteer. After some discussion it was decided to assign her to the University Ambulance Unit, which in turn appointed her to a feeding station in Almería.[14] She arrived in that battered, overflowing port city on 21 February 1937 to find thousands of Malagan refugees sheltering in any nook they could find: under railway arches, in ditches, caves, the cellars of ruined houses. Many of those who had survived the journey were 'in the last stages of starvation and in the extremity of exhaustion', Sir George Young wrote – 'families without fathers, children without parents, mothers without children.'[15] The city lacked every kind of food. While it had orange trees, vines and date palms, it was hemmed in by 'parched and bladeless mountains' and had no hinterland.[16]

By the time Mary arrived, a plan to set up a hospital was already well advanced. The ambulance unit's commandant, Violetta Thurstan, had wasted no time. With the help of the town's governor she had secured a suitable building a few miles outside the town, the

Villa María, which was being converted into a hospital and clinic. It had its own grounds and gardens, was comfortably furnished, and was soon catering for twenty-five children at a time. It was Mary's first hospital posting in a career as a volunteer that would span nine years and two of the worst wars in twentieth-century Europe. The women she met in those first months of the Spanish Civil War were courageous nurses and volunteers whose composure had been developed while working on the front lines of the First World War, with refugees in North Africa and in famine-stricken post-civil war Russia. She would prove to be just like them: clear-headed, unsentimental and focused in the chaos of war.

———

Over the next four months, Mary moved from the feeding station to the villa-hospitals that were being established by the ambulance unit. There were enormous challenges, but with them came visible rewards. The first food station to open in Almería was soon feeding up to three hundred children daily. 'If the kind people who sent the stores could have seen the toddlers with their whole faces buried in a bowl of milk,' one unnamed member of the unit wrote in a letter home to London, 'small boys tearing wolfishly at the bread, often trying to cram it all into their mouth at once, women crying for joy when they saw the hot meals provided, they would feel rewarded'.[17]

The description was quoted in one of many newspaper articles aimed at raising awareness and much-needed funds. Sir George Young, a former journalist, was acutely aware of the need to keep the Spanish conflict in the minds of those donating food, money and supplies. He provided newspapers with regular updates of the unit's progress and wrote many articles himself, evoking the suffering of the Spanish people in vivid prose and providing readers with a political context.

Lady Young too kept the issue alive with constant updates and regular letters of thanks for the 'generous and widespread' response from the British public. In a letter to the *Manchester Guardian* dated 16 March she wrote: 'We have received gifts and subscriptions from those who could least afford it, from the unemployed, from miners' wives and from children as well as many others.'

Sir George Young could have established the ambulance unit and handed it over to younger volunteers, but he was determined to lead it into the war zone himself. He knew the country well, having worked there as a diplomat. Years earlier he was even credited with introducing polo to Spain, and was said to have won King Alfonso's admiration for his horseriding.[18] In the intervening years he regularly visited his house in Torremolinos and became known to Spanish customs officials as 'the English lord' (*el hidalgo inglés*). He certainly dressed the part, often venturing out in flowing cape and broad-brimmed hat.[19] He wore an old white bow tie, which he dyed by dipping it into coffee, and he used brass paper clips as waistcoat buttons. But, as his son said of him, 'he wore whatever it happened to be – my mother's motoring veil tied over an old squash hat, or under his eyes as a yashmak, a shawl thrown over his shoulders – with such an air that it was never simply ludicrous.'[20]

Sir George was unconventional in many more ways than appearance. He was a writer, artist, intellectual and linguist who could turn his hand to anything. He was an ingenious mechanic and was able to fashion a contraption for any occasion out of materials to hand. A British nurse, Frida Stewart, recalled him arriving in Valencia 'clinging to a wicker chair, strapped to an antiquated motorbike ambulance . . . There's no doubt about him being courageous and cracked!' she said.[21]

Over the course of the war he and his wife proved to be selfless humanitarians who used the support garnered in Britain to finance an extremely effective relief and medical service. While he was a socialist and an advocate of federalism – 'the drawing of diagrams to prove political theories was a favourite game of his' – he advised volunteers to avoid expressing political views in Spain's tense political atmosphere.[22] His volunteers were not paid, but they got personal expenses and were trained and treated well.[23]

The unit's overland convoy arrived in Almería on the same day that Lady Young's supplies came ashore from the British destroyer *Boadicea*. A food station was set up within hours, and tons of food – milk, bread and soup – were distributed to initially suspicious refugees. 'The milk distribution was especially useful in enabling us to find sick children and destitute families,' Sir George wrote. 'Some women or children would come to get a supply for the sick, and helpers would be sent back with them to verify and investigate. Later, when they found we were not officials, they would come for help for themselves.' [24]

He set up food stations, at 20-mile stages, 'over that awful wilderness of the Sierra Alhamilla'. Then he set out on horseback to establish a front-line medical service of hospitals and casualty clearing stations. He rode over the most hostile terrain, often spending up to ten hours in the saddle. The facilities were soon treating guerrilla fighters wounded in the fighting taking place high in the mountains. On one occasion the unit's overloaded ambulance was crawling up over a 6,000-foot pass in the Sierra Nevada when it came across 'some young *milicianos* lying in the ditch half-dead from exhaustion and exposure'. They were sheltered and revived and then all, bar one whose feet were frozen, started again on foot for the front. Sir George recalled the incident as an illustration of his belief – mistaken, as it turned out – that the war was nearing its end, but it also gives an insight into how the ambulance unit ventured into the most inaccessible places. [25]

Back in Almería, the rainy season was unusually cold. The harsh weather took a heavy toll on refugee children, already weakened by their ordeal. Epidemics of flu and measles took hold. Another hospital was needed urgently. On her one-woman reconnaissance the previous month, the authorities had asked Violetta Thurstan to take a special interest in child welfare, and they were quick to help now. They assigned a Spanish doctor, José Soriano Romero, to the ambulance unit. He helped to secure a villa, the Villa San Juan, which was quickly converted into a twenty-bed hospital. Mary left the Villa María to start work in the new hospital on 1 March, but she had hardly begun there before it was overrun with sick children. The severe overcrowding meant that the volunteers were forced to make unthinkable decisions: lack of space compelled them to turn away 'obviously hopeless cases' and admit only those infants with a chance of survival. [26] In the first weeks many of those children died too, but the death rate dropped significantly as the unit got to grips with the backlog of cases and the epidemics subsided.

Soon, with the help of the city mayor, another nearby villa, the much larger Villa Elena, was converted into a hospital. It offered a welcome sanctuary. The two-storey building was set high up in an enclosed garden and was guarded day and night by government soldiers. 'It was protected by high brick walls, framed by tawny mountains and overlooked the old Moorish city of Almería,' wrote Elizabeth Burchill, an Australian nurse who arrived at the villa at the same time as Mary.[27]

As before, Mary and her colleagues were faced with the daily challenge of tending to the young, traumatised victims of the war. Elizabeth Burchill wrote:

Day and night the routine, bustling atmosphere of our hospital could be interrupted by the noisy, ominous sound of the 'peto', the air-raid siren. Its screeching tones caused sick children, denied the warm security of family life, to leap from their beds in terror and run to us for protection, clutching at our uniforms and exclaiming, with fear in their eyes, 'Franco, Franco, *Señorita!*' as if living again the horrible experience of the Retreat from Malaga.[28]

But there were times of unexpected joy, too.

Never will I forget the unexpected, exhilarating visit of a gypsy troupe which comprised six lovely teenage girls who lived with their tribe in rock caves north of Almeria. They came shyly to our quarters one siesta time and offered to dance for the English *señoritas.* And what a treat we were in for! They wore the traditional gypsy costume of red, swinging skirt, white blouse, black velvet bodice, red head scarf, dangling earrings and soft black shoes; the epitome of grace and Latin beauty as they treated us to a private exhibition of graceful, rhythmic dancing that enthralled us.

For brief, precious moments we entered into an avenue of 'escape' where these modern exponents of a centuries-old art moved with lightning speed and appealing lithesomenness; their black eyes flashing with the swishing of their billowing skirts and the haunting sound of hand castanets keeping pace with the swift movements of light feet. The gypsies' visit appeared like a good omen and we interpreted their happy performance as a demonstration of goodwill towards the foreigners who came to help their country in its hour of need.[29]

If Mary Elmes was at the Villa Elena that day – and she very probably was – the graceful elegance of those Roma dancers must have reminded her of the stories told by Walter Starkie, her former lecturer in Spanish at Trinity College. He had written vividly about his own adventures as a holidaying vagabond fiddler who followed the trail of the Roma in Spain, Hungary and Romania.

There were other stolen moments of peace too.

In quiet times, the traditional practice of *siesta* was a rejuvenating experience if all was quiet. Even in war-time Almeria, it could be observed with totality. During this welcome two-hour afternoon period, shops closed, blinds were drawn, and people rested and slept as if there was no war on. In our upstairs living quarters it was always a treat to snatch a brief respite from nursing, remove our uniforms and lie supine on our inflated rubber mattresses on the flat roof during *siesta*, feeling the southern sun gently tanning our skin and watch the fleeting shadows created by the dark green leaves of nearby trees.[30]

The war, though, was never far away. In the early hours of 30 May, German warships pounded the town with high-explosive shells. One of Sir George's hospitals was hit during the bombardment. He and four members of the ambulance unit were in it at the time, and his assistant, Peter O'Donovan, was struck above the eye by flying glass as they were evacuating patients to an ambulance.[31] 'The other hospital had shells of high explosive with time fuses and shrapnel burst all about it,' he told reporters, 'but escaped with little damage. The staff of nurses behaved with great coolness and courage, dealt with the many casualties brought in, and kept the children, native staff and the refugees that crowded in quiet by preparing them a good meal.'[32]

He kept a souvenir: a splinter, a foot long, from a shell that missed the main ward by a few inches. He told the *Egyptian Gazette* how those shells, which had a time fuse that exploded some moments after contact and then scattered shrapnel laterally, wounded or killed all living creatures within many yards. 'Hundreds of innocent people will now drag through the remainder of their lives with mangled bodies from which bits of steel have been taken.' Asked whether the work the hospitals were doing in saving life justified the risk to the lives of the English staff, he said that he had put that to them himself and that they had unanimously refused to return home.[33] Of course his volunteers were not only English: they came from America, New Zealand, Switzerland and Ireland. Mary Elmes was not the only Irish volunteer; Kathleen MacColgan, a BA graduate of Oxford, was Irish or at least of Irish descent. She and Mary certainly met and must have been friends, because a book with Kathleen's name inscribed on the flyleaf found its way into Mary's collection – a present, perhaps, or a request to hold on to it while Kathleen was stationed elsewhere.[34]

Meanwhile at home in England, Lady Young again wrote to the newspapers:

The recent bombardment of Almeria has put an added strain upon the British University Ambulance Unit there. Its two children's hospitals are full and the clinic is working day and night. One of its hospitals was hit during the bombardment and one of its members was hurt. Almeria has so continually been bombed from the air that refugees have lately been evacuated to Murcia, some 200 miles east, where 100,000 men, women and children are camping in conditions of great misery.[35]

A British Quaker volunteer was the first to arrive in Murcia. She was so quickly overwhelmed that she sent an SOS for help to Sir George Young. He responded by sending a number of his team; Mary Elmes was among them.

Chapter 5 ∾

AN ABYSS OF MISERY

'They broke down the doors, they flung down the sentries, they surged into the room … It was not a breakfast – it was hell. They couldn't believe that there would be enough to go round.'

— Francesca Wilson, English Quaker

When the English Quaker Francesca Wilson first tried to distribute food at the biggest refugee shelter, the Casa Pablo Iglesias, in Murcia in April 1937 she felt there was something odd about the place: 'It was like an anthill that has been stirred up – the whole building was alive. We had to lock and bar the kitchen door and . . . when we tried to let in the children in relays to their breakfast, we were stormed out and had to give up the attempt.'[1] Some four thousand 'ragged, wild-eyed' refugees (though she doubted that anyone had ever counted them) had been packed into an unfinished nine-storey apartment building, without windows or doors, on the outskirts of the town. 'The noise was terrific: babies crying, boys rushing madly from floor to floor, sick people groaning, women shouting . . . They surged around us, telling us their stories, clinging to us like people drowning in a bog.'[2]

The shelter was one of five that had been set up to house the torrent of refugees, some 20,000 or more people, who had fled to Murcia, a garrison town with a peacetime population of 60,000. While conditions in the other shelters were slightly better, Francesca was shocked to find a family of four living in a wall cupboard in one of them. 'They refused to budge,' she said, and explained that they had known such 'bitter poverty' around the countryside in Málaga – some of them had been living in caves – that this was 'only one degree worse'.[3]

In those early chaotic days at the Casa Pablo Iglesias it was impossible to set up feeding stations. Every time Francesca tried to set up a canteen she was overrun. While some men and women were happy to help her establish order for the price of a cup of cocoa, the pregnant and nursing mothers were like 'wild animals', she wrote.

> They broke down the doors, they flung down the sentries, they surged into the room, dipped their tin mugs into the scalding vats, fought with each other, tearing each other's hair and the clothes off each other's backs. They shrieked and gesticulated. It was not a breakfast – it was hell. They couldn't believe that there would be enough to go round.[4]

'Where have I heard before of five thousand being fed?' Francesca wrote afterwards, recalling the miracle of the loaves and fishes with playful humour. She would need a similar miracle now if she was going to distribute aid in Murcia, she said.[5]

There was one person who had already achieved not quite a miracle but the improbable by bringing food and medical aid into remote areas where others had failed: Sir George Young. Francesca sent him an urgent request for help; he responded by sending two of the unit's experienced nurses. Soon, breakfast at the shelter was 'like Sunday School treats followed by a mothers' meeting tea – or very nearly'.[6]

What was urgently needed now was a children's hospital; the infant death rate in the shelters was approaching 50 per cent. 'Numbers and numbers of children were dying, and I saw dreadful things,' Francesca said. 'It was almost the greatest misery I have ever seen in my life.'[7] Again she turned to Sir George Young. He agreed to help if she could find a suitable premises. With help from the town's authorities, she identified a modern villa that would make an ideal hospital, and felt little remorse when its occupants were evicted. 'I did not feel as sorry for the owners who were turned out of it as I might have done,' she wrote in an article in the *Manchester Guardian*, 'because they had another villa to go to, and besides it seemed ludicrous that such a place should be inhabited by a handful of people when it might be housing 30 sick children'.[8]

Frantic preparations followed. 'The week spent in equipping the hospital was feverish but thrilling,' Francesca recounted in character- istically buoyant prose.[9] 'Buying pots, pans, beds, bowls, combs and card-indexes, all in Spanish, was in itself an amusement. The refugees were wonderful. They made all the sheets and mattress-covers, the nightgowns and clothes for convalescents at lightning speed and just for the pleasure of it without any charge.' She mentioned, in passing, that the local chemists had been 'ransacked' for medicine and equipment, and she turned a blind eye when local people arrived with furniture, cutlery and crockery looted from the abandoned houses of the wealthy.[10] Needs must.

When the Hospital Inglés de Niños (English Hospital for Children), as it was called, was ready she got hold of a huge hotel bus and collected sick children from the shelters, 'from their straw and flies,' and brought them to the hospital. 'They came with mothers attached,' she said, explaining that Spanish women were very re- luctant to part with their children. It felt like a maternity hospital at first, but then the typhoid cases began to pour in, 'in all stages of fever, delirium and sickness'. Once they were given proper care and nursing they recovered quickly. 'In a week, the "dying" babies recovered and were restored to rejoicing mothers,' Francesca noted, complimenting the two nurses who had done so much to save lives. 'Nurse Shaw was wonderful and Frida Stewart was a perfect brick,' she wrote.[11] However, Nurse Shaw said the correct ratio for the treatment of typhoid patients was one nurse to three patients; she had thirteen in her care alone.[12] More help was urgently needed.

When Mary Elmes was posted to Murcia in mid-July she arrived to find a hospital beset by difficulties. Sir George and the British Quakers were no longer able to meet the rising cost of running a fifty-bed hospital. It had expanded rapidly because, as Francesca Wilson had pointed out, 'when needs are great, risks have to be taken'.[13] But the money had run out. Francesca, who represented the British Quakers, called on the American Quakers to help.

The American Friends Service Committee had been founded in 1917 to help the civilian victims of the Great War. Its volunteers stayed on in Europe to help rebuild many ravaged communities, and now it was distributing food, aid and medicine to civilians on both sides of the Spanish conflict. The committee agreed to take over and finance all three hospitals set up by Sir George Young. Although his personal resources had been significantly reduced, he continued to work for the victims of war and vigorously campaigned against Britain's policy of non-intervention.

The children's hospital at Murcia had secured financial backing, but there was another pressing issue: growing discord among its staff. When Mary arrived, the hospital's Spanish doctor was on the point of resigning. The friction between the English nurses and the Spanish paediatrician, Dr Amalio, had become so acute that the latter was threatening to leave. He complained that the English nurses were extremely uncooperative. For their part, the nurses were deeply critical of Spanish medical practices, including a complete disregard for the nursing profession. Spanish doctors had no tradition of working with nurses: they usually worked with *practicantes* (medical students) and male orderlies, and relied on injections as a means of administering after-care.

Sir George had noted the clash of medical cultures in one of his reports: 'They do not at present, with rare exceptions, know how to use nurses, and our nurses do not consider injections a satisfactory substitute for nursing – especially combined with a complete carelessness about hospital routine and sanitary regulation.'[14]

The language barrier had made things even worse. One American volunteer, Esther Farquhar, spelt out the reasons for the worsening tension in a letter to the Quakers' head office in Philadelphia:

> I think I shall tell what the doctor said, because he expressed a feeling which has been manifest in the other hospitals also. He said he never felt at home in the English Hospital. They served him tea and said 'thank you – thank you – thank you,' but he never felt that his orders were being observed.[15]

She went on to explain that the English nurses felt they were 'far above' the Spanish doctors in their knowledge of hygiene and were very opposed to the constant use of injections. 'You can easily understand that this attitude on their part has made it very difficult for the Spanish doctors who give their time and service to our hospitals.'

A New Zealand nurse, Dorothy Morris, arrived in Murcia a short time after Mary to take over as the new Quaker-appointed hospital administrator. None of these tensions was new to her. She had worked with Spanish doctors and nurses in the mobile hospitals on the front line with Sir George Young's ambulance unit. 'The Spanish girls are good, although some of the things they do make my blood run cold,' she had said, commenting on their indifference to hygiene. When a doctor suggested that she might try to teach them something of 'real nursing', she remarked: 'However, you can't teach a Spaniard anything.'[16]

Yet that experience on the front line proved invaluable in Murcia. Dorothy and Mary spent the late summer of 1937 working to establish a new routine in the hospital. It is not clear if they were directly involved in the tricky staff negotiations, but after 'a rather difficult session' Dr Amalio agreed to stay, while three of the four nurses involved returned to England. Esther Farquhar told the American Quakers that she was very optimistic about the hospital's future:

> I am happy to say that the new administrator, Dorothy Morris, has worked with the Spanish doctors at the front enough to realise that even though their methods are different, they are good doctors and she thinks the English nurses should adapt themselves to the physician under whom they work. I believe that Mary Elmes also has more of this attitude, and so feel easy about our future relationships.[17]

Mary was not a trained nurse but she was already gaining recognition as an able administrator, calm and capable in a crisis. Her love of Spanish people and culture had brought her to Spain, but once there her organisational skill came to the fore. 'I liked to make people do things,' she explained many years later. 'But I didn't just give orders. I did things myself. I got things done. I had a fixed point of view and I went on with it. I was not emotional but rather clinical, like a doctor, or a soldier, I suppose. Luckily, I became hardened. It allowed me to work constantly.'[18]

Like the thousands who travelled to Spain to fight on both sides of the conflict, relief workers volunteered for many different reasons.

Dorothy Morris was blunt about the nurses who had recently left the Children's Hospital to return to England: they 'had come for fun and adventure and hadn't attempted to see the Spanish point of view and had gone back ill or just dazed after a few months', she said.[19] Francesca Wilson, the British schoolteacher who had established the hospital at Murcia, even admitted that she had come to Spain for adventure. '[My] motives do not sound very sublime, but once on the job other emotions quite often come into play – compassion perhaps, or the desire to help, affection for the people helped, or if it is mainly ambition to do a piece of work properly, there is still some merit.'[20]

Others had qualms that their presence among people in the greatest distress might be intrusive or patronising. In a letter to Mary an American volunteer, Emily Parker, said she would never again go to a refuge just to see what it was like. 'If I can go to help in any way I will go gladly but those whose homes have been shattered have quite enough of misery and bitterness to bear without the additional embarrassment of having people gaze upon you even though it may be with great sympathy.'[21]

Many had deeply held political convictions too, although Sir George and the Quakers made a point of being apolitical and offered help to anybody who needed it. Volunteers were advised not to air their views publicly, or even in letters, which were regularly censored. That did not stop Dorothy Morris, though: she did nothing to water down her deep contempt for Franco in the letters she wrote home. She was vehemently anti-fascist and railed against the political leaders of France and Britain who chose to stand by while fascist rebels tried to oust a democratically elected government.

If, like Dorothy, Mary Elmes expressed her political views in letters home, that correspondence does not survive. The two women became the closest of friends and must have talked privately, at least, about the complex allegiances on both sides of the conflict. Mary would certainly have been well acquainted with the country's political history, which she had studied at Trinity and later at the London School of Economics. She must have had lively discussions with Sir George, who was said to know everything there was to know about Spanish politics. When asked about the Spanish Civil War many years later, Mary simply said she 'disliked Franco of course', but she didn't say what she thought of Ireland's strong pro-Franco stance in the 1930s.

In Ireland, the Spanish Civil War was seen as a religious rather than a political conflict, a war between Christ and anti-Christ. In September 1936 Cardinal Joseph MacRory, primate of all Ireland, said there was no doubt about the issues at stake: 'It is a question of whether Spain will remain as she has been so long, a Christian and Catholic land, or a Bolshevist and anti-God one.'[22]

Mary would have seen reports of a rally in her native city in 1936 when 40,000 people attended a meeting of the pro-Franco Irish Christian Front to protest against 'church burning and priest slaughter', as the organisation's manifesto put it. The *Cork Examiner* published a visually arresting photograph of the demonstration showing thousands of people raising their hands above their heads to make the sign of the cross. Given the public mood, it was not surprising that the number of Irish volunteers who fought on Franco's side outnumbered those on the Republican side by three to one. The 700 or so Irishmen who fought with General Eoin O'Duffy's pro-Franco Irish Brigade returned home after a short, disastrous campaign; in contrast, the 200-strong Connolly Column had more success with the International Brigades, fighting at several battles, including the Ebro, between 1936 and 1938.[23]

Despite the fervently pro-Franco sentiment, the leader of Fianna Fáil, Éamon de Valera, succeeded in staying neutral, and the Spanish Civil War (Non-Intervention) Bill passed through the Dáil in 1937. Those in favour of the bill hoped that staying out of the war would prevent it spreading, but many others – including Dorothy Morris and perhaps her colleague Mary Elmes – believed the Spanish conflict was just the first act in a far greater tragedy.

Carl Geiser, an International Brigade volunteer, was in no doubt about that. He spelt out the danger very clearly in a letter to his brother in Ohio in May 1937:

The reasons I am here is because I want to do my part to prevent a second world war, which would, without doubt, draw in the United States and seriously set back our civilization. And secondly, because all of our democratic and liberty-loving training makes me anxious to fight fascism, and to help the Spanish people drive out the fascist invaders sent in by Hitler & Mussolini . . . In the time I have been here, I have been able to ascertain without doubt, that the fight here is between democracy and fascism, and not between communism & fascism or democracy.[24]

While politics loomed large in the background, relief workers put the welfare of their patients first. The Children's Hospital at Murcia was now running smoothly. In a single year it had treated more than four hundred children, and another five thousand had passed through its examination and milk clinic. Dorothy Morris was pleased to report that she had found it in 'deep waters' but had turned it around within months.[25]

Meanwhile, the American Quakers had established another hospital, and a modern, well-equipped facility opened in Alicante on 1 September 1937. When it came to appointing a new administrator they looked no further than Mary Elmes, the woman who had done so much to restore order at Murcia Children's Hospital. By early January 1938 she had taken up her new position, though she had little time to settle in to the role.[26]

News of her father's unexpected death reached her shortly after the New Year. Edward Elmes died on 27 December 1937 after a brief illness during a Christmas family break in Killarney. The following day the *Cork Examiner* published a notice to say the funeral was strictly private: 'No flowers and no mourning by his wish.'[27] That must have struck Mary Elmes with a cruel irony, because, despite her efforts, she was unable to return to Cork. She had a travel permit and had been assured that her job in Alicante would be held open for her; however, she refused to abandon the hospital unless somebody could be found to replace her. That replacement never materialised.

Four months later Mary's mother, Elisabeth Elmes, travelled to Friends House, the Quakers' head office in London, requesting that Mary come home. Dorothy Thomson of the Quakers' Spain Committee wrote to the American Quakers in Spain to outline Mary's mother's concerns: 'Mrs. Elmes called in here yesterday, and is very anxious for Miss Elmes to come home, as she has been in

Alicante for 15 months.'[28] (In fact Mary had been in Alicante for only a few months, but she had been in Spain for fifteen months.) The letter went on to say that the London office would try to find a replacement, though Mary herself had made it clear that she wanted to return to Alicante after any time off.

In June 1938 Mary and her friend Dorothy Morris finally managed to take that holiday, but Mary didn't succeed in getting as far as Cork. The two friends had leave to go to Paris for a week, and it is likely that both went on to London. Mary's mother may have met her there; if she did, she would have seen that the war was beginning to take its toll.

One of the volunteers noted that Mary Elmes was in need of a break. The nights without sleep, the strain of the daily fight with death, the emotional tension, had 'wiped away the difference of years and made the young older and the old younger', Augustina 'Gusti' Jirku, an ambulance driver working in Spain, had said of the pressures she witnessed.[29]

Earlier in the war, Dorothy Morris had described herself as 'a living corpse', having lost 22 pounds in weight. While conditions at the Children's Hospital in Murcia were easier than those on the front line, her health was suffering. She had a 'bad cold with other complications'.[30] There were constant dangers. Hospitals were seen as legitimate targets, and aid workers regularly described how rebel bombers chased ambulances as if they were hunting animals; it was one of their favourite sports.[31]

More fundamentally, though, food supplies were also diminishing. Emily Parker, an American colleague of Mary's, noted with a certain resignation: 'Whenever I get a small-boned animal [to eat] I always try to believe it is goat or rabbit and not cat, but these are no days to be fussy!'[32]

A typical day's fare for a relief worker consisted of breakfast, at 7:30 or 8 a.m., of porridge and cocoa with milk powder, and lunch, at 2 p.m., of soup with a plate of beans and lettuce. Sometimes there was corned beef, or something 'that looked like a fried potato but was not'. Supper was late, in the Spanish tradition, at about 9 or 9:30 p.m., and was similar to lunch, followed by a dessert of oranges or nuts. On Sundays, as a treat, dried cod and potato were served.[33]

There were times when food was stolen or when supplies were blocked for weeks. Dorothy Davis, a nurse at the Children's Hospital in Murcia, once recalled opening a case of corned beef to find that the top layer was intact but that thieves had substituted bricks for the layers underneath. 'We hope that the pilferer was hungrier than we were!' she remarked.[34] As for delays, after the war the Quaker director of European aid, Howard Kershner, wrote a long account entitled *Odyssey of a Shipment of Flour* to explain how one shipment took three months to go from Le Havre to Valencia via Casablanca. He blamed the hold-up on red tape, diplomatic arrangements, blockades, fighting and business chicanery – people taking advantage of the war to make a fast buck.[35]

Meanwhile, back in Alicante the fascists were gaining ground. Mary's new and well-equipped hospital was under attack. The terrified children hid in the basements as rebel destroyers shelled the town from the sea. It was time to evacuate once again.

Chapter 6 ∿

THE CHILDREN OF WAR

*'When one sees so many cold, ragged, dirty, homeless
orphans one realises that there are many things worse
than death.'*

— Emily Parker

'Have I spoken to you of Palmira?' Mary Elmes wrote in a letter to her friend Rose Duroux many years after the Spanish Civil War. In it, she recalled a 'beautiful little girl of 21 months' who was badly wounded in a bombardment at the market place in Alicante in May 1938.

Her mother was holding her in her arms at the time of this happening. In the confusion which followed, she lost her daughter. The child was very severely wounded in the left leg, of which the foot was only held on by a few strands of flesh. The surgeon who was responsible for her wanted to amputate the foot. Fortunately, the doctor of our little hospital who was a paediatrician, opposed this and brought her to our place where she lay on a plank for three months, at the end of which she was able to get up and eventually to walk normally.

It was a triumph for Doctor Blanc and the English nurses, who should be admired for their devotion and patience. Being so young, she was not able to explain who she was and her family didn't find her for many days – what tears and what joy when finally her father found her![1]

The letter is a rare surviving example of Mary's personal experience during the Spanish Civil War. There are few written accounts of her two years in Spain, but she left behind a detailed photographic record, a carefully captioned album with pictures of the children she cared for in the hospitals and feeding stations in southern Spain. There's a picture of her holding Palmira, the bandage and splint on her left leg still visible. Another shot shows the little girl up and about, sporting a floppy hat, the picture of health.

The photographs are among a series taken by Mary's close friend Emily Parker, an American who worked in Spain with the American Friends Service Committee. Her photographs provide an unrivalled insight into how, despite the war that was raging all around them, an international group of volunteers created sanctuary for the victims of war, particularly the children. It was the memory of those children, and their fate, that remained with Mary Elmes all her life. When, at the age of eighty-eight, she spoke to the author John Baskin, who was interviewing her for a book, the details of other aspects of her volunteer work had receded in her memory, but she still specially recalled the child victims of the Spanish Civil War.

She would tell her own children, Patrick and Caroline Danjou, about little Tato, a toddler who had been found wandering alone on the battlefield. Nobody was sure how he got the name. She thought he might have invented the name himself; or it may have been a corruption of 'Ignacio', or maybe a nickname carved out of the surname 'Tatay'. In any case, he quickly became the 'pet of the hospital' and shortly afterwards 'Mary's orphan', because she hoped to adopt him.

Tato features in several of her album photos: joyful images of woman and child sharing a special bond. In the final days of the war, when the hospital buildings at Murcia and Polop were likely to be reclaimed by their owners, Sir George Young suggested transferring the facilities to his house at Torremolinos. He thought that perhaps Dorothy Morris would be willing to work there – 'as, I expect would Mary Elmes, as it would solve the difficulty of the small orphan refugee she has taken an interest in.'[2] Sir George, a committed humanitarian to the very end, said he would even be prepared to pay the taxes and rates if the Quakers could take over the running of the transferred hospital.

During the war he had rallied some fifty international volunteers who worked, without pay, to bring food and medical aid into the most remote regions. His efforts and those of his aid workers saved many lives. Now all those volunteers were forced to leave Spain as the fascists swept to power. Mary stayed longer than most volunteers but finally left in May 1938, and without 'her orphan', Tato. There was too much red tape; too many insurmountable obstructions. The authorities said she was too young. As her son remembers it, she was told she had to be at least forty years old. She never found out afterwards what became of Tato.

There's a picture of Pepe too, a long-term patient who is sitting up in a bed with a book within reach. Mary and the other nurses brought books, games and toys to the children, but at first they weren't quite sure what to do with them. They weren't familiar with the games, and they didn't know how to play. Mary's friend and colleague Emily Parker, a play specialist, observed an 'apparent lack of play culture'. Yet, she said, the children soon got the hang of it.[3] She later described bringing a brightly coloured ball to a little boy of about two and said it was the first time she ever saw anything like light on his face.[4] That little boy died a short time later, like so many others who were carried out, sometimes two and three a day, in little coffins made from powdered-milk boxes. 'It's the war!' Emily wrote later. 'When one sees so many cold, ragged, dirty, homeless orphans one realises that there are many things worse than death. But . . . I keep saying, What if it were Ann or Freddie or Louis? It seems very different when you do that.'[5]

The photographs in Mary Elmes's album tell a poignant story, one that was fleshed out in words by her colleagues who wrote deeply moving accounts of how war affected its most defenceless victims, children. The American nurse Martha Rupel, for example, mentioned the Pepe of the photograph, explaining that he was a boy of twelve who had been in the Children's Hospital for about a year. In December 1938, he must have been feeling relatively well, because Martha said he had made most of the Christmas decorations that year. 'These articles were made of paper, cardboard, tinfoil and tin cut in various shapes, and a few balloons which added color,' she wrote. 'It really looked lovely when finished.'[6] Pepe had even written, directed and made costumes for a play that was performed by the older girls in the hospital. Before New Year he was busy again, this time making a card to wish Mary a happy new year. It reads: *Miss Mary Elmes, Hospital Inglés, Feliz Año Nuevo* [happy new year], *Pepe*. The tiny card and its handmade envelope are still in the family archive, along with the last photo of Pepe Puelles Varillas. The final caption reads: *Died 11 January 1939.*[7]

Losses of this kind were not uncommon. The American Quaker volunteer Florence Conrad described the typical 'war baby' in a letter written in Murcia on 27 September 1938:

> Some time ago I was at the hospital [in Murcia] for supper with the English nurses. After the meal, they slipped into the babies' room to see a little tyke that they didn't think would last the night. The child was supposed to be suffering from kidney trouble, but was actually an excellent example of a typical 'war baby'. It was about six months old, its head one third of its tiny body. Its arms, I'm not exaggerating, were no bigger around than my forefinger and its loosely covered fingers just hung from the wrists ... Already it had begun to gasp a bit for breath, moving its head back and forth on the pillow as though the very motion would give it more air ... No bomb holes, or refugees, or women's tears and sob stories can move me so much as that struggling little life, so helpless against external diabolical forces.
>
> Just a PS, the baby died.[8]

In a letter dated 27 July 1938, Sylvia Pitt, who worked at the Children's Hospital in Murcia, told the stories of two children as an illustration of the experience of thousands of others in Spain.

> Things are not all beautiful in Spain by a long way. I have just discharged a 12-year-old girl Josefa . . . She was telling me her story the other day. She lived with her family at a town M– [Málaga] in fairly comfortable conditions. Food became short and they were living on the leaves of trees, fried! During one of the bombardments their house was hit, the bomb falling about 2 yds from Josefa and she was slightly hurt. They fled with thousands of others by the only way of escape, a road which ran along the seashore, on the other side of the road are high

mountains. Along this road they were bombarded from the air and also from the sea and Josefa and her family were a few of the lucky ones who were not hit.

They walked for eight days and eight nights without food or drink (except sea water) until they reached the next town 218 miles away! The story of the Black Hole of Calcutta is mild compared with this. Josefa's father somehow was separated from them and is now on the other side and they have no news of him. They eventually came to Murcia and it is little wonder that Josefa got typhoid and got it very badly. For three weeks she completely lost the power of speech though she understood everything. Now she is one of our brightest and most intelligent of children.

Another child, Andres, was not quite so fortunate, as Mary's colleague Sylvia explained:

I have had him for about 8 weeks with whooping cough and т.в. chest and he is now quite beyond all hope of living. His mother told me today that she came from the same town M– [Málaga] and having two small children she was given a lift in a lorry along that ghastly road. They went to another town [Almería] which was frequently bombed and they spent much of their time underground. Andres became deaf with the noise. The seven-months-old baby caught a chill and died and his mother brought Andres to Murcia, but the father is somewhere in the war zone still and we cannot get any telephone message through to him about Andres. All the mother's people are on the other side.[9]

A New Zealand physician, Gladys Montgomery, who worked with Mary at the Children's Hospital in Murcia, explained that malnutrition left children vulnerable to many conditions, including pneumonia, diarrhoea and abscesses.

They were miserably thin, and one of them, the famous Bernardo, we seemed unable to satisfy, for at any hour of the day we would hear him calling, *'Pan, pan, pan'* ('bread, bread, bread'). He had an aching void that we could not fill . . . The Spaniards are very kind to their children, though we found parental affection had its drawbacks. The close of visiting hour reminds one of the sounds emanating from the Wailing Wall in Jerusalem.[10]

———

By June 1938 frequent air raids and naval bombardment forced Mary Elmes and her team to abandon the hospital in Alicante. Some thirty young patients were evacuated from a well-equipped facility to an ill-suited hotel at the seaside village of San Juan. The Hôtel Mediterranean was already being used as a holiday colony for healthy children, so it was overcrowded and uncomfortable. The drinking water was poor, and clothes had to be washed in the sea.[11] But at least the children were out of immediate danger, and it gave Mary and her colleagues an opportunity to find another possible hospital site.

They soon found an ideal building – 'the summer residence of a rich man who has fled to a more suitable spot for rich men' – and moved there on 18 July.[12] The villa-hospital at Balsas de Sentelles, Polop, was in a secluded spot in the mountains, about thirty miles from Alicante. And it was safe. Sylvia Pitt noted in a letter: '[The] children are so enjoying some peace at last. The trouble is now they can't stop singing, they are so relieved to be in safety.'[13]

Two weeks later a British nurse, Dorothy Litten, arrived, in blazing heat, at the airport in Alicante to join the hospital as head nurse. An account she sent to the Quakers in Britain about her early days there opens a tantalising window into life at the hospital in the late summer of 1938. Travelling in wartime was fraught. She had landed first in Barcelona in the midst of a bombardment and 'saw a fountain of dust and stones rising into the air'. Then she made her way to Alicante but still had to clear customs, which took time – and patience. 'It was quite difficult to persuade them not to open a package of X-rays films!' she wrote. There had been a raid that morning and, passing through, she saw a half-sunk ship in the harbour and others burning, which 'reminded us that, in spite of its peaceful appearance from the air, this was a country torn by a terrible war'.

Polop, however, seemed like another world. Mary had succeeded in finding a protected sanctuary as far away from the fighting as was physically possible. Occasionally the sound of bombs was audible in the distance, depending on the direction of the wind, but the hospital might well have gone about its business unaware of the war had it not been for the shortages of food and medicine.

On the way there Dorothy was taken by the beauty of the countryside, with its blossoming oleanders, olives, vines and fig trees, but she also saw that the villages were full of refugees. They had fled the fighting but, in the rush to escape, many families had been separated. Some children were found wandering, alone, and one of them, a little boy, had recently arrived at Polop hospital.

> No one knows who he is . . . This latest little admission, suffering from scurvy, is pathetically anxious for affection. Every time I go near him he holds out his arms and points to some new place where he wants to go. He always seems to be searching for something, and I think he must only recently have lost his family . . . It seems very worth while work to try to build up strong healthy children for it is to them that the work of building the new Spain will fall.

The hospital had twenty-three patients that August, though it had capacity for ten more. Two of them, including Palmira, who had injured her leg, had been wounded in the bombing at Alicante, but most of the others were suffering from malnutrition.

Dorothy Litten had been appointed to take over the nursing and treatment of children and had a staff of six Spanish nurses, all of whom were refugees. They had no training apart from what they had already learned on the job. 'They are kind and willing, but very like children and need much supervision', Dorothy said, though as her Spanish improved she was able to teach them. The only person who spoke English and Spanish fluently was Mary Elmes. 'She has excellent Spanish, having studied it at university', Dorothy wrote. She also noted that Mary, 'the responsible in charge of the hospital', was 'marvellous' at planning meals out of very meagre resources. The hospital was due a shipment of wheat from America, as well as medical supplies, but both had been delayed by months.[14]

Dorothy referred in passing to teaching Spanish nurses, but the Quakers considered the medical training of local staff one way of leaving a post-war legacy of improved medical care. One hospital visitor remarked that the work carried out by volunteers had given the Spanish an entirely new view on treating ill children. 'Before, if they got sick, well, they did what they could but now an ambulance comes and gets the child, it is taken to the hospital where it receives good care and when it comes home again it is well and smiling. And they say we never saw such a thing before . . .'[15]

New medical approaches were also developed to deal with the unprecedented number of civilian casualties. Urban centres were being deliberately targeted, which meant that, for the first time, the numbers of civilian wounded outnumbered those of the combatants. Faced with new medical emergencies, aid workers found new solutions. The methods developed during the Spanish Civil War led to lasting medical advances that would save lives in future conflicts, including the world war that followed so shortly afterwards.

There were advances also in the way blood was collected, stored and administered, and significant progress was made in the way gunshot and shrapnel wounds were treated. The use of plaster of Paris was pioneered by a Spanish surgeon, Josep Trueta, for the treatment of wounds and fractures. When Dorothy Morris saw it first she was shocked by it but later said it was very successful – of the 200,000 injuries treated with the new method, the death rate was less than 1 per cent.[16]

After the war, Dr Trueta went as a refugee to London, where he wrote two medical manuals that formed the basis of advice for civilians and the military when the Second World War broke out. He commented: 'So far as I know, the Germans learnt one lesson only in Spain – how to destroy.'[17]

If Polop was a haven for its patients, it also served as a temporary refuge for other volunteers who faced the daily rigours of working in wartime hospitals. At Christmas a number of nurses from the hospital in Murcia spent a few days in the mountain retreat. One of them, Martha Rupel, recalled:

It has a beautiful location and away from town, so it was a delightful rest to be in the country away from the crowds and where there was peace and quiet. It was very cold, but there was a fireplace before which we could toast our shins and we did plenty of this too. After three days of this mountain air we dreaded to return to Murcia and to the realities of life and to the struggles before us.[18]

At New Year a celebration at Murcia hospital brought the volunteers together. Martha Rupel mentioned a number of nationalities – English, Irish, Swiss, American and New Zealand – that were gathered to ring in 1939. Mary Elmes was very likely to have been among them. The other Irish, or partly Irish, aid worker, Kathleen MacColgan, who had worked for Sir George Young, had probably joined the International Brigades medical team by then.

In Murcia, for that brief moment, the war was again briefly put to one side. Martha Rupel described the scene:

It is a Spanish custom to eat grapes as the clock strikes midnight – one grape at the time of each strike and if you succeed in doing it, you are supposed to have a successful year. I succeeded, but when No. 12 had struck I found my mouth was full of hulls and seeds. I guess we did not have the right kind of grapes. We were listening on the radio to hear Big Ben from London, but when 12 came and we could hear nothing we supposed we had the wrong station and as the Cathedral clock began to strike we all hurriedly ate our grapes, then one bright chap remembers that we were one hour ahead of England as we have daylight-saving time here, so we had to count out more grapes and wait until one o'clock for Big Ben and New Years (God's time). With all that my year ought to be successful.[19]

The year got off to a good start for Mary Elmes. Her dear friend Dorothy Morris was visiting Polop for a three-week holiday in early 1939. In a letter to her parents in New Zealand, Dorothy enthused about the scenery and the clear, sparkling air:

This hospital, a small square white country house, 'a finca', rather Moorish looking, has about 35 children mostly convalescent from their ills and running about in the lovely sun. It is run by my friend Mary Elmes an Irish England girl very calm, collected and capable who came to us in Almeria nearly 2 years ago. She is tall, fair reminds me always of Edna. She is giving me a heavenly restful holiday.

Dorothy went on to describe the scenery in almost poetic detail:

It is beautiful wild scenery . . . Hills sloping down to the blue sea with distant views of capes and headlands. Mostly the lower slopes are intricately and beautifully terraced and planted with oranges and almonds, and with crops below. On the unterraced slopes are the rows and rows of grey and black olive trees which stand out so strongly against the tawny soil. The whole panorama is cut by deep ravines of mountain streams . . . now in the last few days all the bare almond trees over the whole countryside have covered themselves with the most delicate blossom pink and white – just soft clouds of colour against the grey brambles. Over it all hangs the sadness of quiet despair of war – the last of the youngish men have all been called up. Today in a village to which we went for fish, the women were all crying – their men had just left and what were they to do?[20]

The war, never far away, was about to shatter the temporary peace. In late January, Barcelona fell to Franco's fascist forces. In the days and weeks that followed, over half a million Spaniards, civilians and combatants, fled towards France in a mass exodus that became known as *la Retirada* (the Retreat). Once again, the displaced refugees faced attack from the air and machine-gun fire on the road as they fled. Those who remained in Spain were little better off. At the beginning of 1939 the International Commission on Child Spanish Refugees estimated that at least ten million people were starving.[21]

Other volunteers were leaving the country as the civil war entered its final days. However, Mary Elmes and Dorothy Morris stayed on to set up desperately needed feeding stations around the province of Alicante. As Dr Norman Bethune had said of war-zone relief work, it was like trying to drain the ocean with a thimble, but that did not lessen the two women's resolve.

Chapter 7 ∾

FOXHOLES IN THE SAND

*'Thank you very much for getting me back into this work
again. I cannot tell you how glad I am to have the prospect
of doing something for my Spanish friends again.'*
— Mary Elmes

On 29 January 1939 Mary Elmes's colleague Edith Pye dashed off
a note to her friend and fellow Quaker Hilda Clark.

No time to write – a tragedy so immense that one hardly sees
how to tackle it. Margarita has a canteen for milk and bread at the
frontier, but the French are only beginning [to let them enter the
country] today. Refugees have had five nights in the open . . . All
our workers [are] safe. Shall not be here long.[1]

Edith was at Le Perthus on the border between France and Spain,
where, as she put it, a solid block of refugees, of all ages, was
streaming over the border from Spain into France.

Seven-year-old Carmen Canadell, her five-year-old sister
Mercedes and their mother, María, were among them. After the
fascist attack on their home town of Girona they fled, along with
thousands more who made up a human tide surging towards the
border. A lorry brought them as far as the Pyrenees, but now they
were on foot, plodding through the snow-covered passes in search
of sanctuary. The enemy planes that Ernest Hemingway had
described as 'mechanised doom' passed overhead; when the bombs
dropped, María pushed her two daughters to the ground.[2] 'Bite the
branches!' she said. It came out like a staccato order; she was worried

that the deafening sound of the blasts would rupture her children's eardrums.

Yet there were moments of excitement too, fleeting though they were. The girls spotted what they called abandoned treasures on the path and picked up the booty, lost or cast off by weary fellow travellers. One day they saw a beautiful make-up kit and rushed to pick it up. However, after a few miles they too jettisoned it in the snow, as their own small bundles of possessions were becoming too heavy.

Mary Elmes was still working in Spain, but she would later be in a position to facilitate the transfer of the Canadell sisters from the hellish French camps awaiting them on their arrival to a comfortable children's home by the sea. For now, she was continuing to administer food distribution in the province of Alicante for as long as Franco would allow it. Further north, on the Spanish side of the border, her future boss, Howard Kershner, saw what was happening to the Canadell family and hundreds of thousands like them. It was an 'ineffable tragedy', he said. He saw 'the wounded being borne in on stretchers, limping soldiers, bent old people, children with their mothers, women alone and children alone – forlorn and bewildered'.[3]

The Quakers were now trying to cope with humanitarian crises in two countries. They quickly established a base in Perpignan, in the south of France, and set up mobile canteens to offer hot food to the endless stream of refugees coming over the Pyrenees in the bitter cold of winter. During the worst days of the flight they gave out more than 120,000 hot rations on both sides of the border.[4]

As the weeks went by it became increasingly difficult for Mary and her colleagues to keep open the Quaker canteens and hospitals in Spain. There were increasing concerns for their welfare. Howard appealed to the Nationalist authorities to guarantee the safety of relief workers, but he got only oral assurances.[5] Many volunteers had already left, but Mary stayed on for as long as possible, leaving only when Franco's forces shut down all Quaker relief centres.

Mary's son, Patrick Danjou, believes she may have delayed her departure in an attempt to adopt the little boy Tato. That is very likely, although in the years to come it became almost customary for her to stay at her post until the bitter end. It is not surprising, then,

that Mary and her equally resolute colleague Dorothy Morris agreed
to stay in Alicante to organise canteens at a time when many others
were leaving Spain. The urgency of the project and the increasing
uncertainty of a civil war in its final days were both evident in a
letter Dorothy wrote to her parents on 14 February:

> Enormously greater stocks of milk and chocolate are being sent
> in and they want to get it out to the people with the greatest
> possible speed. We feel that we have very little time. God only
> knows what these people won't have to suffer inside a very few
> weeks. I am going up today and am to work with Mary Elmes. A
> new car has just been landed and we will work with that. I'm
> afraid I can't write much. My own immediate plans are vague
> now and the future equally so.[6]

A month later, in March, the Quakers became concerned for
Dorothy's safety. 'It was considered that my life and liberty were in
danger owing to the probable change of regime,' she wrote. She had
cared for soldiers from the defeated International Brigades, and the
Quakers feared she might be arrested by the victorious fascists.
'Imagine – for nursing sick men!' she wrote, outraged. She considered
ignoring the warning, but decided against it. 'I thought I'd take the
risk but the Consuls got into flaps – and anyway I felt it might be
unfair to prejudice the Quakers' work "afterwards" – they hope to
continue relief work until need ceases and of course hope to thereby
protect people a little from the horrors that are coming.'[7]

Mary was thought to be in less danger, because she had cared
exclusively for children. She continued to set up canteens all around
Alicante. By April she had opened canteens in Altea, Villajoyosa and
Benidorm. There were plans to do the same at Cocentaina, Pego
and Jijona.[8] Later she said, with characteristic understatement:
'Our situation was most uncomfortable.'[9] She didn't elaborate,
but about this time nurses at the Murcia hospital reported that
food had become so scarce they were obliged to prise open the
beanbags sent from America as toys and use the beans – which were
still edible – to make stew. The cotton covering was then used to
patch children's clothes.[10]

Two months later it was almost impossible to work under the Nationalist regime. Mary's colleague Ruth Cope reported that all kinds of charges were hurled against the volunteers: 'charges of communism, partiality, incompetence, laxness of morality, political bias of employees and of generally being unfit to exist in liberated Spain'.[11] The authorities took over all the hospitals and, shortly afterwards, closed them all down. Sick children were returned to their parents; if they had no families, they were transferred to centres run by the Spanish welfare agency Auxilio Social.

In May, Howard Kershner went to Spain to evacuate four Quaker volunteers: Ruth and Alfred Cope, Jean Cottle and Mary Elmes. By the time they left, their only permitted role was 'inspection', but of the kind that did not allow for any criticism.[12] They drove over the border into France, bringing with them a record of the work they had done in Spain. Among these papers was a letter from General Franco thanking Mary and her colleagues for their assistance. It is still among the family papers.[13] The Quakers had helped victims on both sides of the conflict, although Mary was working in an area where most of those seeking help were defeated Republican civilians.

When she arrived in Perpignan, Mary was reunited with her friend Dorothy Morris, who, with her Quaker fellow volunteer Dr Audrey Russell, had set up a temporary headquarters at the Hôtel Regina in the town's centre to provide aid for the influx of Spanish refugees. Dr Russell had come over the Pyrenees with those refugees and had seen such horrible things during the flight into France that she no longer had the ability to feel. 'I have become a robot,' she said.[14] While Mary did not personally witness *la Retirada*, she had seen many atrocities. She had been in Madrid during bombing raids and had evacuated children under the threat of fire in Alicante. She had also seen the terrible suffering inflicted on the war's most defenceless victims: children.

Now, for the first time in more than two years, she was free to go home to see her widowed mother and her family in Cork. She stayed for about four weeks but was keen to get back into the field to help 'her' Spanish people', as she called them. She was deeply committed to her work, almost stubbornly so, but she also appears to have been remarkably resilient.

Once again she put herself forward as a volunteer, and in July 1939 she travelled to Paris to be interviewed by the International Committee for Child Refugees. Later that month she wrote to the Spain Committee in Friends House, the Quaker headquarters in London, to say that she had been appointed to join her old friend and colleague Dorothy Morris. They were to start a cultural programme in the refugee camps in the south of France in an attempt to make the lives of the thousands trapped there more bearable.

She was excited about her new role:

> I think that the work will be most interesting and I hope that the years that I spent at college in the study of Spanish literature will prove of something more than the purely personal pleasure that they have been so far and be useful now in the choosing of books for the libraries that it is proposed to start for the men . . . Thank you very much for getting me back into this work again. I cannot tell you how glad I am to have the prospect of doing something for my Spanish friends again.[15]

In the meantime, the people whom Mary so admired had been admitted into France under duress by a government keen to send the revolutionary 'indésirables' back to Spain as quickly as possible. The Spaniards believed at first that they had found sanctuary. When they finally made it to the French border, their faces lit up with 'indescribable relief'. Howard Kershner was particularly struck by this. 'The oldest and the weariest . . . threw down their bundles and dropped beside them. Men shouted for joy. Women laughed and cried and hugged one another in ecstasy. Some danced and sang. Others gave thanks to God.' He knew, however, that their elation was misplaced. 'Not yet had even the serious-minded begun to contemplate the difficulties and responsibilities of life in an alien country. The happiness was short-lived.'[16]

The humiliation began at the border itself. Gustav Regler, a German communist commissar who had fought with the International Brigades, reported that Republican soldiers were received as though they were tramps.

The Spaniards were asked what was in the haversacks and ditty-bags they carried, and they answered that in surrendering their rifles they had given up all the arms they possessed. But the French tapped disdainfully on the haversacks and demanded that they should be opened. The Spaniards did not understand. Until the last moment they persisted in the tragic error of believing in international solidarity . . . I have never seen eyes of such anger and helplessness as those of the Spaniards. They stood as though turned to stone, and they did not understand.[17]

The writer and campaigner Nancy Cunard also made a chilling reference to the white-slave traders who spotted an opportunity. The traffickers had come from Marseille, she reported, and had set their 'business-eye' on the many young and pretty women in the Spanish migration.[18]

In three short weeks the population of the Pyrénées-Orientales had doubled. There were schemes for vaccinating the refugees against typhoid, diphtheria and smallpox, as France feared a pandemic, but it was impossible – and expensive – to treat everyone. One contemporary estimate said the crisis was costing the French government £40,000 a day (about £2.2m in 2017).[19] The French authorities were simply overwhelmed. Lieutenant Albert Belloc captured the atmosphere well in a few sentences scribbled on a postcard to his parents from the beach at Argelès, outside Perpignan: 'Drowning, flooded, submerged by Spaniards. It is an absolute torrent, a tidal wave. Since Monday last, I haven't slept and have barely eaten. No time.'[20]

María Canadell and her two daughters finally made it into France. They were moved from town to town and later from camp to camp. María's husband, José, did not cross the border until later, but many of the families who arrived together were being divided and sent to separate destinations. Some 150,000 men were herded into camps along the coast on the beaches at Argelès-sur-Mer, Saint-Cyprien and Barcarès. In fact in the earlier days they weren't even camps, merely stretches of sand along the Mediterranean into which thousands of men were corralled behind barbed wire.

'The men stood about with only the clothes on their backs,' Howard Kershner wrote.[21] There was no shelter, no sanitation, and very little food.

When Mary's colleague Francesca Wilson first saw the improvised camp at the windy stretch of beach at Argelès-sur-Mer outside Perpignan, she was horrified:

It is impossible to imagine what eighty thousand men herded together behind barbed wire looked like if one hasn't seen it. I wanted to cover my eyes – it was a sight so wounding to human dignity. Men penned into cages like wild animals; exposed to the stare of the passer-by, like cattle in the market place.[22]

The men burrowed into the sand, digging foxholes for shelter. If they had luggage they made barricades against the wind or used bits of blankets, rags and corrugated iron to build makeshift tents. Before she arrived to help them Mary would read a Quaker report that described how, in those first days, a bitterly cold wind swept down from the mountains, producing a raging sandstorm. 'The refugees scoop hollows in the sand for protection against the wind, but if they go more than a few metres down it is wet. A number of women who refuse to leave their husbands are living in the camp, and there are at least 89 children, nearly all of whom are suffering from conjunctivitis from the sand.' By the time Mary arrived to work at Argelès, conditions had improved significantly.[23]

Meanwhile, some 300,000 women, children and old men were herded onto trains and divided among the various French regions. Local officials rushed to find anything that might provide shelter: 'sheds behind stores, old barracks, cellars, any available place that would cover the heads of these desperate, uninvited guests,' wrote Howard Kershner, who had counted some two thousand camps at sites all over France.[24]

Mary had seen Spanish people flee under fire on the road from Málaga. She had seen them living in doorways and under bridges in Almería; she had evacuated children from a hospital in Alicante; and now those same people were facing new degradations in an unwelcoming country. They had not committed any crime on French soil, but they were virtually prisoners. They were patrolled by the horse-mounted Algerian Spahis, a bitter reminder to the defeated Republicans of the Moors who had fought so brutally with Franco's troops. One Quaker volunteer wrote:

> The Algerians, who ride nervous Arab horses with their swords drawn, are a terrifying spectacle. The constant wild neighing of their horses adds to the sense of tension, and one of our workers told of several cases in which robbery at their sword's point had been seen by them.[25]

Despite the conditions, the Spaniards soon began to organise themselves in an attempt to boost morale. They had endured horrors on the road to France and further loss of life in the camps from disease, malnutrition and exposure. Now they were held as prisoners, but in body only. In no time at all, to quote one visitor, 'their spirits and minds soar out beyond the borders of the camps'.[26]

For instance, at Argelès – the 'city of 80,000 tent-burrows', as Francesca Wilson called it – a choir had been started. A sports group followed, then workshops, followed by adult classes.

But to run classes you need books; for workshops you need materials; for music you need instruments. The needs of the refugees had already defined the parameters of Mary Elmes's new role. She took to her new duties with an enthusiasm and energy that soon won her widespread recognition and respect among the refugees, who would give her the nickname *Miss Mary*.

Chapter 8 ∾

UNQUENCHABLE SPIRIT

*'Spirit and enthusiasm are the most important things in
life, and these the Spaniards will have for ever.'*
— Mary Elmes and Dorothy Morris

T he Catalan poet Agustí Bartra had not expected to spend so
much time behind the barbed wire at the Agde refugee camp,
but now that he had no other choice he decided to put his time
to good use and study English. He asked about the possibility of getting
hold of a book or a dictionary, and somebody suggested writing to the
Quaker office in Perpignan, 75 miles away. 'I did so, and some days
later received a package,' he explained a few years afterwards.

It contained a Spanish-English dictionary, used, on whose first
page was the signature and address of the person who sent it,
Marie Elmes, TCD Dublin. I will never forget it. Marie Elmes did
not send me a dictionary; she did infinitely more; she sent me *her
own*. This dictionary which has travelled with me during all my
exile, is for me a luminous example of love. I wish she might
know that the Catalan poet to whom she sent *her* dictionary still
keeps it in his work.[1]

That spontaneous act of kindness was one of the first things Mary
did when she returned to France to take up her post in Perpignan in
the summer of 1939. But it was a 'flea-bite in view of the colossal
problem of the Spanish refugees here', as Mary's colleague Dorothy
Morris colourfully put it.

The two women quickly went about organising the distribution
of books to people in the camps on a much larger and more co-

ordinated scale. 'They long for books,' Dorothy said of their joint project. 'Their physical condition is now fairly good – but it is a wretched life, and they are too fine to be left to rot, and their minds must, we feel, be occupied.'[2] Mary made regular trips to Paris, searching the city for Spanish-language books. As a seventeen-year-old she had remarked on the quaint second-hand book stalls with boxes clamped to the quay wall along the River Seine. She passed by those old haunts again but this time concentrated her search on the many long-established bookshops on the Left Bank, where she bought up all the books in Spanish she could find.

Back in Perpignan, her days were spent 'madly typing' on a portable typewriter in a room at the Hôtel Regina, which was still acting as Quaker headquarters.[3] Mary and Dorothy were both employed by the International Commission, a Quaker-initiated organisation formed to lobby governments for relief funds. Friends House in London had provided a secretary, Ruth Cope, and they hired Victor Samarini locally to drive the Quakers' three-ton Bedford truck and blue Ford.[4] Mary, however, was still obliged to write most of the correspondence, as she was the only one who spoke and wrote perfect French and Spanish. And it seems they had only one typewriter; one of Dorothy's personal letters, written in those early hectic days, explains that she had to 'stop this inaccurate rattling', as the secretary needed the typewriter.

The small Quaker office joined with the National Joint Committee for Spanish Relief in an attempt to tackle the enormous challenge facing them. Together they helped several thousand people emigrate to South America or return to Spain, although Nationalist reprisals meant that this was still a very dangerous option. There were constant letters to and from the camps: requests for help in finding missing husbands, wives, children; requests for medical assistance, food, clothing and books. Mary and Dorothy's scheme for addressing the latter was particularly welcome. Schools and classes had begun to spring up in many of the camps; they were 'sketchy and rudimentary . . . but animated by the most wonderful spirit'.[5]

The tent villages were no longer transient holding-places. The camps were now divided into row upon hastily constructed row of wooden or concrete barracks. Inside each basic shell, the inhabitants tried to make them more comfortable; woollen blankets were turned into dividing walls, and furniture was fashioned out of bed frames. Communities developed within the barbed-wire settlements; there were improvised markets, a barber's corner, a wine stall and make-shift sports fields. Some camps even published their own newspapers, while others tried to re-create a home from home. At Barcarès, the 'residents' christened the alley between the rows of shacks 'Las Ramblas', after the famous street in Barcelona. It became a place of reunions and meetings, 'a hotbed of discussion, opinion and tall stories'.[6]

The social structures of civil society soon began to re-impose themselves, as Mary's colleague Alice Resch noted with astonishment: 'To my amazement I saw that the same class divisions one could find on the outside had sprung up inside the camp, and those who were better off paid the poor to be their maids, housecleaners, and hairdressers.'[7]

The camps' professional population – doctors, lawyers, artists – also began to use the skill they had acquired in a previous life to make the present one more bearable. They set up rudimentary medical centres, proto-libraries, workshops. At the Argelès camp a Spanish schoolteacher, Francisco Pons, enlisted Mary's help in lobbying for a camp library for men and a school for children. In his memoirs he recalled that Mary, with the Quakers' backing, had the moral authority and the necessary means to convince the camp directors to support the project.[8] She began by carrying out a survey of the camp's needs to help her in negotiating the necessary resources. Then, on her recommendation, one of the camp barracks was converted into a school that could cater for up to a hundred teenagers (fourteen- to seventeen-year-olds). Four or five others were set aside for younger children, and another was to be used as a nursery for three- to five-year-olds. With funds from the commission, Mary provided all the necessary equipment: tables, benches, stools, books, copybooks, pencils and pens – enough for six hundred children. The camp authorities were happy to back the project, as it reflected well on them.[9]

A library was also established, stocked with the books Mary and Dorothy had bought in Paris. It would eventually hold more than three thousand volumes, an eclectic range of titles in Spanish, French and English. Francisco Pons became the camp librarian, and he recalled how Mary Elmes would often drive into the camp at the wheel of a car loaded up with books and musical instruments. She was a woman of boundless energy and fierce determination, he said.

When the hard slog to get the libraries open was finally complete, Mary asked Francisco if he would like to spend a day in Perpignan. She had succeeded in getting him a special day-pass, but he turned down her offer with a vehemence that surprised her. He explained later:

> She was really taken aback when, having thanked her for the thought, I refused outright to go. I had to explain myself because she insisted the Quakers would cover any costs and that she would take care of the necessary authorisation. I was certainly aware of the good a day at liberty might do me after so many months of being held at the camp . . . but this day of complete and legal liberty, what would I get from it? What would I feel when, once again, I would find myself behind the barbed wire . . . ? The day I left the camp would be the day when I'd never have to return . . . She understood. Or she said she understood, though she couldn't hide her astonishment during our entire conversation. And we never spoke of it again.[10]

When Francisco was finally released from the camps he wrote to Mary to tell her he was free at last, and had a job that allowed him to lead a normal life. 'Miss Mary wrote a very warm letter in response and she said she hoped the future would be better for me.'[11]

Mary also worked to set up schools in the other camps. She organised toys, picture books and paper and pencils for the children to draw with. 'In the beginning, the drawings were tragically revealing of recent experiences, scenes with falling bombs, wrecked houses and dead bodies in the road,' Howard Kershner wrote. 'Later when their bones were better covered with flesh and the events of the pilgrimage to safety a little further in the past, the children's creative imagination turned to happier things. They drew birds and flowers and stretches of fields.'[12]

Soon there were small circulating mobile libraries between the camps. Language lessons got under way. When a refugee wrote from the camp at Bram requesting French lessons, Mary organised the distribution of French grammar books. By August, Dorothy Morris said she was delighted with their progress. Their contribution, she said, was 'one-in-the-eye' for Franco, who had wanted all the 'intellectuals' of Spain to perish in despair.[13] Mary, however, was more interested in encouraging those with few qualifications, or none. In a letter to Margaret Frawley, the International Commission representative in Paris, she said the intellectuals had attracted all the attention, but it would be wrong to forget the 'humbler' people.

I should like to emphasise, perhaps a little more than I did the other morning, that my chief [interest] so far has not been solely in intellectuals. I feel that the Commission can do a great deal more by concentrating rather on groups of men whose cultural opportunities have never been very great, or perhaps even nil, rather than on a very much smaller number of intellectuals . . . The most interesting part of the struggle in Spain was that it was directly identified with the raising of the level of culture for those who were not able to attend universities and have professions, and it seems worthwhile to try to carry on the tradition.[14]

The Quakers also ran a health scheme and found ways of using calcium and fruit juice to boost the nutritional content of the food given to the camp populations. While the French doctors denied the need for such measures, Spanish doctors interned in the camps welcomed them.[15] There were a large number of health workers – doctors, nurses, dentists – among the Spanish refugees, and they were already using their skills to provide care, in difficult circumstances, to the Spanish sick and wounded.[16]

Some of the camp doctors even performed clinical trials. But, Dr Àlvar Martínez-Vidal and Dr Xavier García-Ferrandis explained, 'unlike the atrocities committed by Nazi doctors in the death camps of the Third Reich, they carried out experiments on humans in order to maximise their clinical skills and scant resources for the benefit of their patients.' For example, Dr Joaquim Vinyes Espín, a young Catalan doctor at the Saint-Cyprien camp, asked a pharmaceutical company for free vitamin samples and used them in an experimental way to try to offset the effects of malnourishment. He demonstrated that the symptoms of poor nutrition, such as shin pain, acute adrenal failure and inflammation, improved or disappeared with the administration of a daily dose of vitamin C.[17]

Perhaps that experiment was the inspiration behind Mary's decision a few years later to commission laboratory tests to analyse the vitamin content of grape juice. When tests revealed that the juice was high in vitamins B_2, B_1 and C, the Quakers tried to find a way of giving it in suitable doses to children most in need. They were forced to abandon the scheme, however, as it was too difficult to administer, but it was one of many designed to increase the calorific intake of malnourished children.[18]

Back in the wretched netherworld of the camps, another Spaniard was putting his time in exile to good use: the world's most famous cellist, Pablo Casals. He had vowed never to return to Spain while Franco was in power; in any case, General Queipo de Llano, who had instilled terror in the Spanish population with his radio broadcasts, had threatened to cut off both his arms if he did. Instead the famous musician settled in Prades, west of Perpignan, to be near the people from his own beloved Catalonia. When he saw the conditions in the camps he compared them to scenes from Dante's *Inferno* and concluded that he had only one duty: to organise aid for refugees.[19]

It wasn't long before his path would cross that of Mary Elmes. They would become colleagues and friends, working together over the next six years to address the increasingly complex needs of a people who would soon find themselves in the middle of a world war. Casals organised a number of benefit concerts and donated the proceeds to the camps. Like Mary, he admired the Spanish spirit and, to illustrate it, often told the story of the bravery shown while he was rehearsing at the Liceu opera house in Barcelona when bombs began to fall nearby.

The whole building shook, and the musicians scattered in the hall – as was not unnatural. I picked up a cello on the stage and began to play a Bach suite. The musicians returned to their places, and we continued the rehearsal . . . The miracle was the spirit of the Spanish people. Not only the heroism of the soldiers who were fighting against immense odds but the heroism of ordinary men and women in every block of the city. With what courage and dignity they went about their work! It was an epic . . .[20]

Mary and Pablo often worked together in the camps, distributing food, clothes and medical supplies. 'I visited the camps as often as I could,' Casals said.[21]

Each time I dreaded going, because of the suffering I would see, afterwards I could not sleep at night. But I knew how the inmates longed to see and talk with a fellow countryman from the outside. I started corresponding with many of the refugees . . . I would spend hours each day writing letters and cards, seeking somehow to relieve their suffering by sending them funds and giving them words of encouragement.

He also wrote frequently to Mary; they are the warm letters of an admiring friend. He wrote to thank her for the bedclothes she sent to the wife of a pianist; for the trousers she secured for a Spanish refugee; for the update on camp residents. When his Christmas telegram came back to him undelivered in 1941 he sat down to write a letter straight away so that Mary would know of his gratitude and his good wishes for the coming year. 'How much we owe you!' he wrote in another letter. Whenever he was in Perpignan he made a point of calling to see her. 'Eureka!' he exclaimed in a letter from 1943. 'What a pleasure to see you again – I'm going to Perpignan again in September. I'm giving you notice.' It included a signed photograph, with the inscription: *To Mary Elmes, with my profound appreciation.*[22]

Other Spanish musicians and artists also strived to continue their work in France. A group of painters, actors and sculptors from the camp at Argelès were given permission to move temporarily into the nearby Mas de l'Abat, a farmhouse in the grounds of Valmy Castle. From there they organised exhibitions of their own paintings, drawings and sculptures and ran theatre performances. On 2 September 1939, the day before Britain and France declared war on Germany following the invasion of Poland, Mary and Dorothy Morris took the time to visit the exhibition. On their way out they both signed the visitors' book under a message that read: *Spirit and enthusiasm are the most important things in life, and these the Spaniards will have for ever.*[23]

Meanwhile, at the Quaker headquarters in Paris, the looming threat of war had dampened the relief workers' enthusiasm. The office had been 'stunned into inactivity', Howard Kershner remarked in the days before the war broke out.

> We do not know what part, if any, of our work can be carried on in the event of War . . . In the face of colossal events, the human mind refuses to interest itself in routine or small matters. There is a feeling of why answer this letter, or why do that small thing, when impending events are so momentous as to make it appear trifling, if not altogether useless.[24]

He worried that the Quaker relief operation might be forced to suspend its operations in the event of a new conflict, but he was also infuriated by the 'silly business of war' that he had witnessed so recently in Spain.

> Hitler sent his engines of death and destruction [to Spain] in order to thwart Russia. Seventy five years from now, old men and women who have gone through life blinded and maimed as a result of the ravages of Hitler's planes, will still be alive. I have seen blinded little children being led about; I have seen them come for shoes and require only one, and I have seen them wearing only one mitten.[25]

In Perpignan, Mary and Dorothy went about their duties but with a great deal of uncertainty. They knew that the outbreak of war would have far-reaching implications for their work but hoped to be able to continue. At home in Cork, Mary's mother must have worried for her daughter, who had just returned safely from a civil war but now found herself in the middle of a world war. Mary's friend Dorothy Morris, however, tackled the subject with levity. 'It seems I have now to apologise for getting into another war,' she wrote. 'Wot a world it is to be sure . . . however I have been showering you with melancholy croakings for so long, that you won't have been too surprised by it.'[26]

A month later Dorothy wrote home again to say that she and Mary were allowed – 'by the grace of god, & myriad Permissions' – to continue their work, at least in the short term. They had a monthly allocation of £10,000 (about £600,000 in 2017) and lots of ideas. In early October, Mary went back to Paris to buy more Spanish books for the libraries and schools, which were still expanding. She 'almost cleaned up the entire town', she said, but still didn't get enough to match demand in the camps. 'By the way,' she told Margaret Frawley, 'one author, the translations of whose works into Spanish are greatly valued and are now impossible to get here in France, is Shakespeare. I can obtain translations of all the great Latin, French and Greek classical authors, but the edition of Shakespeare is now exhausted.'[27] The following month, she reported to Friends House in London that the camp schools were also doing well and that the number of students was growing.[28]

Mary and Dorothy's colleague Dr Audrey Russell had returned to London, but she wrote a letter to Dorothy saying she hoped they would be allowed to continue their work.

> There isn't the least doubt in my mind that you and Mary and Francesca will remain calmly organising culture while hell breaks loose all round and I pray to highest heaven that the authorities will let you stay . . . I feel unless you are there nobody will ever know what becomes of the Spanish.[29]

They weren't planning on going anywhere. If the outbreak of war prompted other foreigners to cut short their stay in France, Mary and Dorothy did the opposite: they settled in for the long haul. In November they moved out of the Hôtel Regina and rented a modern apartment in the wide and leafy Avenue des Baléares, an area that had been redeveloped for new housing. 'Our new flat is very satisfactory and we have a larger office – we were simply bursting out of the other one,' Mary wrote in a letter to Emily Hughes in London. 'The new arrangement has many advantages, not the least of which is a very much longer rental.'[30]

The flat became something of a talking-point among Quaker delegates. When they passed through Perpignan on business they were treated to lunch on the apartment's sunny first-floor balcony. The food was prepared by Thérèse, a 'treasure', as Dorothy explained in a letter home. 'Therese our maid is a pleasant and obliging creature – and most important, a true jewel of a cook . . . in both French and Spanish . . . which is most satisfactory of course. I feel that I must soon put on many kilos, to judge by the daily appetites.'[31] The apartment's modern and spacious bathroom also made an impression. One of the many lunch guests, Lois Gunden, even mentioned it in a letter to her mother, saying it made her feel as if she was back in America.[32] But most of all, number 30 Avenue des Baléares provided sanctuary from the relentless demands of the job.

The two women made an extremely effective and courageous team, and they were also the closest possible friends. Dorothy Morris's biographer Mark Derby imagines them sitting on their flower-filled balcony at the end of a long and probably exhausting day in the internment camps, planning what they would do the following day to save as many lives as possible among the hundreds of thousands of desperate Spanish Republican refugees.

> I like to think of them there, in the warm, fragrant Mediterranean evenings, talking about saving the world, not in the vague, idealistic, theoretical way most people do. I imagine they talked about saving the world in a totally pragmatic, costed and realistic way – 'How are we going to save the world tomorrow?'[33]

This pragmatism permeates Mary's correspondence. Thousands of her level-headed and down-to-earth letters were archived by her employers, the American Friends Service Committee, and they give an exceptional insight into a woman who was a tireless advocate for refugees, of all nationalities. She got her point across with quiet insistence, but if needed she could be uncompromising and forthright.

There was one fierce exchange of letters with a colleague when she was attempting to speed up the delivery of a long-overdue prosthetic hand for a Spanish man. She demanded that his case be addressed immediately and suggested that the delay was due to negligence. The recipient, Alan Haigh, who oversaw the prosthetic workshop at Montauban, was so taken aback by the correspondence that he switched from French to English to make sure there had been no misunderstanding. 'I am not the kind of person who is easily riled,' he wrote, 'but quite honestly I felt distinctly annoyed at the attitude you take up in your letter.'[34] He offered an explanation for the delay, denied the charge of negligence, and promised to pursue the case to see what could be done. If there was a response to that from Mary, it was not preserved in the files.

In her personal letters she was warm, open and self-effacing. After a hectic spell during the winter of 1939 and into the spring of 1940 Mary began a long-overdue letter to her friend Emily Parker at the Quakers' headquarters in Philadelphia with a contrite apology: 'Dear Emily, You will never know how abject I feel in starting to write you this long delayed letter or how the thought of you in America sending us messages of friendship and remembrance, which we have left unanswered, has haunted me again and again.' She begs her friend's forgiveness for failing to answer her letters, a telegram at Christmas and a St Patrick's Day card, which had just arrived. But then she was sure that her friend would understand. 'You know so well the storms and stresses of this kind of life we led in Spain that you will be able to imagine the new variants we have to deal with here in France and will therefore understand and forgive our inability to write letters with ease and still less with frequency.'[35]

Mary gave her an overview of her work so far and seemed to have been quite pleased with the progress she and her colleagues had made in the first year of their work in Perpignan.

This has been a year of many ups and downs and difficulties and misunderstandings, but on the whole it has been most interesting. I think that in spite of everything something useful has been done to keep alive and foster the spirit of Spanish culture. It is impossible to point to any one permanent institution that has been founded – indeed no sooner has a school or library been opened and their creaking wheels got to run more or less smoothly than superior orders have caused the camp in which they functioned to be moved, disbanded or enlarged and the work of weeks has disappeared overnight and everything has had to be reorganised and restarted. I suppose it teaches one to be adaptable to have to work in this fashion, but it is often discouraging. One feels as if one lived in a travelling show company which pitches its tents afresh every night and leaves the ruins of its passage behind every morning.

However, she thought that the Spanish refugees were entering a slightly better phase. Many of the men had been drafted into work companies or employed privately, which meant their wives could join them. The commanders of the work groups were very open to the Quakers' cultural work and did what they could to facilitate it. By April 1940 some two thousand children were getting some sort of education at Argelès. They

have at least learned something and have been kept for most of every day from aimless wandering . . . on the cold and windy waste which houses them. It has been a headache for me all the time and I am not even one quarter satisfied with it, but I have not been able to do any better with the best will in the world.

Mary apologised again for being 'the worst correspondent in the world!' and said she was turning over a new leaf. However, another refugee crisis was about to unfold that would leave little or no time for personal letters.

Chapter 9 ᴖ

INTO ACTION

'Dispensing charity in France today means exercising the power of life or death over one's fellows. How does one do it and retain his sanity?'
— Howard Kershner, head of the Quakers in France

On 18 June 1940, Mary Elmes drove right through the night to get her friend Dorothy Morris from Perpignan to Bordeaux in time to board the *Madura,* the last ship out of a country still reeling from a swift and resounding defeat. The journey across France was a hazardous race against the clock. For most of it Mary drove without headlights, as there was a possibility of German bombers overhead.

During the eight months of the so-called 'phoney war', from September 1939 to May 1940, there had been tension but little fighting on the Western front. That all changed on 10 May when the German army swept through the Netherlands, Belgium and northern France. On 14 June, German troops entered Paris. Eight days later France surrendered. The country had fallen in just six weeks.

It was an inconceivable rout and one that gave rise to another mass movement of refugees, but this time on an unimaginable scale. Some half a million Spanish refugees had poured into France after the defeat of the Republicans in the Spanish Civil War, but now an estimated eight million would leave their homes to flee south, or west, uncertain of their final destination.

After a fraught drive, Mary and Dorothy arrived in Bordeaux to find utter chaos. The roads were choked with cars, lorries and carts, all loaded with people and their hastily packed personal belongings. The *Madura,* a British India ship, had altered course to pick up as many British citizens as possible. It was likely to be the last British vessel to leave France, and there was a mad scramble to get on board. Their Quaker colleague Edith Pye joined them in the city, but they still had to make their way to the port, Le Verdon, 60 miles further up the coast. That road too was jammed, and progress was slow. After a nerve-fraying trip they arrived in time.

The port was full of people, cars and noise; overhead there was 'the scream of a dive-bomber, the ack-ack of machine gun fire and thunderous crashing out at sea', as one fleeing British girl, eight-year-old Daphne Wall, would later describe it.[1] Like many others, she and her family had driven south and witnessed the great exodus: cars, bicycles, carts, women pushing prams, people on foot – millions beating a path of retreat. From the back seat of the car Daphne described

> an extraordinary, never-ending procession of men, women and children with bundles on their backs, weighed down with suitcases, carrying babies and toddlers. Most were walking, some riding bicycles, many pushing or pulling carts, piled high with mattresses and a jumble of chairs, buckets and saucepans. Everybody seemed to be going one way, the way we too were travelling, south.[2]

However, the refugees' diaries would later fill with accounts of being redirected, or forced to circle back the way they had come. Nobody knew where they were going: they were simply following the person ahead.[3] In the mêlée many families were separated. The film critic and writer Georges Sadoul was struck by the appearance of chalked signs directing lost family members. He saw one that read: *Edmond, keep going, we are waiting for you in Rouen.*[4]

Those who made it as far as Bordeaux were the lucky ones, although it might not have seemed like that to the Quaker friends in the early morning half-light. Dorothy had to abandon her friend and colleague at the shortest possible notice. Edith Pye, whom both women had known in Spain, had helped to move the Quaker office from Paris to Bordeaux days before. She had hoped to continue to work in the south, but this was no longer possible. It must have been an emotional parting as two committed workers left behind their friend, a neutral Irish citizen, to face a deteriorating situation.

They said their farewells and boarded the ship's launch. It was going back and forth as fast as it could, trying to shuttle two thousand passengers onto a ship built to carry five hundred. Every square inch of the deck was covered, full of the great and the good – Belgian and French politicians, diplomats, journalists – and the rich and famous; the French banker Baron Guy de Rothschild was among them.[5] As the ship was leaving, the leader of the French government in exile, General Charles de Gaulle, made a famous broadcast from the BBC in London, calling on the French to begin resistance against the Germans.

The *Madura* took a circuitous 36-hour route to Falmouth in Cornwall to avoid submarines. The passage was terribly crowded, 'like Blackpool on a bank holiday', Edith Pye reported later, although that had its advantages:

> One night four of us together, taking our shift at sleeping on the deck, were lying very close to keep warm. A ship's officer came out of his cubby-hole and said he thought he could find us another blanket. He brought it out, tucked it very carefully around us, surveyed his work and remarked, 'Now I am the proud father of quads.'[6]

Mary wasted no time getting back on the road to Perpignan, but this time alone. She must have felt Dorothy's departure acutely, as the women had lived and worked together so closely in the intense first months of the war. The separation was made all the more difficult as it would be several weeks before letters were allowed into unoccupied France. Edith wrote a letter to Mary in August but it didn't reach her until the end of October. In it she wrote: 'I want to send you assurance of my constant thoughts and affections. We long to hear such news as it is possible to send as we have felt very cut off the last weeks.'[7]

In the intervening months, Mary had taken over Dorothy's duties as head of the Quaker delegation at Perpignan and faced an onerous task. Her new area of responsibility covered the departments of

Pyrénées-Orientales, Aude and Hérault, a significant area stretching from Perpignan to Carcassonne and Montpellier, further north.

Following the German invasion, the south of France also had to cope with millions of fleeing refugees and attempt to administer aid under the new collaborationist Vichy regime. The Franco-German Armistice of 22 June divided the country in two: Paris and the northern region were in the German-controlled Occupied Zone, while the Unoccupied Zone in the south was run from Vichy under the First World War hero of Verdun, Marshal Philippe Pétain.

Back in Perpignan, Mary's colleagues were delighted to have her back. 'It is a great joy to learn that you [have] returned...' her Danish colleague Helga Holbek wrote from the Quaker office in Toulouse.[8] She asked Mary to outline what she needed to continue her work and told her that she had already been allocated a budget of 250,000 francs (€110,000 in 2017) to help people in the camps.

Mary wrote back to say that she needed a truck, milk, dried foods – and finance. 'I also want money – don't think this statement too blunt – all you can spare and then some! I don't know your possibilities ... so shall not ask for a definite figure.'[9] However, she said she was very pleased with the way the new office was taking shape in Perpignan. Her Catalan driver, Victor Samarini, was still working with her, along with two 'faithful and competent' secretaries. There was also the 'indefatigable' Mme Lliboutry, who, as a native of Perpignan, had very useful contacts. 'Mme. Lliboutry, the French woman who helped Dorothy, is invaluable and my Spanish helpers who have been with us for a long time are loyal and helpful to an unlimited extent – even to giving up their Sunday (unasked) to sorting all the grand clothes you sent,' she wrote.[10] Over the coming months she would mention her staff often. When things became increasingly hectic the following month she wrote: 'I can absolutely depend on these people and as they have been here so long it is easy to direct them as they are so well acquainted with our methods and work in general.'[11]

The new regime brought with it many challenges, as Helga spelt out in a letter to Mary from Toulouse:

We find that all the authorities have an invariable penchant towards storing things, even when the [Belgian] youngsters are half starved ... I may add here for your personal information that there is the wildest distrust and rivalry between all the departments, each of whom claims the honour for all that has been done, accusing all others of all that has gone wrong.[12]

When Mary tried to organise aid to the Belgian camps she found 'inefficiency everywhere' and the recriminations and distrust that Helga had described.

> The Red Cross seems to be the only body that realises the urgency of the situation and is trying to do something about it ... The inevitable result ... of the situation is that the boys are escaping from the camps in large numbers (particularly from Agde) and starting off on foot to return to Belgium ... They are to be seen everywhere on the roads with their miserable baggage on their backs.[13]

The letters back and forth spoke of everything from the humdrum – 'The Belgians do not care for [lentils], but can consume potatoes without limit!' – to the harrowing experiences of the new refugees of war.[14]

Twelve-year-old Joseph Charlier wrote to thank the Quakers for the clothes they had given him and his younger siblings, aged eleven, nine and three, after they fled their home:

> We arrived broken by terror and tiredness because the German planes followed us and bombarded us without pity. We all crouched down on the ground but when we were able to get up to walk again, we had to abandon our poor father who had been killed by a bomb. We had to leave him on the ground, all alone. All mother could do was cry; she was so afraid of losing all of us. She carried my youngest sister, aged three, in her arms.
>
> When we are grown up, we will not forget what America and France did for us when we were so unhappy and had nothing.[15]

A new crisis struck in October when a flood devastated the region, claiming the lives of three hundred people. In the camps the floodwaters reached the roof of some of the barracks, and several women drowned when a truck attempting to rescue them was swept away.[16] At Argelès, the Spanish refugees worked for four days and nights to save the stocks of food. 'There are many unsung heroes in France today whose brave deeds will never be known,' Howard Kershner noted.[17] Although the Quakers did not have the resources to evacuate the thousands of people affected in the camps of Argelès and Saint-Cyprien, Mary Elmes was at least in a position to distribute clothes, food and blankets to the camps.

'We are all so shocked at the news of the flood,' Howard Kershner's wife, Gertrude, said in a rushed handwritten note to her. 'As usual you have handled your part of the situation in your very efficient way.'[18]

In any given day, Mary's routine at her apartment office on the Avenue des Baléares involved a mixture of administrative work, camp visits and endless meetings. A typical day started at about 9 a.m. There were telegrams, cables, letters and phone calls to answer. Then there was a review of any changes in the camps, new shipments of refugees, and aid for the thousands of flood victims. There were endless calls to the police and local government offices to arrange permits, visas, transport and petrol. After that there were meetings with school officials, public health officials and social agencies to arrange everything from canteens to the distribution of vitamins in schools.[19]

'To be ideally equipped for the job,' Howard remarked at the time, 'one should combine the faculties of diplomat, business man and general psychologies, and have [diverse] other mental skills on call.'[20]

To give a further insight into the nature of the work, he listed a sample of the requests that had come in from the six Quaker branches operating in regional France – Auch, Biarritz, Montauban, Perpignan, Toulouse and Lyon – over the previous months:

New born babies are being wrapped in newspapers because there is no clothing.

Two thousand women and children are sleeping on the bare sand, can you send beds, blankets or clothing?

Women and children are perishing of cold in this bitter weather, we implore you to send blankets or clothing.

We receive only 750 calories of food daily and are slowly starving.

'Dispensing charity in France today,' he said, 'means exercising the power of life or death over one's fellows. How does one do it and retain his sanity?'[21]

By the end of 1940, Mary and her team at Perpignan had helped several thousand people in the camps in her district. At the biggest one, Argelès, she had organised a school for two thousand children, set up a library with four thousand books, established a maternity facility in one of the barracks, distributed clothes, blankets, ortho-paedic instruments, reading glasses and hernia belts, established classes for adults, set up sewing and carpentry workshops, distributed food and milk, and set up a hospital, equipping it with medicine and instruments.[22]

She had done similar work in other camps – Barcarès, Saint-Cyprien, Bram and Agde – and had also administered aid in the region's general hospitals and schools.

Ross McClelland, the Quaker delegate who oversaw refugee camp work at head office in Marseille, was suitably impressed. He wrote: 'The record of the volume of work you have done certainly brings my hat off to you. I can see how you feel occasionally about some of the member organizations of the Coord. Comm. who demand this & that when their entire camp activity is limited to a few recent months.'[23]

He was referring to the Nîmes Co-ordinating Committee, which sat every month in the city, bringing together twenty-five relief agencies working in the camps. The meetings could be stormy and acrimonious affairs, as very often there were vastly different opinions between agencies, as well as within them. There was the added complication of trying to operate under the Vichy regime. In the early days of the war, Howard Kershner had issued a strongly worded memo to staff, warning them to 'observe the regulations of the competent authorities'.[24] While the Quakers could legally help those who wanted to emigrate, they had to do so within the rules, he said.

'The one thing that we must not do under any circumstances is to aid or abet any person in trying to leave France without the

French *"visa de sortie* [exit visa]"; Kershner had insisted. He also pointed out that the Quakers received a number of concessions from the authorities, including customs exemptions, free railway transport and warehousing facilities. They also received a large grant from the French aid organisation Secours National to cover expenses in France. That meant the money raised in America could be used exclusively to buy food and clothes for those in need, but it also meant that Kershner was keen to keep his volunteers on the right side of the authorities.

In January 1941 he sought, and was granted, a meeting with the Vichy head of government, Marshal Pétain. He seemed impressed when Pétain sent his private car to the airport to pick him up. The two men spent a cordial half hour together, during which Howard stressed the non-political nature of the work of the American Friends Service Committee in France. He was pleased to get assurances from Vichy that any food sent from America for children would not be taken by the Germans. Pétain emphasised the friendship that existed between France and America and said his country would face famine if the United States did not send aid.[25]

It was not the time to discuss Pétain's first Jewish Statute, passed the previous October, which had deprived Jews of the right to work in the civil service and the army as well as in a range of other professions.

Later that year Kershner met Pétain again. By then his government had passed a second raft of anti-Jewish legislation, although that subject was certainly not on the agenda during a two-day tour of the alpine Haute-Savoie region when Kershner joined, as he put it, a group of 'distinguished Frenchmen'. He seemed almost star-struck by the head of government. In his diary, he recorded with satisfaction that he was the only foreigner invited on tour and mentioned, with pride, that he had spoken to the 'Maréchal' on four occasions.

He gushed about the competent Pétain. His age had become a concern – he was over eighty when the war began – but Kershner noted that he was 'physically and mentally alert' and in robust health. 'His affection for the people and interest in them is unbounded,' he wrote. 'Disabled soldiers of former wars wearing proudly their decorations swelled with pride as they shook hands with their chief.'[26]

Although Kershner did not broach the subject of the internment of foreign Jews, this had been one of the Quakers' central concerns since a new camp at Rivesaltes, outside Perpignan, opened in January 1941.

The new camp was a thorny subject at the Nîmes Co-ordinating Committee. Many relief organisations did not want to be associated with the camp until conditions there improved.

When the camp was first built it had been intended to be a model army camp, but it was soon found to be almost uninhabitable. A smouldering sun beat down on it in summer and it was bitterly cold in winter. It wasn't even fit for horses, the army decided afterwards.[27] However, the Vichy government needed more space for the Spanish refugees as the beach camps closed and for interning the growing number of Jews who were being rounded up under Vichy's anti-Jewish legislation.

Roma were held there too, but at least they were allowed to live as family groups. Spanish and Jewish families were split up, with the men in one block and the women and children in another. At times women were separated from their children. By April 1941, Rivesaltes had more than nine thousand people living within its bleak enclosure. About 40 per cent of those were Jews, who would face increasing threats as the months went by.

Mary was quick to speak out when she saw this danger. However, it is interesting to note that in September 1941 she denied a claim that an 'anti-Semitic movement was afoot in the camp's administrative circles'. She said that many Jews were grouped together in one block, but others lived in a block with Spanish and non-Jewish internees.

> There is nothing of the Ghetto about Ilot B [where Jews and Spaniards lived together] as its inhabitants can circulate in the camp under the same conditions as those living in the other Ilots (blocks). I myself have had the pleasure of working with the Rabbi of the Camp and have been able to observe that he is treated with consideration and respect by the French personal [sic] of the camp.[28]

Her comments were prompted by a concern that the authorities might expel the relief agencies if they were seen to be too openly critical. Mary had been working on the ground since the camp opened, and her approach was conciliatory and pragmatic. She told her friend and colleague Helga Holbek: 'I cannot stress too much my conviction that we will obtain far more of the camp authorities and be allowed to have much more freedom in our interviews with the refugees and in our service for them if we proceed with tact at this stage. I have proved this over and over again at Argelès.'[29]

Those good relations with camp officials would save the lives of hundreds of Jewish children in the months to come.

Chapter 10 ᐁ

EXPOSURE

'While Bram camp was poor, it was lively and gay. The French who came from the North, they were sad, but not the Spaniards. The Spaniards knew how to live. For them, life was stronger than everything else.'

— Gilbert Susagna

The people coming towards Mary Elmes and Marjorie McClelland at Rivesaltes internment camp were walking against a wind so violent it made them stagger like drunks. The air was filled with flying dust and sand, and the glare was blinding. The two women squinted their eyes into slits and walked on. Most of the internees stayed in their unheated barracks, looking out on the wind-scoured vastness of the camp.

Marjorie had asked Mary for a guided tour. She worked behind a desk compiling welfare reports at head office in Marseille and wanted to see at first hand what was happening on the ground. 'I used my imagination as much as I could about it all, but it still was not the same as though I had seen it with my own eyes,' she said.[1]

It took the two women about twenty minutes to drive from Perpignan, but it seemed to Marjorie McClelland as if she was journeying into another world – one in which there was nothing except row after row of concrete barracks stretching out as far as the eye could see. At its peak, the camp held 18,000 people in 150 barracks. When Marjorie commented that there was no green – not a blade of grass, not a single tree – to relieve the monotony of the grey buildings against the bare, stony ground, Mary said there were, in fact, two small trees. From where they were standing, however, they were impossible to see, as the compound covered several square miles of terrain.

The first stop on Mary's tour was at a barracks to meet mothers and their children. The mothers told Marjorie they had been in several camps but the wind made Rivesaltes the worst. It had chafed and chapped their children's faces and there was no protection from the relentless sun. The children's faces had a rosiness that did not come from health, Marjorie thought.

Mary and her visitor pressed on against the wind until they reached a barracks that had been converted into a kitchen. Mary had been in it many times before, but its cheery exterior made her guest stop in her tracks. Unlike all the other barracks, it was whitewashed and painted with bright, colourful pictures. There was a ship, an aeroplane, a lorry and a train, all of them laden with food destined for the camp. Each mode of transport represented a relief agency: the Quakers, the Œuvre de Secours aux Enfants (Children's Aid Society, a Jewish humanitarian organisation), and the Swiss Red Cross. Children queued outside, each one of them holding a tin can or pail, all waiting eagerly for their four o'clock snack of rice (from the Quakers), milk (from the Swiss Red Cross) and fruit paste (from the OSE).

It was the picture of the American flag, 'large and capacious', on the side of the painted Quaker ship that made a particular impression on Marjorie:

> As I looked at it, and then looked at the children standing patiently in line, buffeted by the wind, waiting to receive their daily ration, the tears came to my eyes to think that ships are not coming from America laden with good food for these sad little children. I think that if the powers that arrange these things could have stood by my side and seen the thin malformed little bodies and the wistful screwed-up little faces of these children they might wish to reconsider their policy.

She was referring to the Allied naval blockade, which was designed to cut off supplies from Nazi Germany but also deprived needy children of food.

The two women watched as the children entered the 'clean, good-smelling' kitchen and sat down at a long wooden bench to eat. The thing that struck Marjorie with a force that she was not expecting was not the wretched clothing, the shoes made from strips of blankets, the stooped shoulders or even the sores that never healed.

> I was prepared for the sight of all these things, but what I was not prepared for was the expression on the faces of all these children. The intentness, the deadly seriousness with which they approached their turn to be served from the steaming kettle filled with a thick mixture of rice and milk. With absolute concentration they watched while the big ladle full of rice was put into the container which they held forward to receive it. And if a few grains of the precious rice got on the outside of the pail they immediately licked it up, so that they should lose not one grain . . .

When they sat down to eat it they did so in silence. There was no joking, no jostling, talking, laughing, just silence and the sound of the spoon scraping in their tin cups. 'It was an entirely absorbing and completely serious business,' observed Marjorie; '. . . it was the brooding anxious faces of these little children scraping up the last bit of the small ration which we can give them that really moved me the most of all.'

The visit continued with a tour of the espadrilles workshop recently started by Mary. After that there was an inspection of an adolescents' feeding station and then a visit to a section of the camp that left Marjorie at a loss for words. The two women went to one of the eleven barracks that were set aside for treating severely undernourished people. 'The barracks of these men, old and young, is a sight which one cannot easily forget, and I simply cannot attempt to describe it to you,' she said.

Mary was more matter-of-fact in a report, written about the same time, in which she described the care administered to the 'cachectiques', those suffering from cachexia, a wasting of the body. 'In many cases, there are men over 5 feet 10 weighing between 40 and 45 kilos [6½ and 7 stone],' she wrote.[2] 'The patients are unable to maintain standing position for longer than a few minutes and are incapable of all other forms of effort. Death occurs frequently for no special cause.'

She outlined the rations they were given and also described a short-term medical experiment that was being carried out on those less ill, a group known as the *pre-cachectiques*.

In a special barracks, a number of men were divided into three groups. One was given the normal camp ration; a second, the camp ration plus a food supplement; and the third, the camp ration, a food supplement and a special vitamin preparation that the Unitarian Service Committee had obtained from Switzerland. Mary said the experiment had yielded 'interesting results': the men in the first category gained weight slowly; those in the second group gained a considerable amount of weight in a short time; but those who got the vitamin supplement fared best, gaining weight steadily with a rapid return to health.

However, the Swiss Red Cross nurse, Friedel Bohny-Reiter, who lived within the camp enclosure, was very uneasy about the manner in which the experiment was conducted. She said the camp doctors would not allow her to nurse the men in the experimental barracks. Patients were forced to stay in bed, even though she had observed that those who were allowed to move about were doing much better.

'I can hardly bear to go into the barracks any more,' she wrote in her diary.[3] 'It seems to me that those looks, which are full of reproach, are directed at me like accusations – "Why don't you help us? Why are you leaving us to die of hunger?"'

Mary and Friedel were colleagues and would remain lifelong friends, but they appear to have had differing views on the vitamin experiments. It was not usual for relief workers to disagree, and Mary was convinced by the seemingly solid evidence to support the experiments. However, if Mary thought there was a problem she was never slow to point it out. She had little time for those who visited the camp briefly and then made sweeping statements afterwards. Asked about one such visit from two noteworthy do-gooders, she said they were just 'protest-standing', a phrase she coined to mean the attitude of those who made vocal protests but essentially did nothing.[4]

Mary had grown used to the harsh conditions too. She didn't notice any of the things that Marjorie McClelland later wrote about in a moving account of her visit to the camp. She must have apologised for being hardened, because Marjorie later assured her:

I do not think that you should feel that you fall short at all because you have gotten used to the conditions at Rivesaltes. It is particularly because it is so striking as a first impression that I wanted to write something about it before it dimmed in my mind. We get used to everything if we see it often enough.[5]

In her report she also recorded that Mary was widely recognised and loved among the camp population.

Everywhere Mary went she was greeted with great warmth and affection and we could not walk very far without being stopped by someone who wished to talk with her. One could see very plainly that 'Miss Mary' as they all call her, brought joy to many people on her regular frequent visits to the camp.[6]

———

'Miss Mary.' Even now, nearly eight decades after he first met her, Gilbert Susagna's face changes when he says the name. He stresses each syllable for effect and uses words such as 'mythical' and 'courageous' to describe Mary Elmes and her work at Rivesaltes camp.

He was only four years old when he met her in 1940, so he doesn't recall her features: she's a silhouette at the edge of his memory now. Yet her name has been a constant in his life, ever since the dark days of the Spanish Civil War, when he and his mother fled their home town in Catalonia in north-east Spain to put themselves at the mercy of their reluctant French hosts. Like hundreds of thousands before them, they were sent to live in wretched conditions in the refugee internment camps that had been hastily built to house the stream of refugees coming over the border from Spain.

Mary Elmes, he says, gave them hope, and did everything possible to ensure that they were transferred from the barbed-wired camps to a comfortable, well-equipped children's home by the sea. For years afterwards his mother, Manolita Susagna, 'spoke about Miss Mary, Miss Mary, Miss Mary,' Gilbert, now eighty-two, says. 'And when she spoke of her, it almost brought tears to her eyes. Miss Mary never once let her down.'[7]

He is happy to speak about it now, so many years later. To this day, however, he regrets that his mother never thought to look up Mary Elmes after the war.

> My mother died in 2010 and Miss Mary in 2002. We were all in Perpignan since 1945. I regret that they never met again. One time when I was at secondary school, my mother and I passed in front of Café de France [an imposing red-brick building in the centre of Perpignan] and my mother said, 'I have a great memory of that café – I have never set foot in it again, but that's where Miss Mary once brought me to have a coffee.'

Mary did much to help the people in the camps, but what stands out in Gilbert's memory are the coveted snacks she distributed weekly, without fail.

> Miss Mary came in her car and she always gave the women in the workshop something while she was there; a snack of, maybe, three dried figs. Or a prune, or a little bit of chocolate . . . a few biscuits. When my mother came back from the workshop, I remember rifling through her pockets. I was five years old and I would ask, 'What do you have?' Physically, I can't remember Mary Elmes. I can just see her outline, but my impression of her is through my mother's good opinion of her.

Manolita Susagna and her son arrived in the camp at Argelès-sur-Mer, now a popular seaside resort, in early 1941. By then they had already been on the move for almost a year. Gilbert wasn't yet a year old when his father joined the Republican side after the Spanish *coup d'état* in July 1936. Francisco Susagna didn't hesitate to join the fighting. He left his wife, then aged twenty, his infant son and his job at the mayor's office to fight in a war that foreshadowed the horror of the world war that would follow it. News of his whereabouts filtered through in irregular despatches. He was badly injured at the Battle of Madrid, but he recovered to fight in the Battle of the Ebro.

He was in Barcelona too when Mussolini pounded the city and its civilians in March 1938, 'leaving the street littered with body parts, which also hung from the trees', according to one eye-witness.[8] After that he made it into France just before the border closed.

Meanwhile at home, Manolita continued to run her own business: she had opened the very first hairdressing salon in Almenar some years before and worked in it right up to the day it was ransacked by the Requetés, the right-wing militia who took over the town in 1939.

They knew the Susagnas as a left-wing family and meted out punishment accordingly, destroying the hair salon and imprisoning Manolita's father. Gilbert's paternal grandfather advised his mother to join her husband in France.

'Her place was beside him,' he said. The family found a *passeur* – one of the many who were smuggling people, weapons and goods into France during the war – to help the mother and son cross the border. They joined another woman and her seven-year-old son at La Jonquera on the Spanish side of the border. They walked for three nights, crossing into France above Le Perthus, and then headed towards a little town, Saint-Génis-des-Fontaines, in south-west France.

It was early 1940. Gilbert isn't sure of the month but he knows it was winter. He has several 'flashbacks', as he calls them, of that journey: there was the log cabin in the mountains where they were put up for a night, the French gendarmes who requisitioned all his mother's jewellery and money at the border, and the unspeakable, bone-chilling cold.

After reaching Saint-Génis-des-Fontaines, they were taken to the town of Le Boulou and then on to Perpignan railway station. They camped there, with other refugees, for the best part of ten days. Again, the cold looms large in his memory. Their travelling companions, the other mother and son, were no longer with them and they would never hear what became of them. Eventually Gilbert and his mother were taken to Bram, an internment camp that housed up to 17,000 people in sub-standard shacks surrounded by a high barbed-wire fence.

Manolita Susagna succeeded in making contact with her husband, but on his way to join them he passed through occupied territory and his working papers were invalidated. He too was interned at Bram, but at least the family was together again, unlike so many others. They were also in relatively good health – and the Susagnas had another advantage: 'My mother could read and write,' says Gilbert. 'She could sew; she was a hairdresser. She was resourceful. The doctor [at Bram] saw that she could be useful and asked her to join the infirmary.'

The job came with better lodgings and conditions, and life settled down for a short time. But soon they were on the move again. The camp closed in 1941 and the family was moved to Argelès-sur-Mer. There Manolita Susagna met Mary Elmes, who, like the doctor before her at Bram, was quick to see Manolita's potential and appointed her director of the camp's sewing workshop.

With Quaker funds, Mary supplied it with thread, needles, material – anything she could secure in the lean months of 1941. 'From time to time, Miss Mary would bring her to Perpignan,' Gilbert recalls. 'My mother had a travel permit because she cut the camp director's wife's hair, so together they shopped for material and needles.'

In February 1941 Mary brought Howard Kershner, the Quaker director of aid in Europe, on a tour of the camp, where he commented on the quality of the work coming out of the sewing workshop. A diary entry for 19 February reads: 'Working with materials we have supplied, and under our supervision, much excellent work is being accomplished in the sewing room. Young women are taught to sew and thousands of useful garments are made for distribution within the Camp.'[9] He was equally impressed by the toys, furniture and 'beautiful articles' that were coming out of the men's workroom.

The camp workers presented some of those 'beautiful objects' to Mary as a gesture of thanks. Her children still have a perfect miniature anvil given to their mother by a fourteen-year-old refugee. The craftsmanship is astonishing. The same is true of a delicate sculpture of a leaping deer carved from bone. It bears the inscription, À Miss Mary, Francia 1941 [To Miss Mary, France, 1941], and is signed A. Gomez.

And yet, the conditions were appalling. Gilbert recalls the widespread horror among the camp population at Argelès after a little boy was bitten by a rat on the earlobe. 'After that, my mother slept with me tucked in beside her and with a stick by her side; she would hit the side of the bunk during the night to scare off the rats.'

In his report, Howard Kershner also noted the inadequate diet, the severe overcrowding and the 'pitifully meagre and inadequate' equipment in the camp's hospital. 'Overcrowding is very serious,' he wrote. 'I saw one *baraque* [shack] where eight people were sleeping in a space not much larger than an ordinary double-sized bed. In many of the *baraques* the women and children have no beds or mattresses at all and sleep on a little straw on the sand.'[10]

Perhaps the worst thing was the complete lack of washing and bathing facilities, he wrote. 'There are four out-door pitcher pumps for a population of 4,000 women and 2,000 children. From the time it is too cold to bathe in the Mediterranean in the Fall until it is warm enough in Spring, there is no way for these people to bathe or even to wash. In the men's Camp . . . the Mediterranean is the sole supply of water for bathing and washing.'[11]

For all that, both Gilbert Susagna and Howard Kershner recalled the inextinguishable spirit of the Spanish people.

'While Bram camp was poor, it was lively and gay,' says Gilbert. 'The French who came from the North, they were sad, but not the Spaniards. The Spaniards knew how to live. For them, life was stronger than everything else.'

Howard too was heartened by the morale and character of the Spanish people at Argelès-sur-Mer. He said the women and girls in the kitchens who were busy peeling turnips – 'and often dropping a good many into the sand' – were cheerful and appeared healthy, even though they were eating less than half the daily calorie intake recommended for health. But it was the children, happy and interested in their work, who impressed him most.

There is a singing school conducted by a master of unusual talent. I think I have never heard such beautiful singing done by children in any land, and in any language. The master had a group of perhaps fifty children who had unusually beautiful and well trained voices. They sang in Spanish, French and English. Having just inspected the living quarters of these children, which were

... like ordinary dog kennels, one could scarcely believe that they could appear so happy, healthy, and sing so beautifully. It is one of the miracles of the Spanish race. I was overwhelmed with the thought of human wastage that is taking place in this Camp. Much excellent material for fine sturdy citizens of the next generation is about to be lost. It would be hard to find two thousand more promising children anywhere, and yet the health, morale and character of these young people will be permanently injured or destroyed if they must continue year after year to live in such conditions.[12]

That thought must certainly have weighed on Manolita Susagna's mind too. She and her husband, who was now working with other refugee labourers outside the camp, were applying for release papers in an attempt to establish some kind of normal life. Mary Elmes, however, advised them against it, explaining that the bureaucracy was insurmountable, and the camp authorities were reluctant to allow people to leave, as it was not in their interests to do so. She promised them she would have mother and son transferred to a different camp and from there to a children's colony, where their chances of release would be better.

She was true to her word. In July 1941 Manolita Susagna and her son were transferred to Rivesaltes camp and from there to the children's convalescent home, La Villa Saint-Christophe, which looked out on the Mediterranean. 'Beside what we experienced, it was paradise,' Gilbert says.

They were there for a very happy two and a half months, until their papers finally arrived and they were free to join Gilbert's father, Francisco, who had found work at a mill. It was a bitter-sweet day at the Villa. The colony's Mennonite director, Lois Gunden, recalled the tearful departure in her journal: 'She put her arms around us, kissed us, and cried; it was extremely touching; Helen [Penner] and I walked back from Canet village in time to see practically the whole colony bringing her down to the station; wholesale kissing after tram had come in . . .'[13]

After the war the family moved back to Perpignan, and Gilbert and his brother Josef both went to school, despite the financial constraints.

It was a real miracle. I owe it to my mother. She said, 'I don't see why my son can't study just because we are poor and we are not in our country.' I went to Montpellier [University] and became a Spanish teacher in the *lycée* [secondary school].

Looking back now, Gilbert Susagna says that Mary Elmes, Lois Gunden and Helen Penner, who also worked at the children's colony, were exceptional women who should be recognised and remembered. 'To quote [Louis] Aragón, "they didn't look for glory or tears" [*Vous n'aviez réclamé la gloire ni les larmes*]. What they did was not proselytising. They didn't want anything. They were happy to do what their consciences dictated. I am delighted to talk about La Villa Saint-Christophe and to thank those women on behalf of all the children who passed that way.'

Chapter 11 ~

EVERYBODY KNOWS
YOUR NAME

Dear Mademoiselle,
All of the pupils in my school, even the littlest ones, know
your name – Miss Elmes. Those words will always conjure
up for us the idea of snacks that we have been without for
so long: chocolate and jam.
Thank you so much for all that we owe you.

— Francine Delmas

Francine Delmas, a pupil in the village of Cases-de-Pène, north-west of Perpignan, was nine years old when she wrote those words, but her elegant script, beautifully spaced on a copybook grid, belies her years.

Another note, from seven-year-old Marcelle Mas at the same school, reads: 'Please, Mademoiselle, pass on lots and lots of thanks-you to our friends in America.' Yet another, from twelve-year-old Rosette Arnaud, said: 'In exchange for all your good things, we have nothing to offer you but our friendship, but we do so with all of our heart.'[1]

Mary Elmes and her colleagues received thousands of similar letters from grateful French schoolchildren and their parents who wanted to convey 'truckloads of thank-yous' for the food, medical aid and clothes received during the war years and afterwards. As well as helping the refugees in the camps, the Quakers did what they could to alleviate the acute suffering that also affected the French population. Food shortages were already severe in the first winter after the fall of France. In November 1940 the mayor of Carcassonne, Dr Tomey, warned that the region was facing 'near-famine conditions'.

The mayor happened to mention to Mary, in passing, that the local council was no longer able to finance the school feeding scheme that it had run in crèches and nursery schools for years. She was said to have been 'profoundly moved' by the news and immediately contacted her superior, Howard Kershner, asking him to intervene. He was able to rally fifty days' worth of food supplies and sent 1,600 kilos of rice, 128 kilos of cocoa and 512 kilos of sugar to Carcassonne, the makings of a comforting chocolate-pudding snack. Some days later a local newspaper published an account of the Quakers' generosity, praising Mary Elmes in particular. The mayor said he was 'profoundly touched' by the gesture.[2]

During her tenure, Mary and her Quaker colleagues provided school snacks or a midday meal to more than 84,000 children in schools in the south of France. The most common – and most popular – snack was the famous Quaker chocolate pudding, made from rice, chocolate and sugar. It was a favourite with schoolchildren, but delegates also spent considerable time trying to work out the right proportion of ingredients to maximise the nutritional content. They also wanted it to taste good and on occasion sampled it for themselves.

'I tasted the pudding and found it quite palatable,' Mary's colleague Donald Stevenson reported after one school visit. 'The children evidently liked it for it disappeared very rapidly. I wish that the ration for each child could have been larger. Double the amount would seem to me to have given them more of a meal.'[3]

But food was increasingly scarce, and children in the region lost a tenth of their weight in one ten-month period in 1941, Howard Kershner reported with alarm in a letter to Mary.[4] Her office in Perpignan monitored the crisis by distributing weight charts to schools. They noted each pupil's weight increase – or loss – after the distribution of food aid. Some gained weight, but many remained the same and many lost weight.

The Quakers responded by issuing millions of doses of vitamins incorporated in little squares of chocolate. Each one was done up in a small wrapper explaining that it was a gift from the American people which was delivered by the Quaker workers as a symbol of friendship. In every school, grateful recipients wrote postcards and letters of thanks, like the ones written personally to 'Miss Elmes'. A pupil was chosen to say a special word of thanks; then everyone would shout *'Vive l'Amérique'* and *'Vive la France'* before tucking in.[5]

There are hundreds of surviving examples of children's poems, drawings and handwritten notes of thanks. From a school at Elne, south of Perpignan, Marguerite Chalverat addressed her note to the 'dear Americans' and told them that she had gained two kilos (4½ pounds) because of their gift and was now in good health.[6] Her classmate Simone Baile wrote: 'Thank you for the good things that you have sent us and that do so much good. I am always very happy at 4 o'clock when we are given our snack.'

Meanwhile, the class at the Jules Ferry school in Montpellier was inspired to write a poem:

We, the little children of France
We salute our faraway friends

We thank with all our hearts
Our generous benefactors,
Who give us every morning
A good American meal.

Please accept the gratitude
Of all the mothers in France.
They will never forget
Your goodness.[7]

However, the letters and cards were not only touching expressions of politeness: they were a vital part of a well-oiled publicity machine that was designed to keep American donations flowing. Howard Kershner frequently reminded volunteers that propaganda in America was of the utmost importance for replenishing the funds.[8] He knew the burden of the workload on volunteers but said it was vital to send stories and pictures of the children who benefited from American largesse.

One Quaker delegate, Katrina McCormick Barnes, put it more bluntly in a letter to Mary Elmes: 'The London and Philadelphia offices have been howling for human interest stories. I know how swamped you are with work, and so I don't dare to set a date in the month for the stories and pictures.' But she added: 'I can't stress too much the importance of these two items.'[9]

Some of those stories were written on postcards with studio-produced images of idealised French children: unrealistic representations of perfect boys and girls. The contrast between those images and the contemporary photographs taken of schoolchildren eagerly drinking from bowls could not be more marked. The head office of the American Friends Service Committee in Philadelphia was particularly interested in the latter, as they were more likely to provoke a generous public response.

In January 1942 the committee's executive secretary, Clarence Pickett, issued a press statement to warn that the conditions of malnutrition and starvation throughout Europe were becoming increasingly acute.

> The results of hunger are already manifest not only in arrested growth, pale and ashen complexions, thin legs, and lack of resistance to contagious diseases, according to Quaker workers. They quote a principal of a large school who states: 'A rule understood and known the day of the lesson is forgotten the next day, and absolutely forgotten as though they had never learned it, and this by painstaking, studious pupils. There is less [gaiety]. A badly nourished child is a sad child. What will become of our school children if this keeps on? The future of our race is at stake.'[10]

Until food could be sent from America, Europe's people would live in misery. 'If Europe is ever to find her way back to enduring peace we must find some way to save her children.'[11]

However, getting that food from America to Europe posed another problem. The delivery of food was being severely hampered by the Allied blockade, which had been implemented to restrict the supply of goods to Nazi Germany but was causing widespread hardship. The English Quakers pointed this out in a declaration to the office of the British prime minister, Winston Churchill, in April 1942:

Hunger is a weapon that affects an entire population, taking no notice of gender, friend or foe, age or youth, but ravages the young to the greatest extent. The food blockade does not only contribute to hunger, it also creates and encourages a heartless attitude in those responsible for the blockade. This results, in the end, in the destruction of our Christian values, such as charity, empathy, etc. Values our land is fighting for.[12]

The Quakers acknowledged the 'serious political and technical difficulties' that could be caused by food parcels but urged the British government to find a solution so that food and clothing could be delivered to the countries that were cut off. Their appeal did not lead to any concessions.

There was the added complication of trying to stay on the right side of the Vichy and German authorities, a point made on several occasions by Howard Kershner in France. In one memo in 1941, he warned the staff to be careful of what they said when it came to publicity.

Nothing should be said that might make it more difficult to carry on our work in cooperation with the many authorities of different nationalities with whom we have to deal. For instance, not a can of milk comes from Switzerland without the approval of the German control. Without going into details, I think you will see, therefore, the necessity for preserving strict neutrality and speaking most respectfully for all. When we remember further-more that our life-line goes through Spain and know all the influences that are at work there, we are reminded that we must not allow anyone who is supporting us to make statements or engage in activity which is not directly in accordance with our well known principles of impartiality in conducting relief work.[13]

———

If hunger was an issue among the French population as a whole, it was even more so in the camps. In January 1942 Mary Elmes's report on the Rivesaltes camp told of the 'terrible hunger' among the

Mary Elmes as a baby with her mother, Elisabeth Elmes.

Mary's parents, Elisabeth Elmes (née Waters) and Edward Thomas Elmes, who worked as a pharmacist on Winthrop Street, Cork.

Mary when she was about
eight years old.

Mary and her brother John as children.

A sketch by Avis Coburn of 'Culgreine' in Ballintemple, Cork, where Mary grew
up. (Courtesy of the house's current occupant, Jacinta Ryan.)

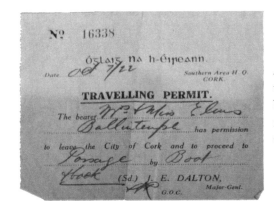

A travel permit issued during the Irish Civil War. It is signed by General Emmet Dalton, the man who landed in Passage West, Cork, with 450 Free State troops.

A passport photo of Mary in the late 1930s. She left her fur coat in storage when she volunteered to work in the Spanish Civil War. Almost ten years would elapse before she collected it.

Mary (first row, second from the left) at Trinity College Dublin, where she excelled in her chosen subjects, French and Spanish.

Mary (second from the right) was assigned to run a feeding station in Almería when she volunteered as an aid worker during the Spanish Civil War.

Mary (first on the left in the back row) with fellow volunteers working for Sir George's University Ambulance Unit. Sir George is in the front row wearing his trademark bow tie.

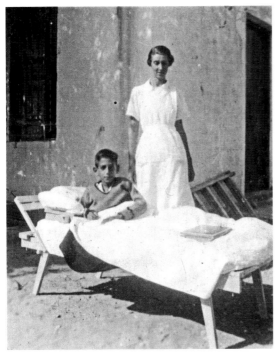

Mary with Pepe, a long-term patient at the hospital she ran in Polop. The picture was taken by her co-worker Emily Parker. (From the archives of the American Friends Service Committee.)

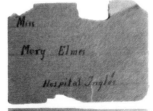

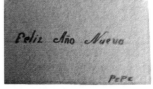

A tiny New Year's card and envelope made by Pepe for Mary Elmes. He died weeks after making it.

Mary with some of her young charges on the steps of the hospital at Polop, located in the mountains about thirty miles from Alicante. (Photo by Emily Parker, from the archives of the American Friends Service Committee.)

Mary with Palmira, a little girl of 21 months who was badly wounded during the bombing of the market place in Alicante in May 1938. Doctor Blanc managed to save her leg which the surgeons had wanted to amputate. (Photo by Emily Parker, from the archives of the American Friends Service Committee.)

Mary with Tato, the little orphaned boy she hoped to adopt.

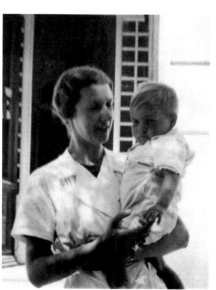

Mary and José Luis, a patient at Polop hospital in Spain.

Driver Juan Arce Donaire, Mary Elmes and Dorothy Morris delivering aid on behalf of the American Friends Service Committee in Spain. (From the archives of the American Friends Service Committee.)

Mary's Quaker ID. She was head of the Quaker delegation in Perpignan during the Second World War.

Mary on the flower-filled balcony of her apartment in Perpignan, which acted as her home and office during the Second World War.

A Christmas card for Mary made by Spanish Civil War refugees while they were interned in a camp at Saint-Cyprien in the south of France.

Joyeux Noël
Saint Cyprien 1939

Joyeux Noël - Bonne Année

A greeting card to Mary showing the barracks where Spanish Civil War refugees were held in the south of France. These camps would later hold Jews and Roma.

A handmade deer carved from animal bone by Spanish Civil War refugee A. Gomez for 'Miss Mary', as Mary Elmes was known in the camps.

A painting of Mary by well-known Spanish artist Balbino Giner.

Gilbert Susagna and his mother Manolita. Gilbert recalls: 'Miss Mary never once let my mother down.' (Picture courtesy of Gilbert Susagna.)

Gilbert Susagna: 'Mary Elmes was an exceptional woman who should be remembered and recognised.'

Brothers Mario and René Freund (now Michael Freund and Ronald Friend) in 1943. Mary Elmes saved their lives by extracting them from the camp at Rivesaltes while deportations were in full swing. (Picture courtesy of Michael Freund.)

Mario and René Freund at school in Marssac where they were mixed in with local schoolchildren. Mario (now Michael) is third from the left in the back row with his hand on his younger brother René (now Ronald Friend) in the second row. Guy Brunet, who coincidentally bumped into Ronald in Marssac seventy-one years later, is on the extreme left in the second row. (Picture courtesy of Guy Brunet.)

Professor Ronald Friend with two bowls that Mary's children presented to him when he attended the Righteous Among the Nations award ceremony in France. (Picture courtesy of Ronald Friend.)

Charlotte Berger-Greneche, who was taken from the camp at Rivesaltes days before her mother was deported. Mary Elmes hid her and other Jewish children at the Quaker-Mennonite children's home La Villa St-Christophe at Canet-Plage.

Georges Koltein, who, with his brother Jacques, was taken to relative safety at La Villa St-Christophe. Mary Elmes arranged for the transfer.

The Koltein family survived the war, although several of their relatives did not. Georges is on the left. (Picture courtesy of Georges Koltein.)

Mary Elmes and her daughter
Caroline, who was born in 1946.

Mary many years after the
war at her home in Perpignan.

Mary's son Patrick Danjou presenting a book originally from Culgreine to its current owner Jacinta Ryan. The inscription reads: 'Coming home after 70 years.'

Caroline Danjou in June 2014 at a ceremony in France to honour her mother. (Photo courtesy of Jean Duroux.)

The medal presented to the family when Mary Elmes was named Righteous Among the Nations at Yad Vashem. The inscription reads: 'Whoever saves a life saves the world entire.'

Mary Elmes was honoured by Network Ireland in Cork in September 2016. From left to right: Bernard Wilson, Patrick Danjou, Network Ireland President Deirdre Waldron and Mark Elmes, Mary's cousin. (Picture courtesy of Darragh Kane.)

internees (968 men, 1,833 women and 1,209 children): 'They never can eat their fill even of the miserably unpalatable and un-nourishing soup served to them twice daily.'[14]

The memory of those deprivations stayed with Carmen Canadell for the rest of her life. She had fled her home town, Girona, in 1939 with her sister Mercedes and her mother, María, while Mary was still working in Spain. Mary would later play a role in their lives, but in the intervening two years Carmen's family endured untold suffering.

When they arrived in France they were moved from camp to camp. In February 1941, at Récébédou camp, south of Toulouse, María's mother gave birth to her third child, Josefa. Her husband, José, worked on a farm, but, like so many other Spanish refugees, the rest of the family had to apply for documents to be able to join him, a process that could take years. In June that year María and her three daughters were moved to Rivesaltes, where they were separated. María and her baby were interned in the improvised nursery in Block J, while her older daughters were left alone in Block K.

Carmen's daughter Brigitte Twomey recounts her mother's memory of that time:

Carmen and Mercedes could only talk to their mother through a wire fence. To go from one Ilôt [block] to the other, they needed a pass. There was no adult supervision and the children were left to fend for themselves. It was sweltering hot in summer and freezing in winter. The conditions were desperate. There were rats and lice; latrines without doors; thin mattresses made of straw always damp; not enough blankets, no tables, chairs, toiletries. The ground was very rocky and hard to walk on for kids without shoes, or just cloth wrapped around their feet. My mother and aunt didn't have any shoes and only very few clothes. Kids were left to themselves with nothing to do all day. Idleness weighed heavily upon them.[15]

But, she says, what stayed with her mother most forcefully was the memory of hunger:

Starvation was the worst, always the worst. During the war, the French people did not have enough food for themselves; refugees had even less and always came last. When my mother was nine and living in one of the camps, she would go out at night to steal fruit from local orchards. One farmer chased her and shot at her with his rifle. When I asked her if she had been very scared, she told me that it did not matter, she was too hungry. Starvation took over everything.

Brigitte's mother also related stories of seeing the bodies of the many who died of malnutrition and other diseases in the camp. She and Mercedes would visit the dead and pinch their toes: they believed that could bring them back to life.

When both sisters contracted scabies they were sent to the Hôpital Saint-Louis in Perpignan. They have memories of mould on the hospital walls and having to scrounge in the bins for food. They also spoke about the terrible pain of having their scabs buffed with hard brushes as part of the treatment.

In January 1942 the sisters were sent back to the camp at Rivesaltes and were moved to the infirmary. The register at the children's home, the Villa Saint-Christophe at Canet-Plage, has a note of their arrival later that month. Their transfer to the home would have been overseen by Mary Elmes, although it was her colleague Friedel Bohny-Reiter who drove them from the camp to the home on the coast.

Their six-month stay provided a blessed reprieve. 'My mother remembered the long walks along the water's edge,' Brigitte says.

She would dig her feet in the sand to feel its silkiness. Once they were allowed to go swimming. It was her first time. When it was windy, she would hold her sister's hand and they would run against the wind and feel its resistance. She remembered the organised games on the beach; leapfrog and ring-a-ring-o'roses.

And, of course, she recalled the food. Many years later the thought of the big bowls of vegetable soup and thick crusty bread and the four o'clock snack of bread and chocolate brought a huge smile to her face.

As adults, neither sister spoke much of those painful times, but the experience of being deprived of so much – food, shelter, security, parental support – in their early years had a lasting effect. Brigitte says her mother made sure that food was always available in their house, and in great quantity.

> After so many years of starvation, she always bought way too much. Her relationship with food was not about eating it, but having it. I have never experienced hunger, but this feeling was passed on to me. When I was a child, I would daydream that I would hide in the local supermarket and get locked up inside for the night. I would go up and down the aisle and cradle all the food. It was not to eat the food, but to revel in its presence.

Meanwhile, the Quakers and other relief agencies were attempting to distribute scarce resources as widely as possible. There were increasing tensions within the organisation about how aid should be allocated: to the needy French population or to the refugee 'undesirables' in the camps. In a reply to Mary Elmes, Howard Kershner said he was against asking the already overburdened government at Vichy to improve conditions in the camps. However, he agreed to support Mary's efforts to provide assistance to the camp refugees and gave her permission to go 'full speed ahead' to do everything within her power.[16]

His attitude was a source of disquiet among volunteers. Mary's colleague Helga Holbek had furious exchanges with him on the subject of food. Another colleague, Ross McClelland, head of refugee camp work in Marseille, accused Kershner of making ridiculous general statements to the effect that 'many children in the camps are better fed than lots of children outside'.[17] He said that Kershner was interested in French children only because it might bring him positive publicity.

> If I could only really feel that he was sincerely interested in the lots of French children, rather than in getting a little 'red ribbon' [the Légion d'Honneur, the highest decoration in France] for himself, it might be different. One is always suspicious that his propaganda for aiding French children is motivated by a desire to receive favourable personal publicity (which helping the camp children certainly would not bring him).[18]

Mary wasn't prepared to mince her words either. When Noel Field of the Unitarian Committee singled out Rivesaltes as 'the sore spot' after a week-long tour of the camps, she wrote a fierce rebuttal, tackling his accusations point by point. She didn't accept his charge that the internees were practically on a starvation diet.

> He doesn't realise that the situation with food is bad for everyone. For the last several days there have been no vegetables of any kind on the market and I myself have been eating the food which I have the privilege of buying from our stores here . . . Usually my evening meal consists of some soup and some potatoes of which I have been given a present. Without this advantage I would be probably as badly off as the internees at Rivesaltes as the opportunity of purchase on the open market [is] practically null.[19]

An incident described by Marjorie McClelland opens another window on what was happening in the south of France in late 1941 and early 1942. By then many of the Spanish refugees had been contracted to work in France; others had joined the French army, and some were being repatriated to Spain. In a letter to Margaret Jones at the Quaker headquarters in Philadelphia, Marjorie described meeting a convoy of about twenty Spaniards as they were being repatriated to Spain. They begged a gendarme to call at the Quakers' office in Toulouse, as they had heard there was a chance they might get something to eat. The gendarme called at the office and was told to bring the group of men immediately.

> Well, we rushed into the kitchen to see what we could find to give our guests. A Spaniard and an Austrian who sleep in the building were summoned, and we set to work, setting the table, building a wood fire in the stove, and opening immense cans of beans, which, to our intense joy, turned out to have little sausages liberally mixed in. While preparations were getting under way, the men arrived and were seated around the table. The three or four gendarmes accompanying them were placed at a little table at the back of the room.

Marjorie was struck by the desperation of the group of wan men who ate what they were given in silence. She said their eyes lit up when plates of steaming beans were put in front of them; for many it was the first real food they had seen in months. At least, she thought, the Quakers had been able to provide a little oasis between two lost existences: the miserable camp they had left and the uncertain future that awaited them when they returned to Spain.

> The men, on leaving, looked quite changed from the group that had come in – their facial expressions were so different. Each one had to shake hands and thank us separately, stammering it out in poor French, which was the common language we used.
>
> 'But, how to thank you?' one of them said. 'I have come out of the night, and you fed me. For 22 months, I have eaten out of a tin pail with a rusty spoon, and you have set me down at a clean table with a china plate and a knife and fork, and you have served me with your own hands. But how to thank you for this?'
>
> After our guests had all gone, carrying with them crackers and cans of meat to eat on the trip, Helga and Ima and I scarcely had anything to say to each other. I think we were all too moved by our supper party and the reactions of our guests. How I wished you and our other friends could have been with us to see this small but concrete example of Quaker work in France.

The Spanish refugees were repatriated to Franco's Spain. The Quakers were not able to say what became of them.[20]

Chapter 12 ∾

MARY'S LIST

'Today is Arnold's 12th birthday and I don't know where he is. It seems that he is leaving for New York ... one part of me found it very difficult to be separated from him, but the other part is pleased that at least one Niedermann will end up there.'
— Friederike Niedermann, Arnold's mother

Eleven-year-old Arnold Niedermann was too ill with mumps to make roll call, but his mother, Friederike, didn't want him to be transferred to the camp infirmary at Rivesaltes. She wanted to avoid that at all costs. She was a trained nurse and felt he faced certain death if he was moved into a barracks with people who were suffering from more serious illnesses. Instead she decided to hide him in her own lodgings, under the loose straw that served as her bed. But there was still the problem of roll call.

For once, the policy of separating Jewish families had a positive side. Arnold's older brother, thirteen-year-old Paul, had been assigned to a different block with his father, Albert. It was forbidden, and difficult, to go from one block to another, but Paul had worked out a route that allowed him to visit his mother and brother unseen. This would prove to be a blessing, along with the fortuitous timing of roll call. It was held at different times in the men's and women's quarters, which allowed Paul to be present at both.

'I just raised my hand and said, "Present",' he recalls, now aged ninety. 'The head of the barracks didn't know us and wasn't able to tell the difference between one young boy and another.'[1] For days he ran back and forth while his mother nursed Arnold back to health in the relatively germ-free environment of her own barracks.

That memory is one of many that Paul has spent his life recounting so that the next generation will never forget what happened in Europe in the late 1930s and 40s. He and his family were arrested in Karlsruhe in western Germany in October 1940. With more than seven thousand other German Jews they were put on a train and interned at Gurs camp in the south of France. In March 1941 they were transferred to Rivesaltes, which would become the holding centre for Jews in non-occupied France a year later.

His first impression of the camp set the tone for the rest of his stay there:

> When we arrived . . . and went into the first barracks, the one where men and women were separated, I remember that a kind of red cloud fell from the beam overhead. It was a mass of hungry fleas; for months, nobody had been in that place. They descended on us with a vengeance.[2]

Like so many others at Rivesaltes, he recalled the lack of food and the fights between men over a morsel of bread. 'I even saw people smoking vine twigs to chase away hunger pangs,' he said.[3]

Given those hardships, it is easy to understand why the visit of a woman promising to transfer the brothers to a holiday camp stood out as 'a very important event'.[4] The woman, Vivette Hermann (later Samuel), told his parents that she could transfer the boys to a children's home if they gave their permission.

He doesn't recall a visit by Mary Elmes – 'I didn't speak a word of French so there was a lot I didn't understand' – but she also went to see the Niedermanns that year. She sought parental permission to add Arnold's and Paul's names to a list of children destined for America in 1941. The United States had agreed to accept five convoys of refugee children under an agreement arranged by the Quakers' executive secretary, Clarence Pickett, with help from the wife of the American president, Eleanor Roosevelt. To facilitate their emigration, the Quakers set up a rescue organisation, the United States Committee for the Care of European Children. During the war years it brought more than a thousand children to America from France and Britain.[5]

Mary was asked to select camp children for the fourth convoy. At the end of August 1941, she interviewed parents and children to begin the slow, tedious process of preparing dossiers for seventeen children.

'You will be glad to know that Paul and Arnold Niedermann . . . are amongst the 17 children whose particulars we took yesterday,' she told the Quaker delegate J. J. Champenois after a series of interviews at the camp. However, she gave no indication of why he might have been glad.[6]

In any case, it was of little use to Paul, because candidates had to be over six years of age and under twelve. Paul was already thirteen. Subsequent letters from Mary about the convoy mention only Arnold, although she may have made a case to have him included. She certainly tried to convince her colleagues at Marseille to bend the rules in several other cases. She made special appeals for children who had lost a parent, or parents, and pleaded that siblings be kept together even when they did not fulfil the criteria; but without success. For instance, she said that Herman and Tobias Weitman, aged thirteen and fourteen, should be included, as they were alone in the camp: their mother was in Germany and the whereabouts of their father was unknown. She also pleaded the case of Henri Mass, who was too young at five and a half. She didn't want him to be separated from his seven-year-old sister.[7]

There was another issue. Howard Kershner was unhappy with the number of Jewish children in the previous convoy. Ross McClelland wrote to inform Mary in September 1941, and he said he hoped all her work in compiling a list would not be undone.

> We all hope they will be able to leave, although I understand that Mr Kershner's reaction to the group which just left . . . was not favourable. He did not feel that we were doing the States a great service by sending over these children. He felt that if it was to turn into a 100% Jewish affair that it should be handled by the Jewish organizations rather than ourselves.[8]

Mary responded, saying she hoped that her children would be allowed to leave, if not in this convoy in the next one: 'I am not concerned about the amount of time and work it has taken to make the dossiers, but I am afraid that the parents and the children will be bitterly disappointed if it is not possible to send them to America after all.'⁹

She was also put out by Howard Kershner's attitude:

I am rather troubled to learn that Mr. Kershner feels that the Quakers should do no more in the matter of 100% Jewish emigration. It of course would seem more reasonable if the Jewish Organisations took it over entirely, but I sincerely hope that he will make a very strong recommendation that the children whose papers we have taken some trouble to arrange should be included in any future convoy.¹⁰

In the meantime, one Jewish organisation took action rather than wait for visas. The Œuvre de Secours aux Enfants moved both Arnold and Paul to one of its children's homes. The transfer to children's homes was often done with the approval of the authorities, but the brothers escaped some time in late March or April 1942, Paul recalls. In the early hours of the morning, Vivette Samuel gathered eight children, including the brothers, and assembled them near the perimeter fence. An old van, spluttering and noisy, made its way through the vines towards them. Paul was surprised at the racket it was making. The driver got out and cut the wire. Eight children crawled underneath it and were driven away.

'I noticed a guard at 200 m who clearly turned his back to us,' he says. 'He didn't flinch once and we left.'¹¹ The camp guards were French and were easily bribed, many internees and aid workers said afterwards. Others were happy to turn a blind eye, and in some cases they even helped children to escape.

The brothers were moved to a children's home in Palavas-les-Flots, near Montpellier, and shortly afterwards the convoy of young refugees was ready to leave for America. In late April the children earmarked for emigration were assembled in Marseille, waiting for the final go-ahead. Eleven of 'Mary's children' – as they were called – were on the list of those departing, including Arnold Niedermann.¹²

Before the departure, the children's parents made a series of 'desperate and piteous pleas' to be released from the camps so that they could see their children off.[13] The OSE agreed to pay for their accommodation in Marseille. Mary was asked to seek special leave from the camp authorities at Rivesaltes so that Arnold's mother and ten others could travel the 190 miles to Marseille to wave their children off. It is not clear why, but only two of those mothers travelled to the port in May.

Arnold's mother was not one of them.

Shortly after her son sailed on the *Maréchal Lyautey* on 14 May 1942 en route for Casablanca, she wrote:

> Today [20 June 1942] is Arnold's 12th birthday and I don't know where he is. It seems that he is leaving for New York today or the day after tomorrow. That thought raises two contradictory emotions in me. One part of me found it very difficult to be separated from him, but the other part is pleased that at least one Niedermann will end up there.[14]

The convoy of children left Casablanca for Lisbon and from there went to New York. Arnold was met by his maternal aunt and uncle, Gertrude and Albert Strauss, who raised him in Baltimore. Arnold's brother was still at the children's home, his mother was at the camp in Rivesaltes, and his father, Albert, had been transferred to another camp, Récébédou, near Toulouse, after spending eleven months in hospital.

From early 1941 to mid-1942, even before deportations began, children's lives were at risk. Relief workers drew attention to the high mortality rate in the camps, caused by malnourishment and disease. The youngest were particularly vulnerable, and they pressed to have them released from the camp. When asked later to describe the effect on children's health, Mary wrote:

> It is only what can be expected after two or three years of camp life with inadequate food, bad housing conditions and lack of hygiene. Many of the children are riddled with vermin and all of them undernourished. It is only due to the fact that they have received a regular supplement of rice from the Quakers and other supplements from the Swiss since about a year that many of these children are still alive. As for their clothing, it is in very bad

condition. A large number of them have no underclothing what-soever. Their footwear is also very bad.[15]

What was termed the 'liberation' of children could happen in two ways. The first was by securing them a place on a refugee convoy to the United States, but that was 'unbelievably complicated', according to Marjorie McClelland. It was a lengthy, bureaucratic process and it obliged parents to agree to allow their children to leave the country on their own. Sometimes the children went to relatives, but not always.[16]

The second way of getting children out of Rivesaltes was by sending them to one of a number of 'colonies' that were dotted around the Pyrénées-Orientales region. They operated like holiday homes and were intended to give children temporary respite from the harshness of camp life for up to three months.

When Mary Elmes established a colony on the coast at Canet-Plage, some twelve miles from Rivesaltes, in March 1941, a local paper sent along a journalist, Théo Duret, to observe the daily routine. He wrote an article full of enthusiasm for the premises, with its brightly painted walls, nourishing food and happy atmosphere. Another article concluded: 'The Quaker formula works very well because it restores to health those children who have been stalked by voracious misery.' The article also made a point of stressing that the Quakers did not exert any religious influence on those staying there.[17] Local people were happy to help when they could. That year the winners of the local *boule* competition donated their aggregate prize-winnings of 470 francs (approximately €120 in 2017) to the upkeep of the colony.

A month later, Mary set up a second colony nearby. La Villa Saint-Christophe was a summer-season villa that the Quakers ran with the Mennonites. Together the homes could cater for more than a hundred children, and they were soon full of Spanish and Jewish refugees taken from the camp at Rivesaltes. These homes would later play a vital role in saving the lives of Jewish children when the deportations began, but that spring they were principally seen as respite centres.

'Woke with noise of happy children outside the window; children singing, playing games, and running on beach,' Lois Gunden wrote on her first day as the new director of the Villa Saint-Christophe.[18]

In another diary entry, in February 1942, she described a visit
from the parents who were released temporarily from the camp to
visit their children:

> It always thrills me to see how happy they are to find their children
> being so well taken care of. There are times when my heart almost
> bursts with joy at being able to be among them and to give them
> this bit of release from the un-homelike atmosphere of the camp.
> We have some dear youngsters under six years old again, but it is
> an entirely different group than at first when we arrived. Often I
> think of Doris and Ruth in comparison with some of the girls of
> the same age. Imagine what it would be like to have been refugees
> away from home and all the advantages of security, comfort, and
> school privileges for three years! All of them are eagerly looking
> forward to the end of the war so that they can again have a settled
> life. Yes, I'm glad over and over that I am here for these months
> are giving me rich experiences.[19]

However, despite the attractions and the comfort of the children's
colonies, the demand for places had fallen off. People in the camps
were under the impression that things were looking up. In mid-April
1942, four months before the first camp deportation to Auschwitz,
Mary Elmes spent three days at Rivesaltes, going from barrack to
barrack, trying to persuade parents to allow their children to go on
holiday to the Quakers' children's colonies. She set up a temporary
office, posted notices all around the camp, and asked for announcements
to be made in the camp refectories. But she was having difficulty
coming up with a list of names. Fewer than sixty had signed up for the
scheme, although there were up to three hundred places.[20]

Part of the reason for the reluctance was that the weather had
improved and, along with it, spirits, she told Gertrude Kershner in
Marseille.

Also, the German Commissions were again taking men away to
work, and several women had applied to join them, although those
applications had been pending for several months. Other women
believed they might be released with their children if they applied
enough pressure, but Mary tried to tell them that this hope was

unfounded. 'The women have got the idea that, if they insist sufficiently that they also must be taken out of the camp with their children . . . however, I have spoken very seriously to many of them and hope that perhaps in some cases this attitude can be changed.'[21]

She went on to say that it would be 'very desirable' to remove family groups into homes, but that wasn't possible on a large scale. She was working as hard as possible to find a solution to this 'new problem' that had presented itself and which almost immobilised the removal of these very needy children into better conditions of living.

Meanwhile, the American head of the Quakers' operations, Howard Kershner, and his wife, Gertrude, left France that April, along with many of Mary's American colleagues. When the United States entered the war after the Japanese attack on Pearl Harbor in December 1941, American citizens in France faced growing uncertainty. Before he left, Howard Kershner wrote to Mary to thank her for her work: 'If we do not see you before we leave, Mrs Kershner and I would both like to register again our great satisfaction in working with you during the past years.'[22]

However, Mary's forthright colleague Ross McClelland, himself an American, was cutting about some of his colleagues, who, he felt, were too 'jittery' and too anxious to leave. In a letter to Mary in December 1941 his rebuke of 'our rabbity friend' (a member of another aid organisation) was merciless.

[He] immediately rushed around in small circles trying to get visas to leave the moment things began to look a little difficult. He was all ready to run for Lisbon in a blue funk . . . When Marj. & I bid him farewell he was looking pretty sick. He is afraid of being bottled up in Switzerland for an indefinite period, although I can think of worse places to be stuck![23]

Ross McClelland stayed on in France and recorded, in detail, what was about to unfold in the summer of 1942 and the many steps the Quakers took to stop it.

On 11 June a meeting was held in Berlin to discuss the implementation of Hitler's Final Solution: the Nazi plan to annihilate the Jewish people. Targets were set for the numbers to be deported from Belgium (10,000), the Netherlands (15,000) and France (100,000). In France, the Germans knew that they would not be able to round up, intern and deport that number. They did not have the personnel: there were no more than three thousand German police in both zones of France in 1942.[24] They were going to need the collaboration of the French authorities.

The Vichy government agreed to the deportation of all 'stateless' or foreign Jews 'as a first step' (*pour commencer*).[25] The implication was that it was somehow stalling the deportation of French citizens, although there was never any formal agreement for such a measure. Almost a third of the Jews deported from France were French.

According to Michael Marrus and Robert Paxton, from the summer of 1942 'the Jews' great peril was the policeman's knocks at the door, the midday round-up or arrest at the frontier.'[26] On the morning of 16 July, the biggest of those round-ups got under way. Some nine thousand French police, comprising gendarmes, *gardes mobiles*, bailiffs, detectives, patrolmen and student policemen, arrested and interned 13,000 Jewish men, women and children in the Vélodrome d'Hiver, an indoor sports arena in the 15th arrondissement of Paris.[27]

News of the forthcoming arrests was leaked by some French policemen. A Jewish newspaper had advised people to flee. People had no idea what lay ahead of them. As many as one hundred committed suicide and thousands fled towards the unoccupied zone. Many of them were arrested and interned at Rivesaltes and other camps.

From Perpignan, the relief workers at Rivesaltes noted that the Jews were now confined to Block K and that a barbed-wired fence had been erected around them. In July a detailed census was taken of all the inmates in the internment camps. All leave was cancelled.

'The compiling of this data went on day and night,' Ross McClelland wrote.[28] The results were entered on master lists, which had to be handed in to police stations by a certain date. They had been told that the authorities were reuniting families (*regroupement familiale*), but the Quakers were sceptical.

On 21 July 1942, a new order meant that foreign Jews leaving France had to make a specific request for an exit visa in Vichy. Those who already had a visa would have to reapply, as visas granted under the old system were now invalid.

Shortly afterwards, the Quakers received the first definite information about deportations in the occupied zone. There was an initial plan to deport 10,000, and people were to be taken from a number of camps in the south of France – Rivesaltes, Gurs, Vernet, Les Milles, Récébédou and Noé. The first trains were scheduled to leave between 6 and 12 August.

The relief agencies immediately convened a special meeting of the Co-ordinating Committee. They decided unanimously to send a delegation to Vichy to attempt to see Marshal Pétain to protest against this action 'formally and emphatically'. If the action couldn't be stopped, the Quakers would seek certain exemptions: children under sixteen, those with a visa or visa authorisation for the United States, and those working for relief agencies.[29]

Howard Kershner's successor, Lindsley Noble, and Ross McClelland were due to make the representations. Before leaving for Vichy, they visited the camp at Les Milles to see what was happening there.

My eye was met by the grim sight of the perimeter of this old brick factory surrounded by a large contingent of the new 'Milice Nationale' [right-wing French militia] in black uniforms (shades of the SS?), steel helmets and carbines slung over their shoulders. This disproportionate display of armed strength contrasted almost ludicrously with the sad assemblage of ill-clothed, under-nourished, half-sick, heterogeneous internees who constituted Les Milles' population. There was an almost constant coming and going through the main gate as the wives, children and elderly relatives of the men interned in the camp were brought in from Marseille and the surrounding area. At one point a small group of children only arrived, followed by three or four heavily guarded busloads of men from the Foreign Workers' Companies in the Bouches du Rhône who had been released from the camp some months earlier . . . and were now being returned for the selection of those to be deported. The atmosphere was heavy with foreboding.[30]

The two Quaker representatives went to Vichy on 4 August, but there was little sympathy for the 'foreign Jews', who were considered 'France's misfortune', Ross reported. They met Pétain's adviser, Dr Bernard Ménétral, who said the problem had started with Blum's Popular Front government, which had let too many of them enter France. They couldn't be assimilated, he said. The German measure was designed to take them back and reunite families.

> We protested that the brutal steps taken in Paris, of which he must be aware, to break up foreign Jewish families and separate them into various categories – the able-bodied, the old and ill, the young girls and children – hardly supported the Nazi contention that they were 'regrouping families' but seemed to us designed to serve some far more sinister purpose. Based on the information increasingly filtering out of Eastern Europe we said we feared the true purpose was physical annihilation.[31]

Ménétral brushed off the interpretation as 'hysterical exaggeration'.

The next day they went back and met Ménétral and the Vichy prime minister, Pierre Laval. He waved aside fears of the Jews' 'extermination' as 'preposterous' and 'pure fiction'.[32] When they tried to secure exemptions for children, Laval simply said he would consider the matter and was then called away.

Meanwhile, Tracy Strong Senior of the Young Men's Christian Association said he would bring up the matter with Marshal Pétain. The meeting was very unsatisfactory, as the ageing general seemed to be unaware of what was happening. He was primarily concerned with the worsening food situation in France. 'The mention of the deportation measures elicited only the repeated observation . . . "Les Allemands sont durs" [The Germans are hard]!' Ross reported afterwards.[33]

The two men spent a number of days trying to set up meetings, but in vain. Downcast, Ross returned to his office in Marseille, where news of the first deportation at Gurs on 6 August was just coming through:

Helga Holbek telephoned to tell us that the first group of 1,000 internees (ranging in ages from 18 to 86!) from the camp of Gurs had been loaded between midnight and 5 a.m. the night before into 33 box-cars at the station of Oloron-St Marie in the Basses Pyrénées and dispatched towards an unknown destination. Helga was terribly shaken and wept as she told us how the hopeful cry of *'Die Quaker sind hier'* (the Quaker is here) had spread from lip to lip as she drove into the low-lying, dreary camp that had already seen so much suffering among Spanish Republican refugees. Yet, other than pressing departing hands, taking a hastily scrawled message for loved-ones elsewhere, and trying desperately to spread a word of cheer, Helga said there had been little she could do to respond to the anguished confidence placed in her and the Quakers.[34]

Meanwhile in Rivesaltes, the camp administration called a meeting of all the relief agencies on 7 August and told them that children were to be deported along with their parents. The OSE representative, Andrée Salmon, later recalled that 'Miss [Elmes], the Quaker delegate, immediately took a first group with her in her own car and came back the same day in search of others . . . We had to get the children out at all costs.'[35]

Ross McClelland said there were 'several instances of compassion and goodwill on the part of French officials who were forced by circumstances to participate in deportation. When the commandant at [the] Camp of Rivesaltes outside Perpignan, for example, learned that the children would probably also be deported, although they were not to be included at the outset, he simply "gave" children to our delegates with the urgent admonition: "Make them vanish".'[36]

Chapter 13 ~

RESCUE

'The Jews are real men and women. Foreigners are real
men and women. They cannot be abused without limit . . .
They are part of the human species.'
— Jules-Gérard Saliège, Archbishop of Toulouse

Mary Elmes 'spirited away' nine children from the first convoy bound for Auschwitz when it left the Rivesaltes camp on 11 August 1942.

That piece of information – damning in the wrong hands – survives in pencil-written notes jotted down by the Quaker director in France, Lindsley Noble. He described how Mary, with help from the commander of the camp, David-Gustave Humbert, rescued as many as 34 children between them, as 400 people were loaded onto cattle wagons and taken to the notorious holding centre of Drancy, outside Paris, and then to their death in Poland.[1]

Lindsley also explained how Mary intended to hide the children she had smuggled out: 'Mary is going to move some Spanish children out of the Mennonite colony at Canet-Plage to take in foreign Jewish children . . . Telling them to hide seems to me now quite justified in view of complete absence of rime [rhyme] or reason in [the] way they are taking people.'[2]

The children's homes run by the Quakers, the Œuvre de Secours aux Enfants and the Swiss Red Cross in the south of France were no longer only respite homes but hiding places for the hundreds of children the relief workers managed to take out of the camp during the critical period from August to October 1942.

On 9 August, Mary visited her friend and colleague Lois Gunden, director of the Villa Saint-Christophe children's home at Canet-

Plage, to tell her what was going on. Lois recorded in her diary: 'Mary informed me about return of Polish and German Jews to Poland where death by starvation awaits them.'[3]

By 10 August, Mary had already begun to move children out of the camp. Lois noted: 'Miss Elmes had brought us three Jewish boys in an attempt to save them when their parents leave; had quite some time quieting the poor little fellow; but finally his sobs died down.'[4]

In the days and weeks that followed she brought a steady stream of children to the relative safety of the Villa Saint-Christophe colony. She smuggled them in the boot of her car and drove out of the camp, according to memoirs written by two of her colleagues, Alice Resch and Vivette Samuel. The fact that she was a regular visitor to the camp meant that the guards knew her well and probably waved her through the barrier.

She never explained how she managed to get the children into her car unseen, but she may have assembled them by acting in a similar way to her OSE counterpart Andrée Salomon.

'Andrée got a group of 12 out,' the Quaker delegate Alice Resch recalled in her memoir.

They were on their way to a checkpoint when she came along smiling cheerfully, and said, 'Children this way!' and led them neatly out of the convoy. The authority in her voice made the guards think that her activities were just part of the whole plan. She led the flock down a side street, where a truck from OSE was waiting and quickly put the children on board. Andrée climbed in beside the driver, and they drove right out through the main gate where she just waved her 'permit' at the guards as usual. The guards recognised her and the car, and didn't bother to check her papers, and the children were saved.[5]

It is difficult to say exactly how many children Mary rescued from the nine convoys that deported a total of 2,289 Jewish adults and 174 children between August and October 1942. However, Mary's colleague Vivette Samuel estimated that 427 children were saved from deportation that autumn.[6]

Lois Gunden estimated that every two weeks Mary brought between three and seven children to the home at Canet-Plage during that time.

On 11 August 1942, for instance, she recorded the arrival of seven children:

> While we were eating supper Miss Elmes brought seven Jewish children – some of whom can't speak French; [Isidore] Mussoles cooked some extra macaroni; *quelle comédie pour les laver en lavabo!* [what theatrics when we went to wash them in the wash-basin]. *Les garçons ne voulaient pas enlever leurs culottes* [The boys didn't want to take off their underpants]; finally found bed spare for everyone; 43 in house at present . . .[7]

The comedy with the boys' underpants was a chilling reminder of how parents had warned their circumcised sons to keep their underpants on to hide the fact that they were Jewish.

Thanks to Lois Gunden's journal, the arrival of Jewish children at the colony in Canet-Plage is well documented, but Mary brought children to the many other Quaker colonies she had established around the Pyrénées-Orientales region. There was a second Quaker colony at Canet-Plage, with places for forty children. She may have hidden children there too, although documentary evidence for that has yet to emerge.

She herself provided proof that she used the two Quaker children's homes at Vernet-les-Bains to hide children. On 13 August she explained in a letter to Louis Frank in Marseille that the homes there were full. 'We have taken 14 children out of the camp of Rivesaltes recently, under extremely exceptional circumstances, which I may some day be able to explain to you.' She added that 'these were children whom we could not refuse.'[8]

Some months previously, Mary had set up a colony at the Grand Hôtel du Portugal in Vernet-les-Bains, a picturesque town known as 'the Paradise of the Pyrenees' during the Belle Époque years. At the beginning of the twentieth century, it was a luxurious spa town whose pristine mountain site, casino and *haute cuisine* attracted a British elite who contributed to a pre-war boom. The English writer

Rudyard Kipling was a regular visitor; he stayed at the hotel, taking daily therapeutic baths to ease his arthritis.

After the outbreak of the Second World War, the town's fortunes took a drastic downturn. The devastating flood of 1940 also took a heavy toll; many of its fine buildings were swept away. The hotels that remained, among them the Grand Hôtel du Portugal, were in a poor state, which had one unexpected advantage: it meant they were vacant and available for rent. Mary Elmes saw the potential of the hotel and went about renting it. It would be big enough to house up to sixty children, she said.[9] The Quakers also rented the Hôtel d'Angleterre.

The hotels that had once provided a playground for the rich were now safe houses for Jewish children who might not have survived otherwise.

Children were also housed high up in the hidden mountain retreat at La Coûme, near the medieval town of Mosset. In 1933, Edith Pye and Hilda Clark (a doctor from the well-known Quaker family that manufactured Clark's shoes) bought a ruined farmhouse there and later used it to provide accommodation for German refugees resettling in France. The following year two German teachers, Pitt and Yvès Krüger, took it over after they were dismissed from their posts by the Nazis. They opened a youth hostel that became famous as an international meeting-place. In 1939, Mary Elmes asked La Coûme to take in Spanish refugees and, later, Jewish children in danger of being deported.

The number of children she brought there is not recorded, but at the end of 1942 one Jewish child was still at La Coûme. There were seven at the Grand Hôtel du Portugal and a further thirteen in the Hôtel d'Angleterre at Vernet-les-Bains. Mary quoted the figures in a letter that stressed the urgency of trying to place them in French homes, or in children's homes outside the region, because they would have difficulties with the civil authorities if they stayed where they were.[10]

At La Coûme, Pitt Krüger was later arrested by the Gestapo and deported. The Quakers tried to make representations on his behalf, but without success. He returned to France in 1948, and he and his wife continued their work. The Krüger Foundation still operates today as an international education centre.

Other Quaker homes also acted as safe places. Mary sent children to Château de Larade, a children's home in Toulouse.[11] She also transferred pregnant Jewish women from the Rivesaltes camp to La Maternité Suisse, a maternity hospital set up in an old castle in Elne, south of Perpignan. The Swiss Red Cross established the hospital in 1939 with financial help from the Quakers.[12] From the time it opened, Mary facilitated the transfer of Spanish, Jewish and Roma mothers. More than six hundred children were born there. Its director, a Swiss woman, Elisabeth Eidenbenz, was honoured as Righteous Among the Nations in 2001 for hiding Jewish women and their children by changing their names on the register.

Officially, the Quakers were expected to operate within the rules laid down by the Vichy government. The previous head of Quaker operations, Howard Kershner, had warned his volunteers on several occasions not to do anything to jeopardise the organisation's work. The same was true of other aid agencies. After the deportations began, the Swiss Red Cross issued a stark warning to its relief workers, ordering them to remain strictly neutral, politically and ideologically.

'The laws and the decrees of the French Government must be carried out exactly and you do not have to examine if they are in accordance or not with your own convictions,' the circular read. It went on, at some length, to say that while the French Catholic and Protestant churches had spoken out against certain Vichy directives, the Red Cross could not be influenced by this.[13]

Some members of the Catholic Church had been unequivocal in their opposition to the deportation of people from the camps in France. On 23 August 1942, the Archbishop of Toulouse, Jules-Gérard Saliège, spoke out strongly against the Vichy government and the Germans' treatment of Jews.

In a pastoral letter he wrote:

Alas, it has been our destiny to witness the dreadful spectacle of women and children, fathers and mothers treated like cattle, members of a family separated from one another and dispatched to an unknown destination – it has been reserved for our own time to see such a sad spectacle. Why does the right of sanctuary no longer exist in our churches? Why are we defeated? . . . The

Jews are real men and women. Foreigners are real men and women. They cannot be abused without limit … They are part of the human species. They are our brothers, like so many others. No Christian dares forget that![14]

The letter was read in the churches of his diocese and became a manifesto for the Resistance.

The Quakers would have their own internal battles about how best to mitigate the horror of what was happening around them. There was a constant fear that the relief organisation would be dissolved or expelled if it went against the Vichy government. Despite those risks, Quaker opposition to the deportation of Jews was clear. After the first convoy left, Lindsley Noble went to the US embassy in Vichy to send a secure wire to Clarence Pickett at the Quaker headquarters in Philadelphia. He told him of the plan to deport ten thousand Jews from unoccupied France and appealed for help:

Recommend immediate intervention competent organisations to provide asylum in friendly countries for all foreign Jewish children in unoccupied zone. Will cable estimate numbers as soon as possible.[15]

In the camps, officials often turned a blind eye, while others, such as the camp commander, David-Gustave Humbert, actively helped children to escape. Lindsley noted the very difficult lot of Frenchmen carrying out these orders: 'They are doing all they can to be real Frenchmen, uphold the national honour in an affair which is cowardly and without honour.'[16]

Paul Corazzi, a senior official at the préfecture, or civil offices, in Perpignan, kept the relief agencies informed of new orders from the Vichy government. There is a reference in Lindsley's notes to say he had even promised to get Mary Elmes a list of the first four hundred people deported from Rivesaltes.

The numbers, however, could not capture the repugnant nature of what was happening. The Swiss Red Cross nurse Friedel Bohny-Reiter, who lived in her own barracks within the camp, did this with a disquieting description:

The cries and moans of those tormented people are still ringing in the air. I can see them coming out of their housing units in long lines, panting under the weight of their personal effects. The guards are right beside them. They have to line up for roll call and wait for hours out in a field under the full sun. Then trucks arrive and take them away to the railroad tracks. They climb out of the trucks between two rows of guards and climb into cattlecars, some of them hesitant, others listless, a few defiant, with their heads high. This lasts for hours, until finally they have all been packed into the train cars that are stifling . . . Two guards have been placed in front of each opening. I observe the faces. Now not even despair can be seen on these aged, worn down, dreary faces.[17]

After the convoy departed, the letters going back and forth between Mary and colleagues were full of enquiries about the whereabouts of people, many of whom had been deported. In a response to Ima Lieven in Toulouse on 27 August 1942 Mary wrote:

I regret to have to tell you that Mr. Richard Stern left the camp of Rivesaltes with the first convoy on August 11. I saw him shortly before his departure. He was very calm and resigned, although disappointed that he had no recent news from his daughter in England from whom he was expecting a letter and a transfer. I am sorry to have to send you this news.[18]

Arnold and Paul Niedermann's mother, Friederike, was also on the first convoy and was sent to her death in Auschwitz. The boys' father, Albert, was sent to Majdanek in Poland, where he died in the gas chambers. Paul was still in the children's home at Palavas-les-Flots. His brother was safe in America, and for now Paul too was safe, but that would not last.

Meanwhile, the Quakers were still working to get children travel documents to allow them to leave on a planned fifth refugee convoy to the United States. At first as many as a thousand visas were promised to Jewish children.

'Phew, what an awful lot of writing back and forth about my

kids,' Alice Resch wrote in a chirpy, upbeat tone that belied the magnitude of the task.[19]

Apart from the vast amount of paperwork that had to be completed, the aid workers had to ask parents to sign papers entrusting their children to the Quakers' care. One father refused several times but eventually agreed. Then he had just one request before his son left; he wanted to see him. The last time had been more than two years previously.

There were other, more optimistic stories. Alice Resch in particular was always quick to acknowledge a little serendipity. In a letter to Mary she talked about clothes that materialised as if out of thin air. 'The two eldest Vidal girls ... needed coats, and unfortunately we had none. Then to day, as lightning from [a] clear sky, appeared some fine coat specimens, just their sizes.'[20] She even had some left over and was going to send them, by express parcel post, to Mary.

Nonetheless the strain of what was going on around them was evident in the letters. Alice was particularly expressive. In one letter, a few days before the first deportation, she wrote: 'The world is all chaos here on account of the happenings.'[21] In another, she wrote in the margin: 'Phew, this letter was solemn!'

The physical demands of the job were considerable, but they were as nothing compared with the psychological strain of working in Vichy France. What also emerges from the letters between the Quaker volunteers is how much friendship sustained them during the darkest years – that, and an ability to snatch a rushed break or an occasional treat despite the chaos of war. When the delegates travelled between the various Quaker branch offices in the south of France there was often a social event tagged on to the official one. It might be a rushed excursion, a lunch on Mary Elmes's famous sunny balcony, or, as in the following instance, a swim in the heat of June.

Before she was due in Marseille to attend a conference, Marjorie McClelland wrote to Mary to say they were all looking forward to meeting her. 'I hope that you will come early and stay late, and bring your bathing suit and we can all go on a picnic. The water's lovely. Affectionately. Marjorie.'[22]

Mary met the man who would become her husband, Roger Danjou, a forester, about 1941 when he did some work for the

Quakers. He was divorced and had a daughter, Catherine, born in Caen to his first wife. Mary and Roger became a couple about 1942 and his name crops up in the delegates' letters from about early 1943. That correspondence was full of news about the ordinary things in life too: an unexpected coffee allowance, a coffee grinder bought on the black market, the exchange of books. Mary sent a copy of Proust's *Pastiches et Mélanges* to Ross McClelland in Marseille. He, in turn, sent her a Hemingway novel, though the letter doesn't say which one.

There is also an everyday pragmatism in the exchanges. When Ross and his wife, Marjorie, were going on a trip to Geneva, Mary asked a favour: 'I should be awfully glad if Marjorie could bring back a couple of packets of invisible hair-pins (blond). Melle Ruth did bring me two packets, but since her return she has not been able to find them in her luggage and I begin to despair over ever seeing them. They are essential attributes to my general tidy appearance.'[23] They returned with several packets for her.

The week before the first deportation took place at Rivesaltes, Mary invited Lois Gunden to join her on a mountaineering excursion to Canigou. Alice Resch was meant to go too. She was just back from a trip to the Côte d'Azur – 'I'm as brown as a berry,' she wrote – and was all set for an outing. However, at the last minute, she was unable to go. Perhaps Mary and Lois thought to call off the excursion after the harrowing week they had just had, witnessing the effects of the departure of four hundred people on the first convoy. Then again, given the rigours of their work, perhaps they looked forward to it all the more keenly.

The previous June, Lois's colleague at the children's home, Helen Penner, went back to the United States, suffering from what the doctors had diagnosed as 'nervous fatigue'.[24] Given the nature of the work and the increasing difficulty of working in Vichy France, it's surprising that there are not more accounts of aid workers suffering burn-out or psychological strain. During Mary's time in Spain a number of volunteer doctors and nurses returned to England, for various reasons. That didn't appear to be the case in France.

Lois later said her strong faith helped her to continue her work. Mary, however, said she was not particularly religious. 'I am not a missionary,' she said in 1996. 'Never was.' She added – as she had done on several occasions – that she was there because there was work to be done.[25]

Whatever their individual motivations, Mary and her fellow relief workers seemed to appreciate the importance of taking time off. She would do just that with her friend Lois on the holiday weekend of 15 August during one of the darkest periods of the Second World War.

Lois gave a charming account of their day together and the planned hike up Canigou. It turned out to be longer and more challenging than either of them had expected:

Friday morning at 5:15 we set out [by flashlight] on our hike. Each of us carried a knapsack on his [*sic*] back filled with provisions – in way of food and warm clothes – for staying up at the top over night. After quite steady upward climbing, we reached the chalet (a refuge containing dining room, bed rooms, and dormitories) almost at the peak by 12:30. We had seen lots of beauty about us on the way up, especially when we looked out over the valley that lay behind us and identified the villages we saw there. The long stretch through the pine forests during the last third of the trip was lovely. We sat under the trees in the sort of level spot surrounding the chalet and ate our lunches. But because there were more people planning to spend the night in the refuge-hotel than there was room for, we started down at four o'clock. When we arrived at Vernet at ten o'clock that night after almost continual walking down the hill (except for a few rests), you may be sure that beds never looked more welcome to us than they did at that time. It is really too much of a trip for one day . . .[26]

The following Sunday, Mary and Lois slept late and had lunch (fresh trout caught by M. Lliboutry, prepared with butter). After that they went in search of a shady spot and spent the afternoon sitting under an apple tree. They 'felt as spry as ever before returning on Monday', Lois wrote.[27]

The women would need all their strength for what lay ahead. That week, from 18 August onwards, the authorities at Vichy prepared to arrest a total of 15,000 foreign Jews throughout the un-occupied zone. The round-up was planned for the early morning of 26 August. The criteria for arrest were much wider than before, because the French authorities wanted to cast the net as widely as possible; they were afraid they would not reach the quotas set.[28]

It was also much harder to get an exemption. Now the only categories exempt were people over the age of sixty, those too ill to travel, women who were noticeably pregnant, the parents of children under two (this age limit had been reduced from five), and those who had a French child or spouse.

The head of the French police, M. Surville, insisted that families should not be separated.[29] In cases where the children were apart from their parents – as in the Quaker children's homes, for example – there were strict orders to return them to their parents and deport them along with the parents.

Mary wrote to Lois at La Villa Saint-Christophe to tell her the children were in danger. She said they could be recalled to the camp at Rivesaltes, where they would be deported with the rest of the family: 'We are doing everything possible to prevent this, but it is unfortunately still an eventuality,' she wrote.[30]

Meanwhile, the French police were searching children's homes all over the unoccupied zone and returning Jewish children to the camps, to be deported with their parents. Two of those children were sisters, sixteen-year-old Hilda and twelve-year-old Hannah Krieser. They were taken back to Rivesaltes to be deported along with their parents, Perla and Solomon, on one of the convoys leaving for Auschwitz. In 1940 the family had fled Belgium and, with thousands of others, made it over the border into France. However, they were soon arrested and interned in Rivesaltes.

Mary's colleague Friedel Bohny-Reiter helped the Krieser children secure a place in a home outside the camp. She was shocked when she saw that they had been returned and were now waiting in line, with their mother, to board a convoy for Auschwitz. Friedel thought for a moment and then took advantage of a lapse in the guard's attention to signal to them to come to her. She ran to hide them in an unlit storeroom in the camp; then she went back to the train to rescue more children.

After the convoy left, she pleaded with the camp commander to issue exit permits to allow the children to leave. He refused at first, but Friedel kept at him, over a period of three days, until he relented.

The sisters made it safely to a children's home in Pringy in Switzerland, where they stayed until the end of the war. The girls' parents were deported separately, but they were both murdered at Auschwitz.[31]

Back at La Villa Saint-Christophe, Mary Elmes was worried for the three Landemann children, Claire, Jacques and Berthe. On 1 September two French policemen called to the children's home and told its director to have the children ready in an hour. 'That rather upset the others who had come at the same time, because they are afraid of what may be happening to their parents,' Lois noted in her diary.[32]

The next day Lois expected the gendarmes to come back, but they did not. It's not clear what measures Mary took to protect the children, because the story is told in snatches in Lois's diary. However, Lois was clearly worried that the police would return the children to the camp, to be deported with their parents. The following day she received an urgent telegram telling her to have them ready to leave; then Mary telephoned to say their uncle was coming for them immediately.

Lois recorded in her diary that evening:

When I heard of how they were finally snatched from the fate hanging over them, I felt as if God must have had a hand in preventing anyone from coming after them during these 2 days interrupted by calls and telegrams concerning them; had they been taken to camp, likely all efforts would have arrived too late for any good.[33]

A few days later, however, there was some good news. Vichy agreed to exempt all children in the Quaker colonies from deportation – although new arrivals after 13 September would not be included.[34]

Mary continued to work at the camp as deportations continued during September. She had taken over a barracks where people who needed help could come to see her. A Quaker report described the room in detail.

Her reception room has the grey walls of all other barrack interiors, but a Spanish artist has relieved this drabness with garish murals representing airplanes, locomotives and other sports full of colour and motion. There was a little bald-headed man in a ragged sweater standing in the corner . . . He was so retiring, however, that he hung his head and made no reply [when spoken to]. I was surprised to learn that this was the artist, because one would never suppose that such a humble person had conceived all those bold murals that adorned the walls.[35]

The painted walls were the only glimmer of light in that report, which was destined for Quaker headquarters in Philadelphia. It outlined in harrowing, though dispassionate, detail the abhorrent reality faced daily by Mary Elmes. 'A succession of persons came to her for help,' the report explained, giving one example. A Belgian scientist, who had once been in charge of an orphanage, came to ask Mary if he might be considered as an escort for children on the refugee convoy to the United States. However, he said he felt confident that he was not in any danger of being included in any future convoy himself.[36]

Mary, according to the report, had confidential information that his name was, in fact, included in the convoy leaving the following Tuesday.[37] It is possible that she had been advised of forthcoming deportations by Paul Corazzi, a sympathetic official who passed on information to the relief agencies when he could and also manipulated deportation lists when possible. The report doesn't say whether Mary was able to help the Belgian man; however, in other cases the Quakers did change the names and ages of internees to keep them safe.

Lindsley Noble said it had been agreed to change one child's age from two-and-a-half to two in order to save the mother. (Under the new rules the mothers of children under two, rather than the previous age limit of five, were exempt from deportation.) He referred to another case in which a girl, a Russian student of art history, was called 'Aryan', though she had the Jewish surname Katz, so that she might escape.[38]

In his notes, Lindsley also told the story of two elderly women who volunteered to be deported when the quota for one convoy was not filled. 'The Quakers had wrapped them in blankets against the night air,' he wrote. On another occasion the numbers were short because people were hidden or had escaped, and the guards made up the numbers by waking people up in their barracks and taking them.[39]

On the days that convoys were leaving, Mary was able to make sure at least that deportees were well fed. At the last minute, she distributed a slip of paper to each person and asked them to write their name and address. She told them these would be kept in a folder at the International Migration Service in Geneva so that relatives could write there for news of them.[40]

Since August, several thousand postcards had already been received from those who were deported. 'These cards,' the Quaker delegates Ross and Marjorie McClelland wrote, 'came principally from Poland and Silesia, and in general gave very little information other than that the sender had arrived at his destination, was perhaps in a work company and was well. It was very rare that more than one postcard was received from the same person.'[41]

———

Sometimes the real stories were told in the scribbled notes in the margins, or in the postscripts at the foot of the endless series of letters written by aid workers trying to keep people off the convoys destined for Auschwitz. A letter written by the Toulouse delegate Helga Holbek to her friend Mary Elmes on 14 September had two postscripts tacked on. Those two little additions hint at a story of persistence and bravery that we will only ever partly know.

In the letter Helga asked Mary to do what she could to help Dr Bacharach, who had been transferred from the camp at Gurs to Rivesaltes. She asked Mary to visit him to see if he could give her any reasons that might help keep him off the convoy. A little later somebody, possibly Mary, wrote the first PS: 'Le docteur was on the convoy today – we are working frantically to get him off.'[42]

As in so many other cases, Mary and her colleague probably tried to persuade camp officials to take Dr Bacharach off the list of deportees. The case could not have been more urgent: the doctor was already on the train – and on a deportation list. The list of deportees for 14 September mentions a man named Jacques

Bachrach. The spelling is different but it's likely to be the same man. Yet when he left the camp that day it was not on the train to Drancy in Paris. That was made clear in PS number 2: 'He is off! And on his way back to Gurs.'

How the last-minute reprieve came about is not stated. Perhaps Mary or her colleagues were able to rescue him officially; they were intimately acquainted with the rules, the red tape and all possible ways around both. In her memoir, Mary's colleague Alice Resch provided an insight into how the women working in those exceptional times used their ingenuity and wit to save, or to bring comfort to, people being taken to destinations unknown. In the late autumn of 1942, she said that her office in Toulouse was 'drowning' in deportations, and her colleagues did all they could to find out about the trains travelling from Gurs to Rivesaltes by way of Toulouse:

> Helga or someone from the CIMADE [a French charity that helped refugees] would send us a cryptic telegram – something along the lines of 'Happy Birthday' – to signal that a train was on the way. Getting to the train was no easy task. We relied on a fair measure of bravado, and we coaxed information from the French guards by offering them food.[43]

Alice and other Quaker workers gave food to people on those trains, and passed on their final messages to their families.

Back in Rivesaltes, Mary's workload was increasing. In late September the Quaker delegate Russell Richie spent four days with her and reported to their superior, Lindsley Noble, that Mary needed someone to take the load off her shoulders:

> She has her work well-organised, and her methods of doing things, which you know, produce good results. However, when the camp is turned upside down as it has been for the last month, her smooth-working mechanics get tangled and such things as checking transfer lists are put aside in favour of trying to save some worthy cases.[44]

She was going to need all the help she could get, because thirteen of the Quakers' own workers were now in danger of deportation. Those in question were former internees who had been employed at Gurs. They had been rounded up and sent to Rivesaltes sorting camp.

Helga, in Toulouse, was very upset and warned that two of her staff were in danger of being 'sent off at any moment. We are frightfully worried on their behalf still,' she said, and hoped that exemptions would be issued by Vichy soon.[45] It was 16 September.

Nothing happened for two weeks, and the two workers were scheduled to be deported on 4 October. Then Helga got good news, as she explained in a letter to Lindsley Noble on 30 September:

> A number of them were destined for departure on Monday, and only at midday, a 'phone call came through from Vichy giving their names as exempted; did you obtain that? We were most delighted, and as I arrived in the camp ten minutes later, nothing on earth will ever persuade those people that I did not liberate them! I tried to tell them till I was blue in the face that I had nothing to do with it – no use.[46]

Helga thought her boss had a role in helping the Quaker workers at the end of September, but she would be appalled by his inaction in the weeks to come. By 5 October, the Quaker workers from Gurs camp were still interned at Rivesaltes. 'They risk being sent off to Germany,' Helga pointed out to Lindsley in a letter.

> There is one convoy going today (5 Oct.) and we managed to keep most of them off the list. I do not know yet whether it has been possible to save the daughter of our men. I feel very strongly that it is our duty to see that our workers are protected, and I know it can be done, for both the Secours Suisse [Swiss Red Cross] and the Assistance Protestante [a French charity] have obtained it [exemptions] for their people.[47]

Helga also told Lindsley how disturbing it was to witness the absolute despair of those being deported: 'A great many swore that they would not go to Germany alive. Is there no hope of getting it stopped? We heard some time ago that America might give a certain number of visas to adults.'[48] There were many suicides and attempted suicides in the camps when deportations were at their height.

Lindsley wrote back to say that he had met the chief of police at Vichy, René Bousquet, who said he 'was through granting exemptions' to the employees of relief organisations. Lindsley thought it was a mistake to 'irritate' Vichy with requests for individual exemptions, as that might jeopardise requests for large-scale exemptions.

> I know this position is hard to appreciate when a person whom one knows and admires is at stake, but one must remember that there are countless thousands of persons in the same position, many of whom may be equally worthy of exemption, and that the most we can do is to try to bring the greatest good to the greatest number.

Then he appeared to suggest that some of the Gurs workers might even feel it their duty to join the deportees:

> At the same time I also think that the finest personalities, whom we admire so much and would very much like to see exempted, may be the ones who feel it is their duty to stay with their people and assist and comfort them in the trials which lie ahead.[49]

Helga was incensed, and said so:

> I must say to you that I am entirely and completely in disagreement with your position that one should ignore individual cases when there are negotiations with Vichy concerning large groups ... The request for exemption in individual cases cannot be regarded as a 'little thing that irritates Vichy'. Each case is someone's life. It is the duty of the Vichy Office to examine each case, and it is my duty to present each case.[50]

She pointed out that the YMCA had succeeded in getting exemptions for seven hundred of its employees. She said she would do everything in her power to continue to work for those two people,

and that she would now turn to another source for help. She turned
to Mary Elmes, and together the two women worked to get their
employees out of the camp.

Meanwhile in the camp, those workers were trying to stay calm,
but Alice Resch said they 'were white as ghosts and scared to death.
They all knew they were most likely headed for certain death.'
However, she went on to say that Mary and Helga managed to talk
the camp administrators out of deporting them. 'They got the cook
back,' she said.[51]

It wasn't the first time a colleague referred to Mary's powers of
persuasion. She used those qualities to make a case for hundreds of
desperate people who now pleaded for help to get out of the
Rivesaltes sorting camp. In some cases, she sent letters abroad or
helped them to secure the transfer of money from relatives; for
others, she handled the long, tortuous process of completing the
paperwork required for their release. Some of those cases played out
over months, leaving behind a trail of letters sent to any authority
that might be in a position to help.

Sylvia Cohn was one such case. A 37-year-old German mother,
she wanted to join her two younger children on the refugee convoy
to the United States. She explained that she was a qualified nurse
and would be useful on board. Her eldest child was still in Germany,
and her husband was in England. Her last chance, she said in a
heart-rending letter to the Quakers, was to start a new life with her
children in America.

> I beg you from deepest heart, allow me to accompany my children
> . . . I promise that I won't be a burden of the USA. I am healthy,
> and able and willing to work and make my life . . . It is so terribly
> cruel for a mother to be completely separated from all what
> she loves . . . I beg you once more, please do me the kindness and
> give me the position of a nurse to accompany my children on the
> next transport.[52]

Earlier in the year Mary had put Sylvia's younger child, ten-year-old
Eva, on a proposed list for the refugee convoy, but her other child
was too old, at twelve. Mary had prepared papers for forty-eight

camp children, but only eleven were chosen for emigration in May. Eva was not among them, and there was never any possibility that adults would be included. Now her mother had secured a Portuguese Consul transit visa, but she needed a transit visa to get out of France. Mary wrote to Marseille on 22 August:

> I hope that something will be done urgently for her as she has been again already placed in a group of people whose departure is imminent and this time probably nothing will be possible to exclude her, except the reception of her exit visa and other papers in order.[53]

She got a prompt response to say that a Quaker representative had left the previous night for Vichy and was going to put in a strong word on that case.[54]

Despite Mary's efforts, Sylvia Cohn was deported from Rivesaltes on 14 September 1942.[55] She was taken to Drancy and from there to Auschwitz. She died in a gas chamber on 30 September 1942. There is no record of what became of her two daughters.

In the meantime, on 9 October, the Vichy prime minister, Pierre Laval, agreed to give exit permits to a thousand children to allow them to emigrate to the United States. However, he withdrew the offer in a fit of pique after he was criticised in the United States for allowing the deportation of Jews. He later relented and issued five hundred visas.[56]

Criticism of the Vichy government was widespread in the foreign press. The Quaker magazine *The Friend* was openly critical in an article on 23 October 1942. It said that it was known that the head of the Vichy government, Marshal Pétain, 'could not' and its prime minister, Pierre Laval, 'would not' do anything to prevent the deportations.

The number of visas was reduced by half again, to 250. In late October the first party of children were escorted overland to Lisbon, where they were due to sail to America. However, they never got to leave. On 8 November, American and British forces landed in North Africa, and Germany responded by occupying the French so-called 'Free Zone'. The borders closed, and there was no possibility of any kind of regularised exit from France. The children were sent back to Marseille.

Mary and her colleagues reacted quickly to the Nazi occupation to make sure the children in their colonies were safe. At the end of November, she arranged to move all children at the Quaker home in Canet-Plage to the children's home in the mountains at Vernet-les-Bains. 'It seemed a wise thing to do because a colony on the coast is exposed and could face difficulties, even risks,' she said in a monthly report.[57]

Meanwhile, her colleagues were worried about the fifty or so children they had taken from the Gurs camp and placed in an orphanage at Aspet in the Pyrenees.

'Gradually, we simply smuggled the children away from Aspet,' Alice Resch said.[58] They gave the authorities a fictional list of people willing to take the children into their homes and then dispersed them to other orphanages in the area. They doctored the children's papers too, erasing the word *Juif* (Jew). Many of those children remained in the orphanages until after the war. Afterwards, they spoke of living like fugitives and hiding in terror during police searches.

Paul Niedermann, for example, said that he had more than one lucky escape. After his first escape – from Rivesaltes – he spent the remainder of the war hiding in different places in France and Switzerland. He had no idea that his parents, Friederike and Albert Niedermann, had been deported or that they were dead. His brother, Arnold, whom Mary Elmes helped send to America, was safe. Paul, however, was not. In 1944, he was living at the Izieu orphanage in eastern France but fortuitously had left it shortly before a Gestapo raid on 6 April 1944. Under the direction of the Gestapo chief of Lyon, Klaus Barbie, a total of forty-four children and seven adults were taken away on trucks. They were later sent on the first available convoy and on to the gas chamber at Auschwitz.

'I had grown tall and everybody worried that I would attract attention, so I left,' Paul says. 'I owe the Quakers and the OSE my life.'[59] He went to Switzerland and eventually settled in Paris, where he became a journalist and photographer.

I could never have imagined that I would make it to the age of ninety. I am a miracle. I am an old man, but I spent a lot of my life passing on the history of that time. I have used my voice to speak out against injustice and forgetting the past. You can't teach the old anything, but we must tell the young.

He was sustained by the 'ferocious optimism' instilled in him by his parents, he says. He also felt a strong desire to live after the war, because he had things to do for its victims. He later testified against Barbie at his trial in Lyon in 1987, along with the orphanage director, Sabine Zlatin. She survived the raid because she happened to be out when it took place. Barbie, known as the 'Butcher of Lyon', was convicted and sentenced to life in prison. He died there four years later.

The Canadells, the Spanish family who spent six months at the children's home in Canet-Plage thanks to Mary Elmes and Lois Gunden, also had a brush with Klaus Barbie. The family settled in a village in Ain, in eastern France, which was raided by German soldiers in 1944. In an offensive led by Barbie, members of the Resistance were killed when the farms and houses in which they were hiding were set alight.

Carmen Canadell saw Barbie, and she and her family were afraid they were going to be put to death, her daughter Brigitte Twomey recalls. They were spared, and the family lived in France for the rest of their lives.

The experiences of Paul Niedermann and the Canadell sisters show that the children who were saved from the Rivesaltes camp by Mary Elmes and her colleagues faced considerable danger even after their release. Some of them were moved to other orphanages, others were taken in and hidden by French families, and some were smuggled out over the border.

Back in Perpignan in the week following the occupation of the Free Zone, everything was calm and there was no curfew, Mary said in a letter to Eleanor Cohu in Marseille. A week after that, however, she was taken completely by surprise with the unexpected closure of the Rivesaltes camp:

In the end, the camp of Rivesaltes closed very suddenly – all the internees left with just 48 hours' notice. The evacuation took place in the worst tramontane [wind] we have had so far this autumn here and we saw some truly 'Goya-esque' scenes. I am afraid that there will be some mortality on account of the cold and the lack of wood which these people have suffered for a period of almost two days.[60]

After the occupation of Vichy, all Americans were ordered to leave France. The American Friends Service Committee anticipated what was coming and prepared for it by establishing a new French organisation on paper, the Secours Quakers. Before they left, they handed over all responsibilities to the new body so that work could continue in France.

At first they thought their efforts had been wasted, because Vichy disbanded Secours Quakers almost as soon as it began operating. Six months later, it was reinstated following appeals to Marshal Pétain. Under occupation, it was now more important than ever to maintain a good relationship with the authorities and to operate in a way that would cause the least possible disturbance.

Meanwhile, the American aid workers who had not left the country were arrested and interned in Baden-Baden in Germany. Nine Quaker workers, as well as Lois Gunden, the Mennonite who ran the children's home at Canet-Plage, were sent there. The French Quaker director, Lindsley Noble, was among those detained. While they were held under Gestapo guard, they lived in the Brenner Park hotel, were well fed and were even allowed to go outside for walks in the Black Forest. In 1944, they were released as part of a prisoner exchange.

As an Irish neutral, Mary could stay in France. In the Toulouse office, Helga (Danish) and Alice (Norwegian) were also permitted to stay at their posts. It was time for Mary to reassess her position. Many of her colleagues had returned home or had been interned; the camp that had taken all her time over the previous three years was closed, and now she was working under German occupation.

She decided to take a few days off and concentrate her attention on the school canteens, the holiday colonies and the Quaker food and clothing distribution points. She was also exhausted:

I'm starting to feel now that the last four months have been difficult and the fact that the camp no longer demands my daily presence allows me to hope to be able to take a few days of rest before tackling the new challenge that awaits me here. I have the impression, from now on, that will be a considerable change because over the last three years my main preoccupation was 'concentration camps'.[61]

———

The term 'concentration camp' was used in France during the Second World War to describe the camps that had been established around the south of the country. The term originated during the Boer War to mean the concentration by the British army of a large group of people in one place. While the French concentration camps were not the extermination camps run by the Nazis, they were places where people seen as 'undesirable' were gathered – Republican Spanish refugees, Jews and Roma.

After the war the subject of the camps was a very sensitive issue in France, and many objected to the term 'concentration camp'. During the war, however, several comparisons were made between the camps in France and Germany, although it's important to stress that the systematic murder of people never took place in France. However, an estimated three thousand Jewish people died in the French camps from malnutrition and illness. In November 1940, the American magazine *New Republic* called Le Vernet camp the 'French Dachau' in an article that prompted other critical articles in the United States and Britain.

Alexandre Doulut pointed out in his book *Les Juifs au Camp de Rivesaltes: Internement et Déportation 1941–1942*, that Rivesaltes became a holding centre for Jews, and sent them to their death. The camp's history between August and November 1942 was 'that of genocide . . . because 2,289 Jewish camp internees were delivered by France to Germany and its gas chambers.'[62]

In late 1942, a total of 2,313 adults were deported over three months. Some twenty-four people are thought to have escaped before the train reached Drancy in Paris. Of those deported, there were only eighty-four survivors.[63]

At the same time, the Rivesaltes camp is the one most associated with the rescue of children in France. Thanks to Mary Elmes and her colleagues, 84 per cent of the children aged sixteen or under escaped deportation. 'There were an estimated 1,193 children in total, of those 174 were deported. 13 died in the camp because of the conditions,' according to Alexandre Doulut.

How many of those children did Mary Elmes save? If the existing documentary evidence is added to the accounts left behind in memoirs written by her colleagues, it seems she was personally responsible for saving about seventy children while deportations were at their height. However, some of those references may refer to the same children while omitting several others. She told her own children that, on one occasion, she squeezed six children into the boot of her car. She also told them that she hid an Austrian family in her flat in the Avenue des Baléares before they tried to escape over the border into Switzerland.

The Quaker archives also offer solid evidence of her efforts to get adults off the convoys that left Rivesaltes. It is clear that she tried to secure documents or exemptions from deportation for hundreds of people at the camp. She did not always succeed, but it is also true to say that not all her successes were documented.

In occupied Vichy it would become much more difficult to continue her work, but that was not going to deter her. Her Quaker colleague Howard Wriggins wrote afterwards: 'We knew that she had been particularly courageous during the German occupation of southern France.'[64] That courage, however, was also going to bring the wrong kind of attention.

Chapter 14 ∾

THOSE SHE SAVED

*'The one thing that I want to share is that I am truly
grateful to Mary Elmes for the life I might not have had,
had it not been for her brave actions to save us and many
others. She was truly a heroine.'*
— Michael Freund, Canada

Mary Elmes was named Righteous Among the Nations for
her role in saving the lives of Mario and René Freund,
known today as Michael Freund and Ronald Friend. The
story of their rescue can be traced through a number of surviving
documents and is told in detail here. Mary's role in helping other
children to escape was less visible but no less important. She drove
children out of the camp herself or arranged for them to be transferred
to the Quaker children's homes that she ran all over the Pyrénées-
Orientales region. In the case of Charlotte Berger-Greneche and that
of the brothers Georges and Jacques Koltein, she organised their
transfer to the relative safety of the children's home of La Villa Saint-
Christophe on the coast.

———

Michael Freund still remembers the moment Mary Elmes came to
rescue him, at the age of six, and his brother Ronald, aged two, from
Rivesaltes internment camp in south-west France. It was midday or
shortly afterwards on what he now knows to have been 26 September
1942. 'Before I knew anything about it, we were brought to the exit

and Mary Elmes took us away in her car. From that moment on, I started making a big fuss because I was being taken away from my mother. She had her hands full with me making such a fuss.'[1]

Some weeks earlier Michael's father, Hans, appealed to the Quakers to get his family out of the camp. He and his wife, Eva, and the two boys had been arrested the previous July during a failed escape attempt over the Swiss border. 'I remember Ronald and I were playing in the dirt outside the office at the border while my parents were being questioned inside. After that, we were loaded up and taken to the camp in Rivesaltes. That is where the whole nightmare started.'

Even now, seven decades later, Michael Freund remembers the degrading conditions and the terrifying atmosphere in the camp.

There was nothing in the barracks except layers of straw. There were guards at each end with guns. People were just lying side by side. You couldn't go anywhere; you just had to sit or lie down. If you had to go to the bathroom, you raised your hand and the guard would come. He would look at you. You would go in front of him and go outside. Outside, there were gun towers and a barbed-wire fence. You would walk across the mud. You knew you were being watched by people with guns. It was a terrifying experience.

His father, however, never gave up hope and continued to write letters requesting help. It was September 1942, and convoys destined for Auschwitz were leaving every week. Michael remembers the crowds gathering in the yard and his father telling his mother not to worry. On the 22nd of that month, it looked as if help was on the way. The Quakers' office in London sent a telegram to its office in Marseille. It read: 'Special, urgent, request your help through Perpignan office assistance case 88 Hans Freund and family lot K Baraque 35 Rivesaltes.'[2] (Each *baraque* or hut had a number.)

When the office in Marseille received the request, Una Mortished, an Irish aid worker from Blackrock, Co. Dublin, immediately wrote to her compatriot Mary Elmes.

On 25 September, Mary replied, saying she was already aware of the case and that the children's father had signed documents entrusting the children to the Quakers' care:

The two children will probably be liberated this evening from the Camp of Rivesaltes. We are sending them to Vernet [a Quaker-run children's convalescent home]. The father is anxious that the children should go to the United States in a convoy ... They send many messages of thanks to their friends who enquire about them. They are extremely anxious that every possible step should be taken to hasten on the granting of their American visas.[3]

Those visas would never come, but at least the two Freund children were out of immediate danger. Mary made sure the right paperwork was done to secure the boys a place in the Quaker home, and she personally drove them there. She may have persuaded the camp authorities to allow them to leave, as she did in some cases, or she may have smuggled them out, as she did in cases where permission was not forthcoming.

'The intention was for Mary Elmes to take us to a safe house,' says Michael Freund. 'But that didn't happen because I was creating such a situation. Also, Ronald and I were very sick. Ronald and I were covered in boils and pussy [infected] spots – that was one of the things that happened because of malnutrition, I suppose.' Mary took them to the Grand Hôtel du Portugal, the Quaker children's home at Vernet-les-Bains. Later they were taken to the Hôpital Saint-Louis in Perpignan to have their infected scabies treated. They stayed there until 14 November and were then taken back to the Quaker respite home, which was now acting as a safe house for Jewish children.[4]

Letters in the Friend/Freund archives give a fascinating insight into the many stages of one rescue network and how it functioned to save the brothers. Several people were involved in any single escape; each one played a crucial, though hazardous, role. Mary Elmes played a vital part in getting the children out of the camp at Rivesaltes and transferring them to a children's home, but ordinary French people put their lives at risk to hide and house them afterwards. The plan was to return the Freund children to Marssac, where the family had lived before the war. There they would be looked after by French families, who acted as their godparents.

When the children left the Quaker colony they were taken to a house, probably in Toulouse, where a Mme Lobstein took the trouble to write to Dr and Mrs Freund, who had been moved to Gurs camp, to tell them their children were safe. On 18 November 1942, she wrote:

Dear Madame,

... The children are very well. When they arrived, I brought them to a doctor who found them in good health. René still has a little wound/scar on his left heel but it is healing well. Michel [Michael] is perfectly right to say that they are well behaved. They have everything they need.

She went on to describe the details of how they would get back to Marssac, giving another insight into the degree of co-operation that was necessary for hiding and transporting Jewish children to places of safety. She ended the letter on a positive note:

I think that you can put your mind at rest about the fate of your children. We hope, too, that your own situation will improve soon.

With best wishes,

H. Lobstein.[5]

On the back of the letter, Mme Lobstein included a note dictated by the young Michael:

Dear Mama and Papa,

We are very well-behaved. We are very well here. Today or tomorrow, we are leaving for Marssac. I'm sending you two kisses for Papa and two kisses for Mama from René-Marcel ... In this house, I'm very happy and the people are very kind to me and my brother. I'm very happy with it all. Since I got out of camp, I've put on weight. I'm sending you four kisses.

He signed the letter himself, writing his nickname in large, bold capital letters: ALLO.[6]

The local priest at Marssac-sur-Tarn, Fr Louis Bézard, later described that journey. He hid the boys in a suitcase as they made their way through Toulouse to the train station, which was under heavy Gestapo guard. When they arrived at their destination, the children were placed with separate foster families and they were baptised as Catholics so that they wouldn't stand out at school. After their mother, Eva, was liberated from the Gurs concentration camp the family was reunited in Marssac. They resumed the life they had before they were interned, but without their father.

Michael Freund still has memories of that time – fragmented vignettes that vividly illustrate a point that the European head of the Quaker operation, Howard Kershner, made forcefully in a report in 1940:

> One of the greatest tragedies of all times is the separation of families in Europe today; wives in one country, husbands in another, with no possibility of reunion and often no means of communications; babies who have never seen their fathers; scattered fragments of families not knowing whether their loved ones are living or dead, and often without hope of ever seeing them again. There are multitudes of wretched souls for whom it seems the sun of hope has set.[7]

Michael's parents, Hans and Eva Freund, still had some hope when they first arrived in France at the beginning of the war. They left an increasingly anti-Semitic Germany for Italy in 1933 and fled again as that country aligned itself more closely with Nazi Germany.

When they first arrived in the south of France, life appeared normal to five-year-old Michael. One of his earliest memories was of his father teaching him to ride a new bicycle: his father held it, then let go as Michael took off, only for him to fall over and cut his lip. 'He took me to the doctor or the dentist and I was stitched up.' It is a recollection that might sit comfortably in any ordinary childhood. However, it is one of very few normal memories.

Even now Michael Freund's voice falters when he recalls hearing the gunfire, about 1943, that killed a number of local people.

> There were four or five of us playing at the [Tarn] river's edge in view of the bridge across the river. We saw this truck crossing the

bridge. It made a sharp turn and we lost sight of it. All of a sudden, there was a barrage of gunfire and we just ran off. Later on, we heard that the Germans had set an ambush . . . I think there were several French Resistance fighters and they were all killed.

By then Michael's mother had been released and was reunited with her sons. They were all living in accommodation above the school given to them by the town authorities.

The boys' father would never join them. In 1943, following the killing by Resistance fighters of two German air force officers in Paris, two thousand Jews were rounded up from camps around the country in reprisal. Dr Hans Freund was among them. He was taken from Gurs camp to Drancy; he left that infamous transit camp outside Paris on Convoy 50 on 4 March 1943, which was destined for Majdanek camp in Poland. He died there.

Reprisals were a fact of daily life. A short time after the massacre on the bridge, witnessed by Michael, some villagers knocked on the Freunds' door and presented the family with a sack of potatoes. The unexpected windfall had come from the farm of a local man who had been identified as the collaborator responsible for the ambush. He had been killed by members loyal to the Resistance, and the produce from his holding was distributed in the town. The incident stands out in Michael's memory not only because of the violent background to the story but also because food was very scarce.

We had very little to eat. My mother would get up very early every day, about 5 a.m., and walk a long, long way across a very dangerous railway viaduct in order to get milk from a farm. She would come back with a glass full of milk, which she would stand on a window-ledge and let the cream collect. Then, she would beat the cream and we would get a little pat of butter, my brother and I. She would always do everything for us.

But the experience of incarceration and losing her husband had taken its toll. In a letter to her brother Max Wilhelm Brauer in England, Eva Freund confided how hard life had been in the camp and now in Marssac:

All the pain and hunger I went through – the cold and worst was the separation from the children and Hans – and then the absolute worst – the parting with Hans with only an hour to say goodbye.

Also the children went through a lot – the first 3 weeks in the camp and then 7 weeks in the camp hospital in Perpignan, because of an infection in the camp from insect bites. I did not see them anymore after that. Maybe that was a blessing for me. People only later told me about it. They said they came back in bad shape full of lice, famished and undernourished. On my return 8 months later their godparents had fed them well and they looked better than before these terrible times. I took them right away with me but I think they were not thankful for that because as far as nourishment goes they were better off with their godparents. The little one hardly recognized me, he called his godmother 'maman' and treated me like a strange aunt. He spoke no German not a word to anyone, and to this day has not learnt any. He only speaks French. On my return I took a different apartment as I could not face the painful memories in the one I had shared with Hans.[8]

The atmosphere in the village was tense and unsettling. One night two German officers knocked on the door of their apartment, Michael recalls.

They said they wanted to listen to the radio. Radios were not allowed. At first, my mother was very afraid but she let them in and they started a conversation. I was lying in bed listening to them and, at one point, I piped up, 'Hitler ought to be shot.' One of the officers turned around and said to me: 'Sometimes we think the same.' Of course, they weren't the SS or the Gestapo, just the regular Wehrmacht, so nothing happened.

After the liberation of France, the Freund boys finally got visas to go to England, where their maternal uncle and aunt would care for them. They left Marssac-sur-Tarn for Paris but had to say goodbye to their mother there; she would have to wait another two years before she was granted travel documents to join them. At that point Ronald was almost six, and he has clear memories of being tossed about on high seas as he crossed the English Channel. 'That's the part I remember. And I remember my uncle coming to collect us in Newhaven because he had some cherries. He put me in the baggage rack and I was spitting cherry pits down on top of him.'

The brothers settled in to their new life in boarding-school and tried to put memories of the war behind them. Their mother arrived in England in 1947 but found it very difficult to settle there and eventually moved to Uruguay. In 1951 Michael emigrated to Canada, and he was later joined by Ronald in 1962 after he completed his education at the University of London. Michael still lives in Canada, in Nelson, British Columbia, while Ronald moved to the United States, first to New York and then to Portland, Oregon.

Looking back now, it is the elder of the two brothers who says the war experience affected him most.

In earlier times, I was definitely afraid of everything. In those times, they didn't have the trauma help that is there now. To give you an example, if I was stopped for a traffic offence, I thought he was going to shoot me. That kind of a fear affected my whole life. I was afraid of any kind of authority, whether it was the police or my boss at work. And I had very nice bosses at work. I was always afraid. If I had had a more normal childhood, my career [industrial engineering] would have been completely different. I would have much preferred having a career to do with farming or animals – I love animals.

Yet he says that it is very important to remember those dark days.

In the last five or six years, I have really started to think about the past and I have been pretty prepared to talk about it. The one thing that I want to share is that I am truly grateful to Mary Elmes for the life I might not have had, had it not been for her brave actions to save us and many others. She was truly a heroine.

Ronald Friend and Michael Freund made it to safety, but their cousin Richard Freund, a talented violinist, did not. Aged twenty-four, he was deported from Drancy, on Convoy 19, to Auschwitz on

14 August 1942.[9] That was as much as the brothers had been able to ascertain. 'I was always upset that he had died very much alone,' Ronald says. Then, out of the blue, in September 2016, Ronald received a report that included an account of his cousin's final days. Fittingly, the report had been uncovered by Mary Elmes's relative Pauline Morum and her husband, Mack, who were researching the life of 'Aunt Marie', as they called her.

In the report Ross McClelland, a Quaker delegate who worked with Mary, described the sickening realisation that those being loaded onto goods trains in early August 1942 would not return.

The Quakers had arrived, at first light, at Les Milles, an internment camp near Aix-en-Provence, where Richard F – (as he was named in the report) was being held. They ladled soup from a large camp cauldron and pushed it in through the partly open doors of the goods wagons that were about to set off.

> We hate to see some of the old familiar faces again, especially in the clear summer morning light. Here is Richard F., for example, a young and talented German violinist. He has been named 'chef de wagon' and is taking his duties very seriously: helping the old people, cajoling the faint-hearted, trying to establish some order within his special domain, counting the number of parcels to see that everyone got one.

Richard had talked the guards into opening the door so that the night buckets could be emptied. When he saw the Quaker delegates he smiled out at them. McClelland was struck by his shoes – 'high-laced, black, old-fashioned shoes that probably once belonged to some bygone, fastidious relative in comfortable middle-class Berlin where he once lived'.

He said that the Quakers had tried to persuade Richard to take his violin with him, but he was leaving it behind for a friend. He told McClelland that he saw the journey as some sort of liberation from the drab and crowded boredom of over two years of camp life. He wouldn't miss the eternal waiting and hoping to get a visa, the boredom, the hunger, always feeling half-sick and never being alone to practise. 'What fate awaited him now, he seemed to welcome it,' McClelland wrote.[10]

At 6.30 a.m. an engine was attached to the train and pulled it slowly out of the siding. McClelland and his colleagues stood watching as it went. 'Then turned away, heartsick, and walked back into the camp.'[11]

———

In October 1942 Mary Elmes wrote to the Quaker head office in Marseille, enclosing a list with the names of thousands of Jewish people who had been deported from Rivesaltes to Auschwitz. It was a deeply disturbing but complete record of what had just taken place. On the 35th page of that document ten names were listed under the surname 'Berger'. The final one was a woman called Zirl Berger. It gave her date of birth (1/5/11), her nationality (Polish), and the date of the convoy that sent her to her death (4 September 1942).

'They sent her off as if she was a parcel,' her daughter Charlotte Berger-Greneche says now, seventy-five years later.[12]

Her mother was thirty-one when she was loaded onto a cattle wagon and taken away from her daughter, who had just turned five. In fact, Charlotte thinks her birthday may have saved her life. Mother and daughter had been due to be deported earlier, but Charlotte believes the deportation was delayed until after her fifth birthday; that would mean she was eligible to be included in the convoy. However, the delay gave volunteers in the camp more time to plan her escape.

Until recently, the only clue she had about what had happened was a single document. In it, the word *'intransportable'* ('unfit to travel') was written alongside her name, and there was a reference to the Jewish charity OSE. Charlotte later met Vivette Samuel, the OSE volunteer at Rivesaltes, who confirmed that she had helped to get Charlotte out of the camp – though she was not the only one involved in her escape.

What has come to light more recently is that Charlotte Berger spent time at La Villa Saint-Christophe, the Quaker and Mennonite children's home on the coast at Canet-Plage near Perpignan. Her stay there confirms that Mary Elmes also played a vital role in saving her life.

In 1941, Mary negotiated the rental of a large villa that was only yards from the beach, near the local tramway and the village school. She thought it an ideal place in which to offer children respite from the harsh conditions of camp life. At first they were sent there for a period of weeks or months, to regain their strength, and then returned to their parents; however, in the latter part of 1942 Mary Elmes used it to hide Jewish children. She arranged the transfer of several Jewish children to the villa at Canet-Plage and to other Quaker children's colonies.

A few children were lucky enough to be reunited with their parents or extended family. Others were fostered and hidden by French families, while some children, such as Charlotte, lived in children's homes until the end of the war.

Charlotte was an only child – 'my parents weren't given the time to have more children' – and has just one memory of her mother. She remembers being dressed by her, aged four, as she lay on a bed at Rivesaltes camp, though 'bed' is not quite the right word: the internees slept on straw mattresses that were lined up in rows inside rudimentary concrete barracks. The Jews were confined to Block K, which was cordoned off with barbed wire.

The camp is now a memorial, and when Charlotte visited it as an adult, surveying the ruined bunkhouses scattered over bleak, barren terrain, it stirred some sort of a visceral response within her. But that was all.

When, in 2013, she found out that she had spent time at the Villa Saint-Christophe, it made sense of another vague memory that had always puzzled her. She recalled playing in the sand but thought it couldn't be a real memory, as there had been no sand pit or beach at Château Masgelier or Lavercantière, the two children's homes where she spent her later childhood. Now she knows that those very early memories relate to her time near the sea at Canet-Plage.

Despite what was going on all around her, Charlotte has happy memories of that time. She says she felt happy – and more than that, loved – in those homes. Also, unlike many others, her father, Abraham Berger, had been spared. He was employed in one of the working groups that took men out of the camps daily to provide badly needed, and very poorly paid, manual labour in a country at war. When the deportations began in August, the organiser of the work group brought the men further away from the camp. They were too far away to make the daily journey back to Rivesaltes, so they stayed away, a measure that saved their lives, whether intentionally or not.

Charlotte knew that her father was alive, and she knew he would come back for her. She recalls, however, that other children believed they had been abandoned. A letter from Ziegmond Kaufman, another child rescued from Rivesaltes by the OSE, shows the confusion that some children felt: 'Dear Aunt Tekla, I don't know what happened to Mother. She doesn't write to me. I'm angry with her.' He didn't know that his parents had already been murdered.[13]

In 1943, Charlotte's father went to visit her at the children's home in Lavercantière. 'He was taking a huge risk. He travelled without money or a passport – it was very dangerous.' She recalls that he somehow managed to stay at a hotel nearby and, when they met, sewed a missing button on her dress.

The Berger family had been expelled from Germany in 1941 or 1942. Her father was an ironmonger and her mother a dressmaker. Charlotte recalls the journey to France, through Belgium, on foot. She remembers in particular the sense of danger and instinctively knowing that she must not make a sound. Later, when German officers called on routine searches of the children's home – nowhere was completely safe – she and the other children, even the smallest ones, knew not to make a sound. 'We were quiet when we had to be quiet and we hid when we had to hide. We knew not to make a sound. We were as quiet as mice' (or, to translate the French phrase literally, 'We were as mute as carps').

All she really knows about that time is what she has gleaned from documents, photographs and archives. 'What makes me sad today is that I never asked my father any questions. I didn't want to upset him,' she says.

In her personal archive, she still has a little note she wrote to her father in the years they were apart: '10 billion kisses for Papa what I will never forget, Lotti.' She has a photograph of all the young residents standing outside Lavercantière children's home. Charlotte Berger is certainly among them, but she can't pick herself out; she's not sure what she looked like between 1943 and 1944. She has only two pictures of herself as a child, one as a baby and the second a blurry newspaper photograph of her as an eleven-year-old when she emigrated, briefly, to stay with cousins in the United States. Her father was to follow her, but she wasn't keen on life in America, and after a year and a half she returned to France to join him.

'When I went to the US, I didn't have a single word of English, not even "yes",' she says. She picked up the language very quickly and laughs now at the sentimental tone and many inaccuracies in the newspaper article reporting her arrival in 1949. Under the heading 'Little war refugee reaches "home" at last,' a local reporter told how Charlotte ran into the arms of her new 'parents' and that she would never want for anything again.

> The dark shadow that has followed 11-year-old Charlotte Berger all her life dropped away a few minutes after midnight today.
> 'Oh my!' said the motherly Mrs. Feldman, a catch in her voice. 'She's wearing the same snowsuit I sent her two years ago.'

In 1950, Charlotte moved back to France. Her father remarried. Her step-mother had lost her husband and son in Auschwitz and found it difficult to be a mother to Charlotte. That experience, and all those that went before it, have profoundly affected Charlotte – though, she says, she's not one to shed tears for the past.

> I am not speaking as a victim, but to say that we should be on our guard. People are throwing around words now without taking any notice of the consequences. They are using words that are dangerous and hate-inducing. We need to pay attention. What happened is not history with a big 'H'. This is not past. It can come back.

Education, she says, is the key. Education has been a recurring theme in her life. 'If everyone had a good education, we wouldn't be where we are now.'

'It is as if everything – my life – started on the day of the round-up. I can't remember anything before that,' Georges Koltein says some seventy-five years later. He is referring to 16 July 1942, the first of two days during which the French police rounded up 13,000 Jewish men, women and children and held them in appalling conditions, without food, water or sanitation, in the Vélodrome d'Hiver, an indoor cycling arena in Paris.[14]

'That is my earliest childhood memory,' he says, as if the shock of that early-morning knock on the door at his family home in the Rue des Couronnes in north-east Paris, when he was seven years old, obscured everything else. The family was woken abruptly at 6 a.m. His parents didn't answer, as they could see from the window what was happening in the street below. Several people were being taken away in what was to become the most infamous mass arrest of Jewish people in French history. Several of Georges Koltein's extended family were arrested and deported to Auschwitz during the incident that would later become known as the 'Vél d'Hiv roundup'.

When the police got no answer they didn't persist: they simply went away, giving the family some time to decide what to do. But they didn't know where to go – or what, if anything, might keep them safe.

At first, we went to hide in our neighbours' apartment on the floor below. An Italian couple, who had fled from Mussolini, lived on the second floor and they took us in. Some time later, the police came back. They questioned the couple who said that we had gone away. Again, the police did not persist. We went back to our apartment but still didn't know what to do.

Meanwhile, across the city in the Rue Vieille du Temple, Georges's aunt and uncle, Estera and Berk Zloczysta, were taken away and deported on 22 July 1942 on Convoy 9 – 'I always remember the number,' says Georges. However, their two daughters, who were both over eighteen and born in France, were allowed to stay. 'It is interesting to note that the French police gave my aunt and uncle time to pack and get ready. They said they would be back in two hours, which means that they were giving them a chance to flee. But they didn't go; that shows you the faith the people had in the French authorities.'

When the police called again, Georges's relatives were taken away and later deported. He and his family went to their apartment in the Rue Vieille du Temple and, with help from the concierge of the building, were able to get out of Paris. Georges remembers that flight from Paris and passing over the demarcation line that divided France into the occupied and non-occupied zones. Shortly after they crossed into the southern region, they were stopped by the police.

They were far from being the only ones. Mary Elmes and her colleagues noted, with horror, the 'sinister and premonitory action' taken against foreign Jews at the time, although Georges and his brother were French-born. 'One rapid result of this action was the unprecedented influx of terrified Jewish refugees into the unoccupied zone of France, in particular mothers and children, and even some children alone,' Mary's friend and colleague Ross McClelland wrote. The aid organisations were overwhelmed with hundreds of children whom they tried to accommodate in an already-strained colony system.

'Almost the only mitigating news,' Ross added, 'was the information that orders had been given to the guard posts along the demarcation line not to turn back Jewish refugees fleeing to the south.'

Families, however, were being split up, as Georges recalls: 'Father was taken to join a work group and we were taken to Rivesaltes camp. We stayed one week.'

It was a crucial week in the life of the camp, as it coincided with the first convoy of Jewish deportees to leave Rivesaltes on 11 August 1942. They were taken first to Drancy, the notorious detention centre outside Paris, and then to their deaths at Auschwitz.

During that week, Mary and the other aid workers put their own lives in danger to save children from deportation. The children's charity OSE, with help from Mary, arranged for Georges and his brother, thirteen-year-old Jacques, to be transferred to the relative safety of the children's colony at La Villa Saint-Christophe in Canet-Plage, but their mother remained in the camp. The children were moved to the villa between 8 and 11 August.[15]

Mary arranged to have several other children transferred to the villa over the weeks and months that followed. The villa's director, Lois Gunden, noted in her diary on 26 August 1942: 'camp called announcing arrival of eight more children tomorrow; lectured to Jacques Koltein and tried to reason with him in gentle manner showing him that his state of happiness here depended on him – think he will be more disciplined hereafter.'[16]

Discipline was part and parcel of the life of the children's home, she explained in another entry:

> As might be expected, life here has its ups and downs. The pleasant and the unpleasant are plunged together in any day's program. There are the cuts and sores that must be looked after during the morning clinic. There are always some who get into mischief and must be punished. The arrival and departure of groups of children always causes some excitement for both the children and the personnel. The youngsters are eager to see whether the new group contains any from among their friends at the camp while the personnel are interested in seeking out those whose hair and clothing have become the habitat of certain little pests. The delousing process usually leaves in its wake some closely-cropped heads.[17]

While conditions at the children's home were luxurious in comparison with the camp at Rivesaltes, it was still very difficult to get food. Queuing became a time-consuming and frustrating part of life. That August, Lois told her parents in a letter: 'It takes a lot of careful planning to get anything like balanced meals for the children. But they seem to be well enough fed, for they are very healthy looking and are seldom ill.' The children had fruit and vegetables daily, meat twice a week, some cheese and one or two eggs a month.[18]

In stark contrast, Jacques and Georges ate nothing but tomato soup/stew when they were in the camp. It left a lasting memory. 'To this day, I am still incapable of eating cooked tomatoes. I still see the curled-up skins floating on the tomato soup that we got at the camp every day and I just can't eat them.'

In October, two months after the brothers' arrival at the children's home, their mother, Chuma Figa Koltein, joined them. She had been released from Rivesaltes because women who had two or more French-born children were being liberated, Georges says. It was a small concession in a zone that had imposed sweeping anti-Semitic legislation since 1940. The first Jewish Statute, introduced on 3 October 1940, excluded Jews from a range of professions. The Vichy government, under Pétain, went on to pass a series of punitive anti-Jewish laws and decrees, even though there is no evidence that it was under any pressure from the Germans to do so.[19]

In December, Georges and Jacques's mother left and went to join their father, who was working as a tailor in Pierre-Buffière, a village near Limoges. In 1943, La Villa Saint-Christophe closed and the boys went to another children's home, Château Lavercantière, but the family was reunited in July the following year.

'In Pierre-Buffière, we were left alone. We went to school and nobody bothered us,' Georges says.

At the beginning of 1944, however, the foreign work-group scheme was dissolved and all its workers – including Georges's father – were being recalled. Georges's father, Chanyne (Charles) Koltein, knew, however, that he was going to be deported, and went into hiding.

Georges kept his father's identity card all these years. It's in a folder full of documents, some of them held together with strips of Sellotape that have gone brittle and opaque. The word *Juif* is stamped on it in red ink. In the section asking for 'next of kin', his father wrote 'Nobody', to keep his family safe.

His father later told his son how he went from farm to farm for six months. Georges recounts the story again now:

He was a tailor so he would take the family's clothes and refresh and refashion them by turning them inside out. That was what he did in return for being hidden. He was known jokingly as the 'turncoat'. When he ran out of places to hide, he came back to us and hid at home. He hid behind a curtain when someone called. At one point, the French police came to find him and we said that he was not there. They did not insist. The gendarmes did what was asked of them, but without conviction.

After the Liberation, the family went back to their apartment in Paris. Georges's cousins had kept up the rent, so they were able to move back in. For years afterwards, Georges Koltein never spoke about that time. His uncle David was the only one of his mother's ten siblings to survive Auschwitz. He never spoke about it either. 'It was too raw, I imagine,' Georges says.

Georges Koltein put the past behind him and looked to the future. 'I had a lot of luck in life, I have to say,' he says now. He became a chartered accountant and married. He has two children from his first marriage, a son and a daughter, and he now lives with his second wife, Renée Scemama, and their son.

Yet the experiences of the past certainly affected him. 'It is a pain that I have suffered and that has formed – perhaps deformed – my character.'

He recalls the nightmares he had until he was about seventeen – always the same one: hiding from the Germans, who were searching for him.

Of the 13,000 people who were rounded up in Paris [in July 1942], there were 4,000 children, none of whom came back after being deported. I have always thought that I might have been one of them.

To this day, I find it hard to throw out bread. I have flashes of memory too; of the beach at La Villa St Christophe, at Lavercantière [children's home], which was much harder. Twenty years ago, I wouldn't have spoken about it. Now I am one of the last witnesses. I was amazed that my story could interest anyone. I am now a historic monument. It is not very pleasant! On the other hand, it is the time to speak of those things. If we don't talk, people can say it didn't happen.

Chapter 15 ᕙ

BEHIND GESTAPO BARS

*'She told me that she would not have missed the experience
of her time in prison for anything. Anyone who can make
use of such an experience in the way she has, can be
depended on and everyone feels this.'*
— Edith Pye, Quaker relief worker and friend

I n early 1943, Mary Elmes gathered up a sheaf of incriminating
documents and hid them under the bath in her apartment in the
Avenue des Baléares. She was acting on some sort of hunch,
or premonition – one that would save her life.[1] Some days later, on
5 February, the Sicherheitspolizei, the German security police, came
to her door and arrested her on suspicion of espionage. They took
her to the military prison in Toulouse, where she was accused of a
series of hostile acts against Germany. The charges, including secret
border crossings and disseminating propaganda against the Reich,
were described in a letter from the French Interior Ministry dated
1943, which is now in the family archive.

Her Quaker colleagues Helga Holbek and Ima Lieven immediately
went to the police headquarters in Toulouse and pleaded for her
release. When they had no success they walked briskly to the Gestapo
office in the Rue de Maignan, but that didn't go well either, as Alice
Resch, another colleague, later recalled in her memoir:

The doorman who announced them was thrown out with a
thundering *RRRRAUSSS* [*out*]! They jumped. At least they were
allowed to visit Mary and the other prisoners and to send them
packages with a few necessities.[2]

The American Friends Service Committee immediately sent a telegram to the Irish authorities requesting help. It read:

> Request intervention international Red Cross and Irish Minister Lisbon on behalf of Mary Elmes, trusted Quaker relief worker since 1938.[3]

Ima Lieven set out from Toulouse for Vichy to see the Irish minister, Seán Murphy, who in turn said he would advise the Department of External Affairs in Dublin.

At first, Mary's colleagues in Geneva were under the impression that she had been arrested because of something she had written in a letter. 'Apparently,' wrote Eleanor Cohu, vice-chairwoman of Secours Quakers, 'it was a question of having too freely spoken of certain matters in censored letters.'[4] There was speculation too that she might have been targeted because of her relief work with Spanish Republican refugees, many of whom were seen as 'undesirables' or dangerous radicals in France.

Later, the hypothesis that she had been denounced by the wife of a French guard at the camp in Rivesaltes was more widely accepted, although there was never any firm proof. Margaret Frawley at head office in Philadelphia said in a letter to the Quaker Foreign Service secretary, James Vail:

> The story is that she was denounced by someone; yet just for doing what is not known. I can only wish we could do something to help her from here, as I hate the thought of the poor girl sitting in the prison at Toulouse for months and months. If she is released, I hope she can come to Switzerland at least for a period of recovery.[5]

When, as an 88-year-old woman, Mary was asked what she thought of her alleged accuser, she simply said: 'I never wanted to know anything about it.'[6]

Meanwhile at home in Cork, Mary's mother, Elisabeth, was completely in the dark. Mary's brother, John, was told of her imprisonment on 24 February, but Elisabeth's doctor advised him to keep the news to himself: the shock would be too much for Mrs Elmes, who already suffered with her heart, the doctor said.[7] That makes her letter to the Quaker headquarters in Philadelphia on 13 March, five weeks after her daughter's arrest, all the more poignant. She wrote to Margaret Frawley asking for help to get a letter through to Mary in Perpignan. Not for the first time, the irregularities of the wartime postal system had cut off correspondence between mother and daughter.

> I have heard nothing from her since Nov. 11 1942 when she called and have no means of knowing if she gets my weekly airmailed letters. I have protested several times to the Irish Department of Foreign Affairs of this lack of facilities for correspondence. She is a neutral working in a foreign country and should be allowed to correspond with her home people. I should be greatly obliged if you can see your way to enclosing my letter to her when next you are mailing letters to France. I have left the envelope open so that you can see there is nothing the censor could object to.[8]

At this point Elisabeth Elmes thought she was merely out of touch; she had no idea that Mary was behind bars, and this news would be kept from her for months.

Margaret Frawley wrote back, assuring Mary's mother that she would give her letter to Philip Conrad, their representative in Lisbon. She explained that correspondence in and out of France was 'extremely difficult' and could take more than three weeks. 'I knew Mary in France in 1940 and value her as a friend and hope that you will feel that all of us here want to do as much as we can to be of assistance.'[9]

However, she felt uneasy about keeping the most relevant news from Mary's mother, and said so in a letter a few days later to Dr Frederick Keppel at the President's War Relief Control Board in Washington. In it, she appealed to him to apply some 'outside pressures' to get Mary released as soon as possible.

Coincidentally, Dr Keppel and Mary were second cousins: his mother and Mary's grandmother were sisters. He used to visit the Elmes family during holidays in Cork when he was a child. 'Those were the red letter days for us,' Mary's mother said of that time. 'We used to have the greatest fun together and I always remember Fred as one of the kindest and cheeriest of companions to his little Irish cousins.'[10]

Letters continued to go back and forth between France, Ireland and America, but in May something unexpected happened. Mary went 'missing'. Unknown to her employers, she was transferred from Toulouse to Fresnes, a French prison run by the Gestapo. As well as ordinary criminals, hundreds of French Resistance and captured British agents of the Special Operations Executive (SOE) were held there during the Occupation. Many of them never got out. Mary recalled in an interview some fifty years later:

> No one knew where I was at first. The danger was that they could have just sent me off on the train somewhere. We thought they needed prisoners in Fresnes because it was a good assignment for the Germans who ran it. If they hadn't been at Fresnes, they'd have been on the Russian front somewhere. I spent my 35th birthday in Fresnes. Needless to say, there was not much to celebrate.'[11]

She said she even felt sorry for the German soldier who took her from the prison in Toulouse to Fresnes: 'Poor man! He was not inclined to fight the French. He had been torn away from his ordinary life. He was much like everyone else. Conscripted by circumstance.'[12]

When she first arrived at the prison in 1943 Mary might not have felt so well disposed towards the conscripted German soldiers. Noémi Hany-Lefèbvre, a Frenchwoman imprisoned in the same year as Mary, described the sobering effect of seeing the imposing iron bars at the prison entrance. There was a heavy guard and lots of Gestapo milling around, she recalled. Inside, prisoners were led through a series of doors, then along an interminable corridor into an enclosed basement. She noted, with a certain amount of surprise, that the same key opened all the doors.[13]

'It was dark and dank,' Noémi wrote in a memoir published in 1946. 'We were chilled to the bone. An indescribable anxiety engulfed us.'[14]

Mary would have passed along the same corridors on her way to the women's quarters, which, the prisoners observed, were every bit as harsh as the men's. There were three women to each cramped cell. Mary shared her cell with Simone Herail, who had been arrested because her father was active in the Resistance in Narbonne. Simone suffered from polio but received no special concession in prison. However, she was later released.[15]

Mary's second cellmate, Faustine Chiarelli from Toulouse, was not so lucky. She was charged with membership of the Resistance and was later transferred from Fresnes to the prison camp at Ravensbrück. She stayed there until after the war, when she was liberated by the Swiss Red Cross in April 1945. She returned to Toulouse but was suffering from ill health.

The transition to normal life was difficult too. Other women who had been at Ravensbrück said there was a gulf between the hope of liberation and the reality. Marie-Jo Chombart de Lauwe, a member of the French Resistance and former detainee, said the return home after being held in detention was very hard:

> Maybe we had dreamed too much about it. The attitude we most frequently encountered was one of scepticism mixed with an unhealthy curiosity. And then people said such banal things: 'My poor girl, you've lost the best years of your life.'[16]

Faustine and Mary became firm friends in prison and perhaps spoke about those attitudes after they were released. They remained in the closest contact afterwards. Faustine would be the witness at Mary's wedding to Roger Danjou in 1946; she would also become godmother to their first child, Caroline. However, her ill health continued, and she died about 1950.[17]

Back in Perpignan, Mary's future husband kept in close contact with the Quakers and tried to get parcels and messages through to her in jail. In early March he succeeded in sending a food parcel to Toulouse prison: five oranges, one banana, five eggs, one sausage, a piece of ham, one tin of sardines, one pot of salted butter and a jar of jam. He asked the person delivering it to tell Mary that they were taking all possible steps to get her out.[18] However, when she was transferred to Fresnes it was much more difficult to send packages, not least because at first nobody knew she was there.

If there was a place where food parcels were desperately needed it was Fresnes. The rations were paltry. One prisoner remarked: 'If they took the bugs out of the soup – we would all starve to death.' The comment was written into the pages of a torn copy of *Wild Justice* by George A. Birmingham (the pen name of James Owen Hannay, an Irish clergyman and prolific novelist), which was passed around by American and English prisoners. It had filthy blue binding and ragged pages, but it was the perfect vehicle for transmitting messages. The reference to prison food appeared on page 109, but the book was also used to record the comings and goings of prisoners. For instance, on page 101 someone had scratched a more pertinent despatch: *T-Sgt S. Joe Marshall 20932531, Captured June 22-44 still here.*[19]

In the morning, at 6 a.m., prisoners were given coffee – or, as Noémi Hany-Lefèbvre described it, 'a bowl of lukewarm black juice that they called coffee'.[20] That was followed at 10:30 by a 300-gram slice of black bread with a piece of margarine or butter the size of a nut and a similar-sized bit of very solid pâté. At 11:30 a.m. the inmates got a half bowl of soup. The quality varied enormously. 'There were insects in it sometimes, but we still ate it avidly,' Noémi said. At 3:30 p.m. there was another bowl of coffee, then nothing until the next day. On Sundays, prisoners got a little bit of meat or noodles in the soup.

Although the Quakers suspected that Mary had been moved to Fresnes, the authorities insisted there was nobody of that name held there.

'She is now held incommunicado in Fresnes prison,' Quaker representative James Vail told Robert Brennan, the Irish minister in Washington, in a letter on 14 June.

We earnestly request you to make the strongest possible representations to your government . . . Miss Elmes is a person of good will, exceptionally effective in dealing with the problems of distressed people. She speaks Spanish and French without accent and we are convinced that there is no valid reason for her detention.[21]

In an earlier letter to the minister, James Vail had spoken of Mary in glowing terms:

For the whole of her service with us, Mary Elmes has faithfully, intelligently and with signal devotion to humanity in distress administered relief to persons interned in the camps in the Southwestern corner of France and in the Hospital of St Louis in Perpignan. She has kept her affairs in scrupulous order and has done a humanitarian work which commands our unqualified respect and admiration.[22]

By now the Irish authorities were aware that Mary had been moved to Fresnes. Her 'disappearance' was due to a clerical error: she was listed as Mary Henls in the prison register. Seán Nunan, counsellor at the Irish legation in Washington, wrote to the Quakers in Philadelphia on 16 June to say that the Irish authorities had been informed of her whereabouts and that they were doing all they could to help her.[23]

The Quakers were also concerned that her health was deteriorating rapidly. The organisation's president, Professor Lucien Cornil, turned to the French Ministry of Foreign Affairs for help. 'We are very worried about her health, which is already fragile,' he wrote, explaining that she had an infected growth which, if left untreated, could have serious implications for her long-term health.[24] An abscess on her back was later treated, but Mary had good health for the rest of her life.

Professor Cornil appealed to the French ministry to make representations to the German ambassador in Vichy. He said the Irish minister in Vichy had given him the impression, 'rightly or wrongly', of having no interest in his compatriot's situation.[25]

Meanwhile the Irish representative in Vichy, Seán Murphy, had been in touch to say the Irish were doing all they could but he was very put out that Mary's mother had not yet been informed.[26]

The news of her daughter's imprisonment finally reached Elisabeth Elmes on 15 June 1943:

It came as a dreadful shock. Now it appears that my son has known since February 24th . . . but my doctor would not allow me to be told as he thought the months of anxiety would be a strain on my heart. I think a mistake has been made as one or two more things could have been done had I not been kept in ignorance. I would have sent an urgent cable to cousin Dr. Keppel immediately but unfortunately my son did not think of it. He has done everything in his power through the Irish Dept. and certainly they have worked very hard to get Mary released but a powerful organisation such as yours [the Quakers] may have brought more pressure to bear.[27]

As it turned out, the Quakers in Philadelphia had already been in touch with Dr Keppel at the President's War Relief Control Board in Washington.

Elisabeth Elmes's surviving letters show that she was calm and resourceful in a crisis. She wrote letters to the Irish government, the German ambassador in Ireland and the head of the Church of Ireland and contacted Geneva in an attempt to get legal representation for Mary. 'She has fine courage but after five months' confinement the strain must be beginning to tell and for her own sake I trust the ordeal will be soon over,' she said.[28]

Food parcels had been getting through to Mary since April. A colleague, Ima Lieven, included books in a package from Toulouse, and when they were admitted to the prison she interpreted it as a positive sign, as it meant she was not out of favour with the prison authorities.

Afterwards Mary said that what she found most difficult about prison was not the bed bugs, or the lack of food or the fortnightly showers, but the fact that the cell window was boarded up. There was no air, she said.[29] For her prison contemporary Noémi Hany-Lefèbvre it was the glass peephole in the cell doors that guards used to keep an eye on prisoners. 'They covered their shoes with raffia to creep up and peer in at us.' The idea, she explained, was to unsettle our nerves. 'The thought that we might be observed, at any moment, through this silent, faceless single eye . . . underlined our power-lessness,' she said.[30]

The prison had a list of rules: 'No singing or shouting. No knocking on the doors except in the case of emergencies. No communicating with other cells. No talking through the windows' which, in any case, were boarded up.[31] However, prisoners found ways around several of them. They passed newspapers, food and books from cell to cell through the hot-air vents in their cells. They waited for the food trolley to rattle past to mask the noise.[32]

After the war the prison registers were destroyed or taken away, but the graffiti on the cell walls left behind a powerful testimony of what life in Fresnes was like. Prisoners used nails, pencils, pins – whatever they could lay their hands on – to leave messages for posterity. In the women's cells there were messages exhorting the comrades to be courageous. Some wrote notes to say they were leaving for an unknown destination; others used the wall to list the names of those who betrayed them.

In Cell 90, the occupant wrote:

Franz Feuerlich fusillé le 18-8-44
Comme autrichien
Ne m'oubliez pas prévenez mon pays
Apres la guerre
Editz nous a trahis
[Franz Feuerlich shot on 18-8-44
An Austrian
Don't forget to tell my country
After the war that
Editz betrayed us][33]

Mary had been released by the time the prisoner in Cell 90 was shot, but she told her son afterwards that she heard shots when she was in the prison. She didn't say if she had been frightened, but she was certainly conscious that there was a risk of being deported, or being condemned to death. There was also a risk to health from disease and malnutrition.

Meanwhile in Cork, Mary's mother maintained a relentless letter-writing campaign, keeping the Quakers' office in Philadelphia informed of any developments and making suggestions of her own. In one letter she suggested that the Red Cross approach the German authorities and request that Mary be deported to Switzerland. The Geneva office advised her against it, giving her an update on the measures being taken in a cable in July:

We are doing everything possible from here. French Quakers Centre Paris already in touch with Mary. She receiving weekly packages, her health reported better . . . Irish legation Berlin actively pursuing case but unable secure any definite statement from German authorities to date. In view of this information and knowing the Eire authorities are doing all they can in the matter, I feel it is best not to make any other approaches at the moment. Something may result if Mr de Valera sees his way to take up the case himself; therefore, personally I think it is best left as it is.[34]

Mary's mother was not entirely convinced. She said she thought the Quaker offices in London and Geneva had a lot more faith in the various governmental department and legations than she had.

There the letter stopped abruptly; then it continued, in a different pen, with an explanation that just as she was writing it the telephone rang with the good news that a Vichy representative had been given permission to interview the German authorities about Mary: 'In view of that perhaps I ought to take back my remark about want of faith!!'[35]

One week later, on the afternoon of Friday 23 July, Mary was released from Fresnes prison. Roger Danjou was in Paris to meet her, and they planned to leave for his native Normandy on a holiday. The next day she wrote to thank her friends for their letters of support. 'Thank you very much to everyone for your very kind letters. It was a great joy to receive them,' she wrote in a letter that is still in the family archive.

It was clear too that she had no intention of leaving the war zone. A month later, the Irish legation in Vichy sent her a note written by the Vichy Ministère des Affaires Étrangères (Foreign Affairs Department) allowing her safe passage from Paris back to Perpignan.[36]

Her mother must have found news that she was staying in France difficult. 'I have my heart set on her going to America for a complete change,' Elisabeth Elmes told Margaret Frawley in a letter. Failing that, she hoped Mary might go to Lisbon or Switzerland.

The fact that you [Miss Frawley] have suggested to Mary that she should move to either Switzerland or Portugal has pleased me more than anything I've heard for quite a long time. I hope she will entertain the idea and choose Switzerland. She loves the country, around Geneva is so lovely that I feel the beauty would enter into her very being and help to wash away the memory of what she has gone through. Lisbon of course would be nearer for a trip home but it won't be so long before travelling is easier again so I am going to tell her if she chooses Geneva I have complete faith in her choice and will be well content.[37]

The first message received by Mary's family was a note sent to her aunt. It said: 'Well, 52 kilos [8 stone]. Wrote mummie today, also week ago. Glad to be back in nice flat with all belongings.' Her mother had asked for her weight in a previous despatch and was glad to report that Mary was no lighter now than she had been when she went to France in 1939.

The Quakers at head office in the United States were still concerned for Mary's future safety and said they would welcome her services in Geneva or Lisbon. But Mary had no intention of leaving Perpignan. She took a break of a month and then went straight back to work.

In a letter to her mother, Margaret Frawley wrote: 'It is like her to go back to Perpignan, and we can't persuade her to come out if she had made up her mind. I should still welcome her in the United States and will try to get word to her. They would have changed her job to Lisbon or Switzerland where she would have been safer.'[38]

Mary's Quaker colleague Edith Pye later wrote to Elisabeth Elmes to say that her daughter had managed to draw something positive from her prison experience:

She really is a wonderful person and the work she has done and the steady way in which she has remained at work in spite of all the misfortunes that she has suffered is really remarkable.

She told me that she would not have missed the experience of her time in prison for anything. Anyone who can make use of such an experience in the way she has, can be depended on and everyone feels this. It must have been very hard [for] you to be so long without news of her, and we owe you our thanks as well as hers for the possibility to continue the work she was doing in France up to now.[39]

Elisabeth Elmes might have been disappointed by her daughter's decision to continue working in Perpignan, but she cannot have been surprised by it. Mary had not abandoned her humanitarian work once since starting in Spain in 1937, and she wasn't going to do so now. The best Mary's mother could hope for was an account of life in France from another Irish aid worker, Una Mortished, who worked with the Quakers in the Marseille office. Una had intended to stay in France until the end of the war but when her fiancé died at the end of 1942, her plans changed. The letters between Una and the Irish legation in Vichy show how difficult it was to travel in 1943. She was told that it was 'generally possible' for the holders of Irish passports to travel, but she was advised to book her passage from Lisbon and then apply for a Portuguese transit visa, a Spanish transit visa and French authorisation before she could leave. [40] The process took the best part of a year. She was due home in Dublin at the end of 1943, and Mary's mother hoped she would visit her in Cork and 'fill in the gaps', as she put it.[41] However, Elisabeth Elmes was convinced her daughter was now safe.

> It was undoubted all the enquiries backed by so much influence that brought about her release and I feel the German authorities won't interfere with her again. She has too many good friends who can make things uncomfortable, still I am most careful in my weekly letters to her. They are only family chit-chat and never pretend any interest in her recent experience or in the war. I fear they often leave her unsatisfied, however, I have kept all the letters from you and all the other folk who have been so active on her behalf. She will have quite a big file to read through and undoubtedly be very surprised to see what some people have said about her.[42]

A few months after she returned to work, a new préfet (the state's representative in a region) was appointed at Perpignan. On 20 December 1943, he wrote to the police commissioner requesting 'all the information that you can gather' on Mary Elmes.[43] Two days later the police sent a reply, giving Mary's date of birth and details of her work in Perpignan and her time in jail. It said she had been reported several times for 'suspect activity', such as secret crossings, but no charge against her had ever been upheld. 'Mlle Elmes is considered to be of good morality,' the police commissioner said.[44]

The French police may have thought well of her but her eventual release was prompted by the intervention of the German ambassador to Ireland, Eduard Hempel, her children, Caroline and Patrick Danjou, believe. According to Patrick Danjou, he was asked to help, and three days later Mary was free.

Her friend and colleague Alice Resch had a more straightforward version of events: 'Mary managed to talk her way out after only a few months. She arrived in our office [in Toulouse] as attractive and well-groomed as always, as if she had just made a journey like any other. What a party we had.'[45] Mary would later say when asked about her time in prison: 'Oh, we all had to suffer some inconveniences in those days!'[46]

While she was in prison, six months' salary accrued to her, but she wrote to her employers saying she didn't want it. She returned the money, asking head office to spend it on whatever was needed.

As head delegate, Mary Elmes was the highest-paid worker in her office. She received a monthly payment of 9,000 francs. (Currency values fluctuated wildly in the war years, especially after 1942, but according to an inflation-adjusted estimate from France's National Institute of Statistics and Economics Studies that was worth about €2,300 in 2017.) Some of her wages were also transferred to a bank account in the United States. She left them there. In the 1970s, when her son was on a holiday in America, she told him to withdraw the money. He went along to the bank with her letter of authorisation and withdrew several hundred dollars. It paid for his trip around America.

Although she spoke little about her time in prison, Mary held on to the brown felt blanket she had in prison. Years later, when her children went to throw out what they thought was a disused threadbare item, she stopped them: 'Don't throw it out. It was cold in prison. That blanket saved my life.'[47]

Chapter 16 ~

MISS MARY AND THE CLOWN

*This is the story of Willie Hudets. Nineteen. Deserted by
father, betrayed by friends, imprisoned by country,
disappointed by liberators, jilted by sweetheart, homeless,
parentless, countryless, penniless. Lived in hell. Lived on
hope. . . How many Willie Hudets, how many . . . ?*
— F. Charles Thum, Quaker delegate, Perpignan[1]

W illie Hudets rummaged through the Quaker wardrobe
and found just what he needed for his role at the
delegation's Christmas party in 1945. He made the perfect
clown, with rolling eyes and an amiable smile that eliminated the
need for language. He spoke many languages – German, Hungarian,
Polish, Russian, Croatian – but not the French or Spanish spoken by
most of the six hundred children in his audience. It didn't matter:
his painted face and grotesque mimicry were an unqualified hit –
more popular than the double food rations, the Christmas tree and
presents, Santa Claus and Punch and Judy. The Quaker delegation
later agreed on that.

But then, Willie Hudets knew what he was doing. The circus was
in his blood. His father was American. His mother, a Czechoslovak
trapeze artist, had travelled with the circus in America. Willie had
been born in St Louis. That, at least, was Willie's mother's version of
events. He had been raised with the circus and had learned to eat
pins – hundreds of them; to be the back of a horse; to paint his face
white and make children laugh.

In late 1945, however, Willie Hudets became Mary Elmes's
concern. He had been liberated from Dachau by the Americans that
April and had set out, on foot, for France. He hoped to make it as far

as the United States. His father was American, after all. He got as far
as Perpignan, where he was arrested and detained. That's where he
first met Mary Elmes.

Charles Thum, Mary's colleague and lifelong friend, wrote about
the encounter and Willie Hudets' fate in a four-page document that
might have been taken from the pages of a novel. He was obviously
moved by the story, but in telling it he has also opened a fascinating
window into Mary Elmes's daily work in Perpignan.

Miss Mary visited the city jail each Thursday at eleven. She took
soap and darning thread and oats and other small things to the
prisoners, things they could not get themselves, things this town-
ship could not furnish. She inquired the reasons for imprisonment,
and sometimes could arrange some legal matters, obtain some
needed paper, or aid the prisoner's family. French law is hard on
foreigners with papers not in order and strangers seldom know
where to go for help.

Miss Mary's native Irish was of less use to her than French or
Spanish in this border town, but to-day the guard informed her
gruffly that she had a compatriot behind the bars who badly
needed an interpreter.

'Why is he here?'

'No papers.'

So Willie and Miss Mary met. Willie certainly did not speak
French or Spanish. Willie certainly did not speak Irish either. 'Is
this American?' thought Miss Mary, and settled down to Willie's
story. Willie did have papers, not the ones required by French law,
but important ones to Willie. There was a day pass for the streets
of Freiburg, a residence card for a displaced person's centre in
Paris, a permit for military travel from Paris to Strasbourg. Miss
Mary saw that Willie was nineteen, that he was husky clean and
had an honest though indignant face despite a new and nasty cut
across the temple. She also saw that prison was no place for him.
He did not have the duck's-back character of the Spaniards or the
resilience of the Catalan. She, therefore, contracted to be temporary
guardian and responsible to the State for Willie's actions and
brought him to the Quaker Delegation.

Charles Thum's moving account goes on to explain that the only thing Willie Hudets was certain of was the fact that he was born. After that, it was the fact that his father was American.

Willie was willing to tell any one this any time. In fact, Willie was often more willing to tell this than people were willing to listen . . . The Quaker plan was to trace down every clue towards proof of Willie's birth. Success would mean Willie's eventual right to enter the United States and to claim citizenship protection. No one had any real hope for success. Except Willie. The alternate solution was to get Willie work, so that he could apply for an ID card and be straight with the law and free from arrest or guardianship.

He had to be housed too; and then there was the issue of his girlfriend, Alyse. He had met her on the road to France. She had set out from Poland, on foot, on her way to find her French father in France. They went along the road together, but she left him briefly for an officer in Strasbourg. He persuaded her to continue towards France with him, and later both of them were stopped in Perpignan.

On the way to prison, they were handcuffed. Willie objected and struck the arresting policeman. As Charles Thum recalled, 'Miss Mary knows the guards well and they afterwards said with jovial respect that he had put up a fine fight.' Alyse, however, was disgusted. 'In her moral code it was perfectly proper to tramp all over Europe with a circus clown, temporarily desert him for an officer, be in and out of jail, live on charity, but never consort with a brawler.' She was finished with Willie and eventually made her way back to Poland. 'No more at all was heard of her.'

Willie, meanwhile, continued to be a 'Quaker problem'. The local abbé eventually agreed to take him in. 'Miss Mary gave him a good big piece of soap when he moved in and Willie was not seen till Thursday when his army shirt, his khaki trousers, the scarf around his neck were washed and pressed and clean.'

But Willie needed to learn a trade, and he needed to learn French. He didn't take to either. He saw no need to learn a trade and less reason to learn French, as he believed he would soon be going to the

United States. But he did show a talent for drawing and began to sketch pencil portraits from photographs. Soon, Charles continued,

urgent jobs were found requiring [the] special talents of an artist, a sign of office hours to hang outside the door ... an [inscription] of a star in red and black [the Quaker emblem] and banner bunting announcing distributions, all to hang in the small villages when Quaker food arrived. Meanwhile, Madame Lliboutry [Mary's friend and colleague] tramped the streets [and] asked sign painters if they needed helpers, photographers if they needed tinters, decorators if they needed painters, but found no job for Frenchless Willie.

Meanwhile, the search for Willie's birth records continued. There was no trace of him in St Louis. 'No doubt,' wrote Charles, 'he had been born between the acts beneath an awning, a bareback rider momentarily making herself useful as a midwife.' No trace could be found of his old circus in Austria either. That line of inquiry was abandoned when a dark rumour emerged that his mother had died in an accident – 'a circus calamity of a slip of the hand and a net not well fastened. Willie had known or had guessed. The search for the circus was stopped.'

Everyone worked to secure him papers: Miss Mary, the priest, the police, the consulates, the government. Eventually Willie got papers and passage to South America. The day he was to leave he came into the Quakers' office with a paper rolled under his arm. 'In his new Quaker clothes, he looked handsome and young,' Charles Thum wrote. 'He always was clean but this time he shone.' He wanted to give a painting to Miss Mary; up to now he had copied portraits, but this was his own composition.

'Miss Mary,' he said and unrolled his drawing. In a whirlwind of sand in the mystery and fury of desert, a terrified trembling horse whinnied help for his fallen rider. He said he got the idea at the flics and asked that it be taken in to Miss Mary.

Later he wrote from Dakar in Senegal – the details of his route to America were not explained – to say that visa requirements made it useful to legally take the priest's name, though there was no mention of that name. He wrote again when he had made it as far as Brazil. He had got a job retouching for Technicolor.

The painting of the horse hung over Mary's desk while the Quakers remained in Perpignan – a reminder of the many other Willie Hudets displaced by war.

Thanks to Charles Thum, the story of Willie Hudets and his circuitous journey comes down through the years in almost filmic detail. Many of the people Mary Elmes helped in the years after the camps closed exist as the stark statistics in a report, or as brief mentions in correspondence between the Quaker offices. Yet the letters, reports and documents so carefully kept by Mary and her colleagues give a detailed picture of the suffering of refugees and local people in Vichy under German occupation.

In the end-of-year report for 1944, for instance, Mary spoke of 'the calamities that weighed on the nation'. The winter had been temperate, but there was a sharp increase in the number of those suffering from bronchial infections, and TB was also on the rise. Adults and children were still losing weight. The Perpignan office ran a scheme of aid that delivered food, clothes and medical equipment throughout the region. They continued to work in schools, prisons and hospitals, helping to supplement a diet that was still deficient.

The number of children at the Quaker 'colonies' was considerably less now, but those staying at the two colonies in Vernet-les-Bains were in perfect health, Mary reported. The only issue at the colony was a continuing conflict among certain staff members – and a battle against bed bugs. One report noted: 'The fight against bed bugs continues. The director found about 60 in his room the other night.'[2]

In the background, however, the threat of violence was ever-present. The Quaker archive contains detailed reports of the unspeakable brutality perpetrated by the retreating German army in Cahors, north of Toulouse. Mary was concerned about her colleagues in Toulouse and wrote to Helga Holbek on 4 September 1944: 'I hope that during the awful days that preceded the departure of the German forces that you were not too exposed to dangers. And that you are in good health? Awaiting your good news.'[3]

Helga replied three days later: 'Thank you for your note. Yes, for some time, we have been able to breathe a little easier. How are you? You said nothing. We are working in the prisons.'⁴ Mary was working in the prisons too, delivering food to – among others – the German police who had arrested her the year before.⁵

The biggest challenge facing aid workers, as Willie Hudets' experience so graphically illustrated, was the number of people recently displaced by war. The Quaker delegate Howard Wriggins spoke of the trainloads of people returning from forced labour in Germany. They were all in need of food, clothes and money: 'Of the 800,000 reported French deportees, perhaps 200,000 never returned. Many who did come back were mere scarecrows, dull eyed, half starved from their years of hard labour and short rations.'⁶

A large proportion of those who needed help were Jews who had escaped deportation. A Quaker report estimated that most of them had lost between one and fifteen family members: 'They are the remnants of shattered family groups, their experience has been traumatic . . . As the result of long internment and the fact that they have been hunted, many have lost initiative.'⁷

Mary and her colleagues were working to secure papers and work permits for Jewish refugees but were concerned that discrimination was still prevalent. 'Certainly Nazi propaganda of Anti-Semitism has found its adherents in every country, minority persecution being an infectious disease,' a Quaker report warned. 'Even a country as liberal and tolerant as France cannot immediately shake off the effects of the hate and prejudice which has been incited.'⁸

The workshops that Mary had established in the camps were moved into Perpignan and other towns, where they continued to offer refugees a chance to work and learn a trade. There were distribution depots for food and clothes. And, as before, the aid workers wrote about the work they were doing in the most human way possible in order to keep the vital donations coming in. A report called 'What happens when you give clothes to Perpignan', written about 1945, described the distribution of clothes so evocatively that you can almost feel the crush that Mary and her colleagues felt on the first Monday of every month.⁹

The crowd would begin to assemble outside the office steps long before breakfast. The Quakers now had their own premises: the office moved from Mary's apartment to the Rue Jeanne d'Arc after the war. When members of the staff arrived at work the first thing they had to do was try to persuade the eager crowd to disperse; 12:30 would be time enough to queue for the three o'clock distribution, they told them. Before 3 p.m. the crowd was already five or six deep around the front of the building. Those pushing towards the door weren't even coming for clothes but for tickets that might eventually entitle them to clothes.

On this particular Monday, the head of the workshop thought she would be clever and went to the back of the queue to distribute the numbered tickets. (The writer of the report isn't named, but it seems likely that it was a 'she'.) The strategy backfired:

I was mobbed! They pushed and pulled and poked and tore. Each time a number was handed to anyone it was snatched from her grasp and torn to shreds; I tried dodging, but even my long reach was not long enough . . . so I went inside again, and we all spent one-and-a-half hours longer than we need have done distributing numbers.

The slips of paper gave the day and date of a forthcoming clothes distribution. Many of those queuing could read neither French nor Spanish, so the Quaker staff helped them memorise the vital data by heart. Then the crowd made a day of it by hanging around for a gossip. All attempts to politely ask them to move through the office door failed.

But before any clothes were distributed, each ticket-holder had to be means-tested to make sure there was genuine need. The Quaker 'investigators' often wondered why it was necessary. When they visited their homes, they found badly furnished rooms without wardrobe, chest of drawers or suitcases to hide any surplus clothes. 'Sometimes,' Mary's report-writer said, 'we hear vague reports of people selling clothes, but I am inclined to think that if anyone I have visited has sold things it has not been for lack of needing the clothes but from [the] greater need of the money the things would fetch.'

When distribution day came round it was a far more orderly affair. If a person passed the 'investigation', they were invited to an appointed place and, again, given a number. The profile of the people waiting spoke volumes. On any given day there might be an ex-internee from Belsen, a Spanish refugee family who fled Franco with only the clothes they stood up in, a countrywoman with seven children, a young woman who was to be married next month, or, to quote the eloquent report-writer, 'a family that pleads for clothes not to cover their nakedness or to protect them from the cold, but very humanly *pour pouvoir fair un petit peu commes les autres* [just to be like the others].'

There were certain universal fashion truths that emerged after distribution day. Mary Elmes's office had made a list of them:

No-one likes to wear even the most attractive shades of yellow or green; every girl up to 20 whatever her complexion feels she looks a dream in pale blue; up to [the age of] 30, light colours are pre-ferred, from 30 to 40, only navy or [black] are seemly, and beyond 40, black, and long black is the *only* wear.

There was a box for donations at the door. The hardest-up people were the ones who were most likely to respond. Others brought grapes or figs or, in one memorable case, a rabbit:

One day this week a country woman rang my front door bell before breakfast, produced a bucking rabbit from a basket, knocked it deftly on the head before my horrified and fascinated gaze, made her way to the kitchen where she proceeded in five minutes to skin and prepare it for supper, and vanished equally swiftly. There are advantages in being in charge of the *'Ouvroir'* [workshop]!

Chapter 17 ⌒◡

DON'T LOOK BACK

'Certainly Mary was very greatly loved and admired by the people who worked with her and the memory of "Miss Mary" will long be closely associated with Quakerism in this region.'

— Charles Thum, Mary's successor

Jeanne Lliboutry, second-in-command at the Perpignan office, managed to get her hands on a cask of sweet wine for Mary Elmes's farewell party on 7 June 1946. Mlle Aldebert had been saving up rations to produce 'an almost endless series of magnificent pastries' for the forty staff members who gathered at five o'clock on Friday evening for a party.[1] Mary's fiancé, Roger Danjou, was there too.

It was a send-off with all the usual trappings: a host of presents (a glass dessert set, a porcelain water jug, an electric hot-water heater) and a raft of speeches. Antonio Rafel, the accountant, gave a speech in Spanish, saying that the employees had very much enjoyed working with Mary. The Spanish refugees were particularly grateful for her sympathetic and understanding assistance, he said.

Mary Elmes replied with a gracious speech of her own but asked permission to make a single correction to what Antonio had said. She said everyone had worked together, not as employees but as friends. She expressed her deep hope that the Spanish would all be able to return to their homes, and she looked forward with eagerness to visiting them. Her successor, Charles Thum, wrote:

I have never seen so many eyes filled with tears. Mary was standing at the table with a whole group of Spanish women behind her and when she mentioned her hopes for their speedy return, I was very struck by the heavy effect upon them. Certainly Mary was very greatly loved and admired by the people who worked with her and the memory of 'Miss Mary' will long be closely associated with Quakerism in this region.[2]

The week before her departure had been hectic. Mary worked at top speed to hand over the complicated job of administration to Charles Thum and her case work to Mary Bentley and to tie up all loose ends. On top of that she was making final preparations for her wedding, which was to take place a few days later. She was marrying a Frenchman, a choice noted with satisfaction by her French colleague Mme Lliboutry.

Five days after the goodbye party, the same group assembled at five o'clock at the town hall in Perpignan to celebrate Mary Elmes's marriage to Roger Danjou. Charles Thum later described the ceremony with the eye of a social diarist in a letter to Mary's friend Margaret Frawley at the Quaker headquarters in Philadelphia:

The mayor married them and made a charming reference to Mary's work for the town. The witnesses were Roger's brother from Caen and [Faufau], a wonderful French lady from Toulouse who sells pickles and propagates good humour and whom Mary met in prison. [They shared a cell at Fresnes.] There was a splendid wedding banquet in Mary's apartment, with the biggest lobsters ever seen and a wonderful *piece montée* wedding cake made by Mr. Massot, one of our employees who was formerly a pastry maker in Barcelone. The principal decoration for the banquet was a magnificent basket of flowers[:] Easter lilies, white [gladioli] at least 4 feet long, baby's breath, white roses and a gorgeous wedding vale [veil] bow. This had been presented by the children of the schools of Perpignan, each child had [made] a small contribution and Mary was very touched and pleased by their thoughtfulness particularly because very few people knew in advance she was to be married and a great deal of effort must have been exercised in the tremendous hurry to organise this pleasant surprise.[3]

Charles Thum, however, admitted that he was ill-equipped to cast any light on one crucial detail: 'Not having spent an apprenticeship at a society desk, I do not feel capable of giving you all the usual details of how the bride was dressed.'[4]

Some days later the *Irish Times* published the following notice:

12 June 1946 in Perpignan, Roger, son of Monsieur and Madame Danjou, Caen, Normandy to Marie Elisabeth, daughter of the late Mr. E. T. Elmes, Culgreine, Ballintemple, Cork.[5]

Just two months after Mary's wedding she received news that her mother had suffered a stroke and had fallen on the stairs. It must have come as a terrible shock. On 21 August, Mary's brother, John, sent a telegram that said: 'Regret mother died very peacefully today.'[6]

Mary was also expecting her first child. Caroline Danjou was born that October: in just five months Mary got married, lost her mother, and gave birth to her first child. If she found it overwhelming she never mentioned it later to her children. She just got on with it.

Like millions of women in France, Mary Elmes Danjou settled down to become a home-maker in a country that was encouraging young couples to have more children. In April 1945 elections were held, the first in France to include women voters.

Women had won the right to vote in France the previous year but they appeared, at first, reluctant to register. A public awareness campaign presented voting as a duty, rather than a right.[7] A journalist and later politician, Françoise Giroud, wrote in the magazine *Elle*: 'If you believe that your opinion should not count, if you believe that the local tramp or your caretaker's nephew or your boss or the garbage collector is more intelligent, more reasonable, better informed, better qualified than you, then abstain. Otherwise, vote.'[8]

Later that year, when de Gaulle was elected head of government, he urged women to produce 12 million bonny babies for France in ten years. He introduced a range of policies designed to encourage *familles nombreuses* – families with more than three children. There were tax incentives, special allowances and reductions on public transport and in cinemas. Reversing France's falling birth rate would be a government priority for the next two decades.

The role of women as mothers and home-makers was embraced not only politically but in the mainstream media as well as the so-called women's press. In the immediate aftermath of the war, the women's magazine *Marie-France* called on the government to give women a happy Mother's Day by allowing them to watch their sons grow up:

> [Mothers'] heroism is made of humble courage as they face tasks which have to be done over and over again. The job of being a *maman* is a 24-hour-a-day job, with no Saturday or Sundays off, with no paid holidays.[9]

Mary's former colleagues were keen for her to continue her involvement with the Quakers, at least in an advisory role, but she decided not to do so. Her new husband didn't like the idea of her working either: he was of the view that mothers should remain at home to care for their children, and, it seems, Mary agreed with him. She later reflected, however, that she would have liked to work at the United Nations.[10]

At the Quaker office in Perpignan, she was sorely missed. 'You can well imagine the difference it has made not having Mary Elmes as head delegate,' Charles Thum wrote in a letter in July 1946. He apologised for the delay in answering but said it was caused mainly by Mary's departure and his attempt to try to maintain at least a semblance of the form of the Quaker delegation that had been 'so excellently organised and operated by her'.[11]

Later, he explained to head office in Philadelphia that she had decided not to take on even an advisory role.

> She has quite withdrawn from even a counselling position from her own desire to give her entire attention to her new life. Moreover it is obvious that the longer she is away from the work the less she is in touch with its details . . . We see her of course frequently and always jump at an invitation to her home.[12]

Her home was the spacious top-floor apartment of a grand villa in the Rue Oliva, not far from the railway station in Perpignan. It had commanding views of the river Basse below and in the distance the ever-present peak of Canigou, the Catalans' sacred mountain. She must have appreciated the Spanish influence that is palpable in the border town: in the architecture, the food and the quality of the sharp, clear light. She remained a committed Hispanophile for the rest of her life.

There were reminders of Ireland too. One of the first pieces of furniture she moved into her new home was a grandfather clock that had been a wedding present to her grandparents, James and Marianne Waters. She took the trouble to write a potted history of the clock and stuck it discreetly inside the works, near the pendulum. The clock had graced the Waters' home in Springfield in Cork until the death of her grandparents in about 1900. After that, it had gone from family member to family member on a journey that took it from Cork to London and back again. It was in Mary's birthplace at Ballintemple from 1930, and when that house was sold she had it shipped to the south of France. It is still in the family, at her son's home outside Perpignan.

If Mary was happy to recall her own family history, she shut the door on the recent past. She seldom mentioned her work with the Quakers, although she was happy to attend a ceremony in their honour when the organisation finally left Perpignan in July 1947. The town's mayor, Félix Mercade, presented Mary with a bunch of flowers and officially thanked her and her close associates – Jeanne Lliboutry and Charles Thum – for what they had done.

On 12 July 1947, the newspaper *Républicain* published a glowing tribute. 'Tirelessly, with courage and simplicity, they [the Quakers] brought to the most deprived the food and clothing which prolonged their lives and the hope of survival. Her [Mary's] confident, affectionate and smiling presence kept the memory of happiness and liberty alive.'[13]

In the same year, the American and British Quakers were jointly awarded the Nobel Peace Prize for their relief work during the war. For its part, the French government wanted to pay personal tribute to Mary for her work as head of the delegation in Perpignan and offered her the Légion d'Honneur, its highest honour. She turned it down, preferring instead to put the war behind her.[14]

In July 1948 Mary had a second child, a son, Patrick Danjou. Her husband worked as a forester and managed 50 hectares (120 acres) of land in Canet-en-Roussillon, where he cultivated vines and grew a range of crops, including peaches and artichokes, over the years.

Meanwhile, Mary developed a business of her own. She used the proceeds from the sale of her family home in Cork to buy a *mas* (farmhouse) in Sainte-Marie-la-Mer, a village east of Perpignan. Her former colleague and successor Charles Thum also stayed on in Perpignan after the war, where he worked as an architect. The old friends worked together to convert the building into *gîtes* (cottages), which were later rented out to holidaymakers. The family still rents out *gîtes* at the Mas Oliu today.

The dark years (*les années noires*) faded into the background and were little spoken about. Occasionally Mary shared a memory with her children, but never in any great detail.

'My father didn't want to hear her talking about it, so she didn't say much,' Caroline says.

If the years she spent helping the victims of two of the worst wars of the twentieth century affected her, she never said, although Patrick believes that few could emerge unscathed after being imprisoned by the Gestapo.

'There was Mary Elmes before the war and Mary Elmes after the war,' he says.

The woman described by her colleagues in Spain and later in France as fiercely determined, able and courageous is almost unrecognisable to those who knew her afterwards. Those who remember her from those post-war years variously remember her as 'kind', 'very cultivated', and 'discreet'. Discretion was a common trait among those who had lived through the Second World War. As her colleague Alice Resch explained, 'no one wanted, or could stand, to talk about the war. It was time to think about the future. We thought we were going to start a new life, build a new and better world.'[15]

Mary busied herself raising her two children. She continued to be an avid reader and followed international affairs closely. She wrote updates on Spanish news into her album of photographs and noted the death of Lady Young, in 1988. That was Sir George Young's second wife. The Lady Young who had accompanied Mary Elmes all those years ago had died in the late 1940s. Mary returned once to Polop in Alicante and went to see the house that had served as a hospital towards the end of the Spanish Civil War. Her only comment to an interviewer in 1998 was that the vines had been replaced by peach trees.

Pauline Reckitt, who knew her as Auntie Marie, visited her in Perpignan in the 1960s and remembers her with great fondness. She and Mary's daughter, Caroline, were pen pals, and Pauline was sent to France by her mother to learn French. The family was related to the Waters family, Mary's mother's side of the family. Pauline's grandmother and Mary's mother grew up together in Cork. Pauline's grandmother, also called Mary, stayed with Elisabeth Elmes's family on breaks from boarding school. Her father worked as a missionary in Zanzibar, where he campaigned against slavery.

Pauline visited France again from New Zealand in the 1970s, this time bringing her husband, Mack Morum, and their children. They both recall how Auntie Marie brought them on a tour of many of the places that had been significant to her. They passed near the beaches where thousands of desperate Spaniards had burrowed into the sand, and the sites of the children's homes where she had driven endangered Jewish children to safety, but she never once mentioned what had happened there, or what she had done. They were both astonished to learn the truth much later.[16]

Mary's reticence was not unusual. The French did not always want to revisit those years, especially because the story wasn't always as heroic as it was in Mary's case. In the late 1960s and early 70s, the uneasy subject of how France's own citizens had behaved during the years of German occupation and Vichy rule was broached publicly for the first time. In 1969, Marcel Ophüls' two-part documentary *Le Chagrin et la Pitié* (*The Sorrow and the Pity*) challenged the myth of French resistance and looked at the extent and nature of collaboration with the Nazis. The narrative of valour hid another, less palatable truth: the Vichy government had not only collaborated, it had implemented anti-Jewish policy without German prompting.

In 1972, the American historian Robert Paxton provided archival proof for this charge in his book *Vichy France: Old Guard and New Order, 1940–1944*. He argued that Vichy's anti-Semitism was deeply rooted in French culture. During the war years it was exacerbated by the French government's desire to hasten the departure of newly arrived Jewish immigrants. When Paxton's book was translated into French in 1973 it was heavily criticised. Yet a new generation wanted to know the truth, and thousands of copies were sold.

Less than a decade later, Robert Paxton and Michael Marrus jointly wrote *Vichy France and the Jews*. The authors reiterated the role Vichy France had played in the Nazi plan to exterminate Jews as part of its 'Final Solution'. They quoted Serge Klarsfeld's list, a comprehensive record of the names of the 75,721 people who were deported on seventy-nine convoys from France to their death in eastern Europe.

'His hundreds of pages remind one of the telephone directory of a medium-sized city, the long columns of names a mute testimony to the scale of the Nazi enterprise,' the authors wrote.[17] Almost a third of those deported to their death were French citizens. Only 3 per cent of the entire number survived. A further three thousand Jews died in the appalling conditions of French internment camps.

Henri Rousso coined the phrase 'the Vichy Syndrome' to describe the way in which the memory of Vichy had been repressed and its myths reinterpreted to make them more acceptable to contemporary society. In his book *The Vichy Syndrome: History and Memory in France since 1944*, he argued that it was impossible to get any real distance from the war years: the memory was still too raw and too disturbing. His thesis explained, in part at least, why there was widespread reluctance to talk about the war years.

Yet there were constant reminders. On 25 April 1986, the French treasury sent Mary Elmes a cheque for a risible 24 francs (less than five Irish pounds) to compensate her for the six months she spent in prison. It came from the Direction Interdépartementale des Anciens Combattants et Victimes de Guerre de Montpellier (Interdepartmental Directorate of Veterans and War Victims of Montpellier), an office established to offer compensation to those who were affected by war. She didn't even cash it, nor did she, as many others had done, pursue the matter further through the courts.[18]

A number of years after that, in 1992, Mary's former colleague Alice Resch wrote to her from Denmark. She wondered if she and Mary were the only two Quaker delegates still alive. Alice told her that she had tried to find her some years previously, as a group of children wanted to thank the Quakers for saving their lives. Alice and Helga Holbek, who had both worked at the Toulouse office, were named Righteous Among the Nations in 1982 for rescuing fifty children. They had smuggled them from the internment camp at Gurs and brought them to an orphanage in Aspet in the Pyrenees.

> I have to admit that neither Helga nor I felt that we had done anything dangerous or heroic – neither of us felt deserving of the honour. At any rate it seldom occurred to us that we were risking our lives when we now and then did things that weren't part of the official Quaker work. [The mantra was,] 'We must under no circumstances compromise the Quaker work.' But it was fairly unavoidable. Both Helga and I smuggled people into Switzerland, for example.[19]

When Helga died, in 1983, Alice again tried to contact Mary, hoping she would travel with her to Israel to accept the award. 'I was alone to represent the Quakers,' she told Mary.[20] 'I hoped to find you to come with me to Israel to plant a tree on the Avenue of the Righteous Gentiles at the commemorial institution in Jerusalem, the Yad Vashem.'

Alice contacted the mayor of Perpignan, but too many years had passed since that office had specifically honoured Mary. Nobody remembered Mary Elmes – or if they did, they didn't realise that she and Mary Danjou were one and the same.

Alice was beginning to think she was the only Quaker worker left when she heard that the American author John Baskin had tracked Mary down. He spoke to her as part of his research for a book about Burritt Hiatt, head of the Quaker delegation at Marseille.[21]

He met Mary in her apartment in Perpignan in 1996. He recalled a well-dressed, elegant woman whose swept-back brown hair, good skin and high cheekbones made her look much younger than her eighty-eight years. She was charming, he says, but relatively abstract; she didn't readily recall the intimate details of the camps.

She was tough-minded too, and unsentimental. Like her colleagues, she didn't think she had done anything special by taking

Jewish children to safety. 'There was work to do,' she told her interviewer. 'I came through without any scars. I have no regrets.'

There were other interviews too, and visits from some of the Spanish people she had known in the camps. In the interviews that survive she rarely spoke about what she had done to save Jewish children. That partly explains why recognition of her work came so late. But there was another reason. Her involvement in the rescues, though crucial, often meant that she spent very little time with the children she saved. She either arranged for their transfer or drove them to one of the Quakers' children's colonies herself. Other children had memories of Lois Gunden, the director of the Quaker home of La Villa Saint-Christophe, who was honoured by Yad Vashem about the same time as Mary. However, they had no recollection of Mary, because she was not involved in the day-to-day running of the home.

Throughout her life, Mary visited Ireland often, although she never revisited her former home in Ballintemple. In 2000 her daughter stayed there on the invitation of Jacinta Ryan, whose family bought the house in 1946.

'It was so moving to stay in my mother's former room,' Caroline said. 'And Jacinta welcomed me with open arms, but my mother didn't come in. She didn't dare.' She did, however, write a long letter of thanks to Jacinta and invited her to stay in one of her *gîtes* on the Mediterranean.

> I want to thank you for all your kindness and hospitality to her
> [Caroline]. She much appreciates everything you did for her and
> the souvenirs you so kindly gave her – and so do I. Thank you
> very much from both of us. I am happy to know that you live in
> Culgreine where I was born 92 years ago. I remember your father
> to whom I sold the house . . . I am happy that your family still
> lives in Culgreine and that it has not fallen into the hands of
> people we had never heard of.[22]

At that point in her life, Mary no longer spoke French: she had switched back to English. She and her husband continued to live in their apartment on the Rue Oliva until she died on 9 March 2002, aged ninety-three. Her husband outlived her and died, aged ninety-two, in December 2003.

Mary never sought recognition, but it would come, ironically, partly because of a chance meeting in the desolate remains of Rivesaltes camp, where she had brought comfort to so many.

Chapter 18

HOW THE STORY CAME TO LIGHT

'There can be no doubt that we are alive because of your mother's deed . . . So I am writing to you to let you know the extreme gratitude and admiration with which I hold your mother for rescuing us, and defying the authorities that unfortunately led to her imprisonment.'
— Professor Ronald Friend in an e-mail to
Mary Elmes's daughter, Caroline

When Caroline Danjou saw that the historian Anne Boitel was due to speak at an open day at the site of the Rivesaltes internment camp in 2006, she made a note of it. She thought the historian, whose comprehensive book *Le Camp de Rivesaltes, 1941–42* covers the darkest years at the camp, might know something about her mother's work there. However, when Caroline got around to asking the question, it was the interest of another author that started a process that would eventually lead to Mary Elmes's nomination for Israel's highest award.

The writer Rosemary Bailey was also at Rivesaltes that day. She developed an interest in the unheralded work done by the Quakers while working on a book about the Pyrenees in wartime. When Caroline mentioned that her mother was Mary Elmes, Rosemary immediately recognised the name. She first came across her in 1996 in a four-volume history of the war in northern Catalonia and was intrigued by her life and work.[1] At the library of the Society of Friends in London she found more tantalising snippets of information, but Mary remained a shadowy figure. She longed to find out more.

However, Mary's daughter was unable to fill in the gaps. She was looking for answers herself. 'My mother never wanted to talk about that time,' she told Rosemary. She didn't want any fuss or acknowledgement either.

When Rosemary's book *Love and War in the Pyrenees* was published in 2008 it generated enormous interest among a generation whose lives had been marked by war.

'I heard from so many people; writing letters, sending e-mails via my website, even turning up at the door,' she says.

A daughter of concentration camp victims got in touch to offer Rosemary their last letters. Another contacted her to say that they had found mysterious skeletons buried in Andorra and thought they might belong to people killed by renegade *passeurs*. Then there was the American soldier who parachuted into the mountains to help the Resistance; Rosemary later met him in Paris. But the piece of correspondence that stood out was an e-mail from an English Quaker, Bernard Wilson. He told the author that he and his wife, Janet, owned a house in the region and were fascinated to hear of the Quakers' work in the south of France.

In fact, the way Bernard tells it, that single e-mail changed his life, as it was the start of a seven-year quest that led him to a vast cache of material on the Quakers, their staff in wartime Spain and France and one in particular: Mary Elmes.

I had a holiday home in the south west of France for 15 years before I discovered that back in the 1940s, that beautiful and tranquil area had once been the site of several internment camps where Spanish and Jewish families were held against their will in appalling conditions. It could have been me. I was born in 1933 and if I had been Spanish, I could have been a six-year-old in the Argelès-sur-Mer camp. Or if I had been Jewish, I would have been nine years old in 1942 when the deportation trains ran, week after week, from the camp of Rivesaltes.

At first he was interested in wartime Toulouse, and when he wrote about it in a Quaker newsletter a survivor of Rivesaltes camp, Professor Ronald Friend, contacted him. It was 27 December 2010. The following

January, the historian Katy Hazan at the charity Œuvre de Secours aux Enfants confirmed that 'Mary Elms' was the woman responsible for getting Ronald and his brother out of the camp. From that day on, Ronald and Bernard concentrated their attention on Mary Elmes. Over the next two years, their exhaustive research unearthed unequivocal proof that she had risked her life to save Jewish children.

In the meantime, Bernard and Janet were trying to track down Mary's children. They contacted Les Trajectoires, a local group of teachers who were campaigning to have the camp at Rivesaltes retained as a memorial. Within days the group found Caroline Danjou, a nurse, at Sainte-Marie-la-Mer, a village on the coast. Her brother, Patrick Danjou, a doctor, was living close by at Cabestany, a suburb of Perpignan.

It was too late to thank Mary Elmes personally, but Ronald wanted to thank her family. He wrote to Caroline in 2011 to tell her that he and his brother were alive thanks to her mother's bravery:

About one month ago, I discovered that your mother was responsible for saving the lives of my brother and I. She rescued us from the Rivesaltes camp on September 26, 1942. I was 2 yrs and 10 months and my brother was 5 years 8 months. The convoys from Rivesaltes to Drancy were in full swing at this time when your mother took us to Vernet les Bains and/or Hospital St. Louis in Perpignan. There can be no doubt that we are alive because of your mother's deed ... So I am writing to you to let you know the extreme gratitude and admiration with which I hold your mother for rescuing us, and defying the authorities that unfortunately led to her imprisonment. I only regret that I had not begun this search earlier so that I could have met your mother personally and thanked her.

As for myself, I was brought up in England until I was 23, and then left for Canada where I married a Canadian-Irish nurse! We left for the us in 1969 where I have been a university professor in New York. We have a son who is a physician and my brother has two daughters, a lawyer and engineer in Toronto. So our lives are really a testimony to your mother's deeds, and in a sense refutation to those dark times.

My very best wishes to you and your family,
Ronald Friend, PhD.

Caroline was very moved by the correspondence. She wrote back to say she knew her mother had brought children to safety but had no idea who they were until now. She was delighted to hear Ronald's testimony but sorry that her mother was not alive to meet him.

Shortly after this e-mail exchange in April 2011, Bernard and Janet visited Mary's children to find that they had an extensive archive. There were letters, documents, drawings and photographs. Their mother's portable typewriter was still in the family's possession. So too were the colourful drawings and beautiful objects made by grateful Spanish refugees with the materials she had provided. There were four volumes of a diary from 1926 and an album of photographs taken during the Spanish Civil War. In short, there was enough in the Danjou archive to throw considerable light on the life of a woman who did not like to be the centre of attention.

At first the family were reluctant to talk, given that Mary had spoken so little of that time herself. She had never even mentioned her work in Spain and France to her three grandchildren – Patrick's children Cyril, Marie-Maude and Xavier. However, the family were moved by Ronald and his brother's story and their wish to have her contribution recognised at Yad Vashem. They gave their consent, and Ronald and Bernard set about compiling the considerable number of documents needed in the application.

They already had one document from the OSE archive, but Bernard began to trawl through the American Friends Service Committee archive to find corroborative evidence. It was a Herculean task. There were seventy boxes of documents; each box contained several files, and each file contained hundreds of pages of letters, reports, photographs, lists and accounts. He also succeeded in persuading the archivist to release the entire archive to him personally, as it was too vast to study in a library. He must have regretted it briefly when a parcel arrived from Philadelphia containing six DVDs of material.

Bernard discovered a series of letters from Una Mortished – another Irishwoman, from Blackrock, Co. Dublin – to Mary Elmes discussing the liberation of the Freund children. He told Ronald, who recalls being extremely surprised. 'And exhilarated,' he adds, because it was the most incontrovertible evidence – 'from the horse's mouth' as such – that Mary Elmes had engineered our rescue. The letter was dated on the eve of our liberation, which made it really stunning. It confirmed all the other second-hand documents collected from Perpignan and the ose records.

Ronald sent off the documents to have Mary nominated for an award at Yad Vashem in January 2012. 'By this time, Bernard and I had so many documents we could have asked for two awards for Mary,' he says.

Then there was an unexpected setback. 'I sent the package first class mail, registered, but it never arrived at Yad Vashem. The us postal service said the package left the us, but could not verify what happened to it en route to Israel. So I recopied everything and sent it directly by airmail. The process took a long time, but I was reassured that everything was in order.'

On 13 January 2013, Yad Vashem recognised Mary Elisabeth Elmes as Righteous Among the Nations.

———

Meanwhile another search was under way, at Canet-en-Roussillon, near Perpignan, where two sisters were trying to unravel a mystery. In January 2009, a letter landed on the desk of Arlette Franco, then deputy mayor of the town. It came from Gerlof Homan, a history professor in Illinois, who was interested in a children's home that had lodged Spanish children and Jewish children from the internment camps during the Second World War. The deputy mayor contacted Simonne Escudier-Chiroleu and her sister, Mireille Chiroleu, who say they are not so much bookworms as archive worms.

La Villa Saint-Christophe had been knocked down in the 1970s to make way for a new apartment block on the sea front, but it seemed to have vanished without a trace.

'We asked everybody we knew but no-one, no-one, no-one remembered the villa with its balustrades and towers,' Mireille recalls.

They knew, however, that the Mennonites had been involved, and they got in touch with their archivist. Then the story began to take shape. After four years of meticulous research they were able to reconstruct the daily life of the villa, its personnel and its young population. They found several documents that mentioned Mary Elmes and her involvement with the home.

The Quaker archives had already provided evidence that Mary found the house, helped negotiate the rental agreement and had even tried to persuade the owner to fix a broken septic tank before the first children moved in, in March 1941. Mary was the main intermediary between Rivesaltes camp and the children's home. She arranged for the transfer of the children, and while she did not always personally bring them from the camp to the coast she would have overseen it. During the height of the deportations, she moved Spanish children to other colonies so that Jewish children could be hidden at the Villa Saint-Christophe.[2]

Simonne Chiroleu-Escudier and Mireille Chiroleu were able to identify some of those children. They uncovered a register with the names of some of the foreign children, presumed Jewish, who were taken there by Mary Elmes during the crucial period between August and September 1942. There are twenty-three names on that list, but it is by no means exhaustive.[3]

———

The story of Mary Elmes's humanitarian work in Spain and France cannot be told without telling the story of the American Friends Service Committee, a Quaker aid organisation founded in 1917 to allow conscientious objectors respond to the humanitarian crisis of the First World War. The Quakers, a religious organisation founded in the seventeenth century, are dedicated to non-violence and the belief that there is something divine in everyone.

During the First World War, their relief workers fed millions of children in France and Germany and became known as humanitarians who helped victims on both sides of a conflict. After the war, they ran relief operations throughout Europe, Asia and the

Soviet Union. When the Spanish Civil War broke out in 1936, they redirected their work there and later moved with the fleeing Spanish refugees into France. When Mary Elmes left Spain, she and her colleagues brought with them a record of the work they had done. Those documents are now archived in Friends House in London.

The work that the American Friends Service Committee did was recorded in the hundreds of thousands of documents archived at the committee's central office in Philadelphia, Pennsylvania. In 2005 the historian Marc Masurovsky was one of those who helped convince the United States Holocaust Memorial Museum to microfilm and digitise the collection. He spent years cataloguing, archiving and studying a collection that provides a powerful record of non-profit work in Vichy France, German-occupied France, and in the immediate post-war years. At the time, he singled out the humanitarian commitment and extraordinary courage of two Quaker workers: Mary Elmes and her equivalent in the Paris delegation, Urbain Maes. The latter spent a year helping Jewish refugees in the occupied zone and was imprisoned, tortured and deported to German camps before returning to France at the end of the war.

After working on the archive, Marc was left with an impression of Mary as a woman who never took no for an answer, a formidable individual who was always trying to find ways of buying time to get the maximum done for her charges, despite the many obstacles: 'Mary, in my view, just did what she had to do. She was intent on doing her work as a humanitarian.'[4]

———

It is the standing ovation that stands out for Patrick Danjou. He never thought he would see the day when he would receive thunderous applause from two hundred women. He flashes a smile, still bemused at the attention he received at the Network Ireland annual conference in Cork when the 2014 Rose of Tralee, Maria Walsh, presented him with an award.

'Nothing for decades, then suddenly "*bof!*"' he says, with another smile, referring to the stream of recent publicity about his mother's achievements: the newspaper articles, a piece of street art, a play, a posthumous award in Ireland and a documentary, *It Tolls for Thee*, by Midas Productions.

At the time of writing, the documentary is yet to be released in Ireland, but its executive producer, Paddy Butler, was the first journalist to bring Mary's work to Irish attention. He wrote an article in the *Irish Times* in 2012, and another in 2013 following her nomination at Yad Vashem. At the time, however, there was little recognition of her work in Ireland, with the exception of the Irish Jewish Museum and the Holocaust Education Trust, Ireland, which honours her at its annual Holocaust Memorial Day.

There was more interest in her adopted country, France: a raft of articles and interviews followed the posthumous presentation of the Yad Vashem medal in June 2014.

Like their mother, the Danjous did not court publicity. 'During the presentation ceremony, Patrick Danjou said that her work would not have been possible without the contribution of so many others,' Rose Duroux, a friend of Mary's, recalls. 'He said it courageously, forcefully and against protocol – and I recognised there the worthy heir to his mother!'

Patrick said that praise was due to many and, in particular, to Mary's driver, Victor Samarini, who also took huge risks to save lives.

Mary Jean Gunden, whose late aunt Lois Gunden worked with Mary, was pleased to see both women recognised at last. Mary Jean contacted Yad Vashem about 2010, and while they were generally aware of Quaker relief work in Vichy they knew nothing of Lois or Mary's work. Lois was recognised as 'Righteous' about the same time as Mary. 'It is my belief that part of the reason Mary wasn't recognised sooner was because she spent limited time with the children she saved. The children were under such great stress during the time they needed the help of Mary and Lois, and many were quite young, so they don't really have a memory of Mary.'

Another two years passed before Mary Elmes was honoured in her own country. Network Ireland in Cork and the Smashing Times Theatre and Film Company in Dublin organised separate events within weeks of each other in September 2016.

Smashing Times staged a performance called *The Woman is Present: Women's Stories of wwii*, which included a reimagining of Mary's work, and toured with it in Ireland and Germany. The writer and Smashing Times artistic director Mary Moynihan wanted to pay tribute to a woman of exceptional courage. 'It is not known how many children's lives Mary Elmes saved, however, there is a ripple effect in terms of three generations of people who would not be alive today if it wasn't for the work of this extraordinary woman,' she says.

The president of Network Ireland, Deirdre Waldron, was equally impressed when she heard of Mary's lifesaving work from John Morgan, a trustee of the Escape Lines Memorial Society, which commemorates Second World War escape networks. At the time, Deirdre and John were working to publicise another Irish hero, Monsignor Hugh O'Flaherty, the Irish priest who saved thousands of Jewish children and prisoners of war. To date, there has not been enough documentary evidence for his contribution to be recognised at Yad Vashem.

'People like Monsignor O'Flaherty and Mary Elmes were willing to sacrifice their lives for strangers because a person was in trouble and it was the right thing to do,' John says.

> I just think it's a remarkable lesson. I have very little interest in military history specifically . . . but it's those people's stories that are important. I think those lessons today are as important as they have ever been. That's the importance of remembering. Those kinds of qualities are universal and they are things that continue to be remembered.

Deirdre Waldron said she was honoured to put forward Mary Elmes for the 2016 Trish Murphy award, which recognises people who have made significant contributions to their community.

'She was fearless, she never gave up when times got tough and never let anything get in her way,' Deirdre says. She hopes that other organisations will follow Network Ireland's example in honouring Mary Elmes.

When the mayor of Cork, Des Cahill, heard of the event he did just that and invited Patrick Danjou to a ceremony at the council chamber, where he presented Patrick with the silver brooch of Cork to give to Mary's granddaughter, Marie-Maude. At the time of writing, he was about to table a motion calling on Cork City Council to find a way of honouring Mary Elmes as a true Cork hero.

'Not a day goes by when I don't tell her story,' he says. 'She is a true source of inspiration and shows that a person from a small town at the edge of Europe can have such an effect on the lives of others.'

Mark Elmes, a cousin of Mary's, also hopes to see her memory honoured in her home town. His grandfather and Mary's father were brothers, and at his home in Monkstown he too has a large family archive, which includes pictures of Mary and her brother, John, in their teenage years.

While Mark knew John quite well as an adult, he didn't know Mary.

'She has the Elmes nose,' he says, looking at pictures of her later in life that he has only recently seen. Like many others, he knew little of her work. He knew of her as 'the lady who married the Frenchman', but thinks it is extremely important that her contribution is remembered.

So far the only official recognition of her work is at Yad Vashem, the World Holocaust Remembrance Centre, set in a forest overlooking Jerusalem. The name *Mary Elizabeth Elmes* (spelt with a 'z' rather than 's') is engraved on the Wall of Honour in the Garden of the Righteous; a single entry under *Ireland*. Somehow it stands out because of that, even if it is the very last entry on plaque number 15.[5]

The museum commemorates the six million Jews who died during the Holocaust. The name Yad Vashem means 'a memorial and a name', and this is a place of names. The names and personal details of millions of victims are recorded, along with more than 26,000 rescuers who tried to save them. The name of one of the most famous rescuers, the German industrialist Oskar Schindler, is commemorated on a tree he planted on the Avenue of the Righteous among the Nations in 1962. Mary's colleagues are honoured here too – Lois Gunden, Alice Resch and Helga Holbek among them.

The Shoah Museum in Paris is also a memorial of names. Each of the 76,000 Jews deported from France during the Second World

War is listed on a wall. Shortly before he was elected president of France in May 2017, Emmanuel Macron paused before that wall and said: 'What happened is unforgettable and unforgivable. It should never happen again . . . The homage that I wanted to make today is this duty that we owe to all these lives torn down by the extremes, by barbarism.' The visit took place days after his opponent, the National Front leader Marine Le Pen, claimed that today's France bore no responsibility for the round-up at the Vél d'Hiver in July 1942 and the deportation of more than 13,000 people.

Ronald Friend was watching the coverage from his home in Portland, Oregon. He noted that Macron was standing near 'F', where his father's name, Dr Hans Freund, is listed.

There is another wall of names at the memorial, called the Wall of the Righteous. Some 3,900 French men and women who put their lives in danger to save Jews during the war are listed on the wall, in alphabetical order. A plaque reads:

The names carved on this wall belong to men and women to whom the title of Righteous has been bestowed in recognition of their actions to save Jews in France during the Second World War, at the risk of their own lives . . . Alone or in organised groups these men and women from all political, religious and social backgrounds overcame the indifference that seemed to hold sway in our land and rejected barbarity. They felt a sense of commitment and responsibility toward their fellow human beings. These Righteous, in providing moral and material support, hiding places, identity papers, food and escape routes, helped three quarters of the Jews in France survive the persecutions of the Vichy government and the Nazi occupiers.

Mary Elmes, the Irish-French citizen named as Righteous Among the Nations in 2013, is listed under 'M'. The honour is seen by the many thousands who visit the memorial, but she would almost certainly be much more interested in the hundreds of people who live on because of her.

EPILOGUE
A message delivered 75 years later

Of all the documents uncovered during research for this book, one stands out. It describes the last journey of Zirl Berger, a 31-year-old Polish woman who was deported from Rivesaltes camp on 4 September 1942. Thanks to Mary Elmes and her colleagues, her five-year-old daughter, Charlotte Berger-Greneche, was taken from the camp to the relative safety of the Quaker-Mennonite children's home on the coast at Canet-en-Roussillon.

Meanwhile, the train taking her mother to her death in Auschwitz a week later stopped briefly at Montauban, not far from Toulouse. Zirl Berger managed to get a message to a Quaker ambulance-driver, Nora Cornelissen, who was on the platform of the station with other volunteers to see how they might help those passing through.

Later that day, Nora wrote down Zirl Berger's last words to her daughter: 'While passing through Montauban, Charlotte Berger's mother asked us to deliver a message. She sends her most affectionate thoughts and a thousand kisses to her daughter.'

She left Montauban at 2 p.m. in the direction of Châteauroux-Vierzon, and shortly afterwards the letter was sent to Château Masgelier, a children's home run by the Jewish charity OSE in Creuse in central France. Charlotte would spend time there, but not until several years later. She never saw that letter. If the message was passed on verbally, she has no memory of it.

On 6 May 2017, that letter came to light again and Charlotte read her mother's final message for the first time – seventy-five years later.

'It is the most moving message I've had,' said Charlotte. 'A thousand thank-yous.'

NOTES

Abbreviations
AFSC: American Friends Service Committee (Philadelphia)
FSC: Friends Service Council (London)
OSE: Œuvre de Secours aux Enfants
SFA: Society of Friends Archive (London)

Introduction
1. Ronald Friend, personal communication, several dates between August and December 2016.
2. Guy Brunet, personal communication, 15 December 2016.
3. Guy Brunet, personal communication.
4. Fr Louis Bézard's account of the escape, handwritten for Ronald Friend in 1956.
5. Fr Louis Bézard's account of the escape, handwritten for Ronald Friend in 1956.
6. Suzanna's letter to her father, 1 June 1942 (Ronald Friend's collection).
7. Samuel, *Sauver les Enfants*, p. 97.
8. Ronald Friend, personal communication, 2 September 2016.
9. Wriggins, *Picking Up the Pieces*, p. 143.

Chapter 1
1. *Cork Examiner*, 8 May 1915, p. 8.
2. *Irish Independent*, 10 May 1915, p. 5.
3. *Irish Times*, 8 May 1915, p. 5.
4. *Irish Independent*, 10 May 1915, p. 5.
5. Details taken from reports in the *Cork Examiner* and *Irish Independent*, 8–10 May 1915.
6. *(Guy's) City and County Cork Almanac and Directory, 1913*, 1916.
7. Patrick Danjou, personal communication, 9 December 2016.
8. *Cork Examiner*, 11 May 1915, p. 5.
9. *Cork Examiner*, 11 May 1915, p. 5.
10. *Irish Independent*, 10 May 1915, p. 5.
11. Letter from Field-Marshal John French to Marie Elmes, 2 August 1916 (Caroline and Patrick Danjou's family archive).

12. Jacinta Ryan, personal communication. Ms Ryan, the present owner of Culgreine, had correspondence with Mary Elmes and knows her children Caroline and Patrick Danjou.
13. *Cork Examiner,* 5 May 1908, weather report.
14. *Cork Examiner,* 5 May 1908, p. 1–4.
15. *(Guy's) City and County Cork Almanac and Directory, 1907,* p. 230 (available at http://www.cork pastandpresent.ie/places/ streetandtradedirectories/1907guyscitycountya lmanacanddirectory/).
16. Interview with Dr John Borgonovo, School of History, University College, Cork.
17. Borgonovo, *The Dynamics of War and Revolution,* p. 15.
18. Interview with Dr John Borgonovo, School of History, University College, Cork.
19. Jacinta Ryan, personal communication.
20. Quoted by Borgonovo in *The Dynamics of War,* p. 7.
21. *Cork Examiner,* 15 March 1922, p. 6.
22. As described by Susanne Rouvier Day, quoted by McAvoy, 'Relief work and refugees'.
23. *Cork Examiner,* 20 January 1913, p. 10.
24. *Weekly Irish Times,* 3 May 1913.
25. Letters in Mark Elmes's family archive.
26. Sandra McAvoy, personal communication. Dr McAvoy kindly pointed out the connection between Elisabeth Elmes and Susanne Day.
27. Day, *Round About Bar-le-Duc,* p. vii (available at https://archive.org/ details/roundaboutbarledoodaysrich).
28. Day, *Round About Bar-le-Duc,* pp. 181–2.

Chapter 2

1. Interview with Anne Marie Hewison, deputy principal, Ashton School.
2. St Leger, *A History of Ashton School,* p. 33.
3. Rudd, *Rochelle,* p. 92.
4. Patrick Danjou, personal communication, 5 April 2017.
5. From the admission registers of Rochelle School from 1914 to 1934 (Cork City and County Archives).
6. *Irish Times,* 31 July 1915, p. 1, advertisement.
7. Rudd, *Rochelle,* p. 85.
8. Minutes from Rochelle School governors' book (Cork City and County Archives).
9. Rochelle School, prospectus (Cork City and County Archives).

10. Rochelle School, prospectus (Cork City and County Archives).
11. Minutes from Rochelle School governors' book (Cork City and County Archives).
12. League of Pity register (Cork City and County Archives).
13. Rudd, *Rochelle*, p. 85.
14. *Irish Times*, 31 July 1915, p. 1, advertisement.
15. Rochelle School, prospectus (Cork City and County Archives).
16. Advertisement from Rochelle School governors' book (Cork City and County Archives).
17. Minutes from Rochelle School governors' book (Cork City and County Archives).
18. Rudd, *Rochelle*, p. 85.
19. Admission registers of Rochelle School from 1914 to 1934 (Cork City and County Archives).
20. Caroline Danjou and Jacinta Ryan, personal communication.
21. *Cork Examiner*, 16 January 1922.
22. Admission registers of Rochelle School from 1914 to 1934 (Cork City and County Archives).
23. *Cork Examiner*, 20 and 22 March 1920, p. 5.
24. *Cork Examiner*, 13 December 1920, p. 5.
25. *Cork Examiner*, 14 December 1920, p. 5.
26. *Cork Examiner*, 13 December 1920, pp. 4–5.
27. *Cork Examiner*, 13 December 1920, p. 1.
28. *Cork Examiner*, 16 December 1920, p. 1.
29. *(Guy's) City and County Cork Almanac and Directory, 1921*, p. 202.
30. St Leger, *A History of Ashton School*, p. 32.
31. Rudd, *Rochelle*, p. 85.
32. Rudd, *Rochelle*, p. 92.
33. Rudd, *Rochelle*, p. 87.
34. Rudd, *Rochelle*, p. 87.
35. Rudd, *Rochelle*, p. 91.
36. St Leger, *A History of Ashton School*, p. 32.
37. Letter from Maida Clarke to Mary Elmes, July 1925 (Danjou family collection).
38. Mary Elmes's diary for 1926 (Danjou family collection).
39. Rudd, *Rochelle*, p. 118.
40. *Cork Examiner*, 26 March 1929, p. 8.
41. *Cork Examiner*, 29 January 1930, p. 11.

Chapter 3

1. *Irish Times,* 2 June 1931, p. 10.
2. TCD Life (tcdlife.ie).
3. *Irish Times,* 2 June 1931, p. 10.
4. Frank McDonald, 'Jammet's: A Dublin treasure crowded with gourmets and wits', *Irish Times,* 14 May 1914 (http://www.irishtimes.com/life-and-style/people/jammet-s-a-dublin-treasure-crowded-with-gourmets-and-wits-1.1793827).
5. Caroline and Patrick Danjou's family archive.
6. Parkes, *A Danger to the Men?* p. 112.
7. Olive Purser, *Women in Dublin University, 1904–1954* (Dublin: Dublin University Press, 1954), p. 12, quoted by Pilcher in *Trinity Hall,* p. 26.
8. McDowell and Webb, *Trinity College, Dublin,* pp. 342–9.
9. McDowell and Webb, *Trinity College, Dublin,* pp. 342–9.
10. McDowell and Webb, *Trinity College, Dublin,* p. 347.
11. McDowell and Webb, *Trinity College, Dublin,* p. 342.
12. McDowell and Webb, *Trinity College, Dublin,* p. 349.
13. Manuscripts at Trinity, blog (http://www.tcd.ie/library/manuscripts/blog/).
14. Manuscripts at Trinity, blog (http://www.tcd.ie/library/manuscripts/blog/).
15. Parkes, *A Danger to the Men?*
16. Parkes, *A Danger to the Men?* p. 114.
17. Parkes, *A Danger to the Men?* p. 115.
18. Parkes, *A Danger to the Men?* p. 113.
19. *Irish Times,* 2 June 1931, p. 10.
20. Parkes, *A Danger to the Men?* p. 113.
21. Parkes, *A Danger to the Men?* p. 118.
22. Parkes, *A Danger to the Men?* p. 118.
23. Parkes, *A Danger to the Men?* p. 118.
24. *Cork Examiner,* 11 June, 1930, p. 10.
25. *Irish Times,* 5 August 1932, p. 5.
26. London School of Economics, students' files, Marie Elmes, 8 November 1932.
27. London School of Economics, students' files, Marie Elmes, 8 November 1932.
28. London School of Economics, students' files, Marie Elmes, 8 November 1932.
29. Mary Evans, 'The "hidden" women of LSE' (http://blogs.lse.ac.uk/lsehistory/2016/07/14/the-hidden-women-of-lse/).
30. Dahrendorf, *LSE,* p. 282.

31. Dahrendorf, *LSE*, pp. 274–90.
32. Dahrendorf, *LSE*, p. 297.
33. Dahrendorf, *LSE*, p. 300.
34. London School of Economics, students' files, Marie Elmes, 8 November 1932.
35. London School of Economics, students' files, Marie Elmes, 8 November 1932.
36. London School of Economics, students' files, Marie Elmes, 8 November 1932.
37. From W. Horsfall Carter's review of *The New Spain* in *International Affairs* (London), vol. 13, no. 2 (March–April 1934), p. 287–9 (available at http://www.jstor.org/stable/2603170).
38. Southern Spanish Relief Committee, report by George Young for February, March and April 1937 (Young family archive).
39. John Baskin, personal communication, and from his forthcoming book *A Fierce Light: An Improbable Story of the Good War* (Bresnick-Weil).
40. *Cork Examiner*, 11 and 15 February 1937, shows that Elisabeth Elmes sailed on the *Innisfallen* to England or Wales.
41. *Otranto* passenger list (accessed through Findmypast.ie).
42. Patrick Danjou, personal communication.

Chapter 4

1. Allan and Gordon, *The Scalpel, the Sword*, pp. 177–8.
2. Quoted by Linda Palfreeman in *Aristocrats, Adventurers and Ambulances*, pp. 124–5.
3. Young family archive.
4. T. C. Worsley, quoted by Paul Preston in *The Spanish Civil War*, p. 194.
5. T. C. Worsley, quoted by Paul Preston in *The Spanish Civil War*, p. 194.
6. Letter from Violetta Thurstan to Lady Young, February 1937 (Young family archive).
7. Lady Young received an account of the journey when she was in Gibraltar with Mary Elmes and Mrs Petter. They were all waiting for news of the ambulance unit, so it is reasonable to assume that Lady Young shared the contents of the letter with the two volunteers.
8. Letter from Violetta Thurstan to Lady Young, February 1937 (Young family archive).
9. Letter from Violetta Thurstan to Lady Young, February 1937 (Young family archive).
10. Letter from Violetta Thurstan to Lady Young, February 1937 (Young family archive).

11. Letter from Violetta Thurstan to Lady Young, February 1937 (Young family archive).

12. Article in the *West Australian*, 22 July 1937 (in Young family archive).

13. Southern Spanish Relief Committee, report by George Young for February, March and April 1937, p. 1 (Young family archive).

14. Violetta Thurstan wrote to Edith Pye on 17 March 1937 to say that a worker – Miss Elmes – had come from Gibraltar and she gave the feeding station to her (FSC, 17 March 1937).

15. Article in the *West Australian*, 22 July 1937 (in Young family archive).

16. From an article by 'our correspondent', thought to be Francesca Wilson, *Manchester Guardian*, 18 May 1937 (Young family archive).

17. Article in the *West Australian*, 22 July 1937 (in Young family archive).

18. Young, 'Whence Green Apple Tree'.

19. Derby, *Petals and Bullets*, p. 33.

20. Young, 'Whence Green Apple Tree'.

21. Derby, *Petals and Bullets*, p. 33.

22. Young, 'Whence Green Apple Tree'.

23. Young family archive.

24. Southern Spanish Relief Committee, report by George Young for February, March and April 1937 (Young family archive).

25. Quoted by Palfreeman in *Aristocrats, Adventurers and Ambulances*, p. 171.

26. Southern Spanish Relief Committee, report by George Young for February, March and April 1937 (Young family archive).

27. Elizabeth Burchill, 'Christian insights', in Fyrth, *Women's Voices from the Spanish Civil War*, p. 194.

28. Elizabeth Burchill, 'Christian insights', in Fyrth, *Women's Voices from the Spanish Civil War*, p. 196.

29. Elizabeth Burchill, 'Christian insights', in Fyrth, *Women's Voices from the Spanish Civil War*, p. 198.

30. Elizabeth Burchill, 'Christian insights', in Fyrth, *Women's Voices from the Spanish Civil War*, p. 197.

31. *Daily Telegraph*, 2 June 1937.

32. *News Chronicle*, 2 June 1937.

33. *Egyptian Gazette*, June 1937 (in Young family archive).

34. The book is in the Danjou family collection.

35. Quoted by Palfreeman in *¡Salud!* p. 257.

Chapter 5

1. Francesca Wilson, 'The margins of chaos', in Fyrth, *Women's Voices from the Spanish Civil War*, p. 189.

2. Francesca Wilson, 'The margins of chaos', in Fyrth, *Women's Voices from the Spanish Civil War*, p. 189.

3. Francesca Wilson, 'The margins of chaos', in Fyrth, *Women's Voices from the Spanish Civil War*, p. 191.

4. Francesca Wilson, 'The margins of chaos', in Fyrth, *Women's Voices from the Spanish Civil War*, p. 189.

5. Francesca Wilson, 'The margins of chaos', in Fyrth, *Women's Voices from the Spanish Civil War*, p. 189.

6. Francesca Wilson, 'The margins of chaos', in Fyrth, *Women's Voices from the Spanish Civil War*, p. 176.

7. Francesca Wilson, 'The margins of chaos', in Fyrth, *Women's Voices from the Spanish Civil War*, p. 189.

8. *Manchester Guardian*, 9 July 1937.

9. *Manchester Guardian*, 9 July 1937.

10. Mendlesohn, 'Practising Peace,' p. 261.

11. Quoted by Linda Palfreeman in *Aristocrats, Adventurers and Ambulances*, p. 183.

12. *Manchester Guardian*, 9 July 1937.

13. Francesca Wilson, 'The margins of chaos', in Fyrth, *Women's Voices from the Spanish Civil War*, p. 192.

14. Southern Spanish Relief Committee, report by Sir George Young for February, March and April 1937 (Young family archive).

15. Esther Farquhar, 'The stricken south', in Fyrth, *Women's Voices from the Spanish Civil War*, p. 206.

16. Derby, *Petals and Bullets*, p. 49.

17. Esther Farquhar, 'The stricken south', in Fyrth, *Women's Voices from the Spanish Civil War*, p. 206.

18. John Baskin, notes on an interview with Mary Elmes when she was eighty-eight (personal communication).

19. Letter from Dorothy Morris, 5 January 1939 (courtesy of Mark Derby).

20. Mendlesohn, 'Practising Peace', p. 104.

21. Letter from Emily Parker to Mary Elmes, February 1938 (Committee on Spain, 1938, FSC, SFA, Individuals, Emily Parker).

22. Quoted by Fearghal McGarry in 'Ireland and the Spanish Civil War', *History Ireland*, vol. 9, issue 3 (autumn 2010).

23. Fearghal McGarry in 'Ireland and the Spanish Civil War', *History Ireland*, vol. 9, issue 3 (autumn 2010).

24. Nelson, *The Aura of the Cause*, p. 188.

25. Letter from Dorothy Morris, 5 January 1939 (courtesy of Mark Derby).

26. Letter, 18 January 1938 (FSC).
27. *Cork Examiner,* 28 December 1937.
28. Letter from Dorothy Thomson, assistant secretary, Spain Committee, to Esther Farquhar in Murcia, 26 May 1938 (Friends House).
29. Quoted by Palfreeman in *¡Salud!* p. 224. The observation was made by a Ukrainian-born volunteer, Augustina 'Gusti' Jirku.
30. Quoted by Derby in *Petals and Bullets,* p. 71.
31. Quoted by Palfreeman in *¡Salud!* p. 224.
32. Emily Parker, 'Está la Guerra!' in Fyrth, *Women's Voices from the Spanish Civil War,* p. 209.
33. From a letter from Dorothy Thomson, FSC, to John Reich, 25 April 1938 (quoted by Mendlesohn in 'Practising Peace', p. 534).
34. Dorothy Davis, 'Saving the children', in Fyrth, *Women's Voices from the Spanish Civil War,* p. 203.
35. Kershner, *Quaker Service in Modern War,* pp. 13–17.

Chapter 6

1. Letter courtesy of Bernard Wilson.
2. Young family archive.
3. Quoted by Mendlesohn in 'Practising Peace', p. 308.
4. Emily Parker, 'Está la guerra!' in Fyrth, *Women's Voices from the Spanish Civil War,* p. 208.
5. Emily Parker to Grace Rhoads, 24 February 1939 (Committee on Spain, 1939, Individuals: Parker, Emily, Box 13).
6. Martha Rupel, 'Christmas – once a year', in Fyrth, *Women's Voices from the Spanish Civil War,* p. 218.
7. Danjou family collection.
8. Florence Conrad, 'PS. The baby died', in Fyrth, *Women's Voices from the Spanish Civil War,* p. 211.
9. Letter from Sylvia Pitt, Murcia, 27 July 1938 (Young family archive).
10. Quoted by Derby in *Petals and Bullets,* p. 47.
11. Quoted by Derby in *Petals and Bullets,* p. 47.
12. Report written by Nurse Dorothy Litten in August 1938, shortly after she arrived in Polop, Alicante (Young family archive).
13. Letter from Syliva Pitt, Murcia, 27 July 1938 (Young family archive).
14. FSC, copy of report received from Dorothy Litten, 2 August 1938 (Young family archive).
15. Quoted by Mendlesohn in 'Practising Peace', p. 130.
16. Quoted by Derby in *Petals and Bullets,* p. 54.

17. Palfreeman, *Aristocrats, Adventurers and Ambulances*, p. 225.
18. Martha Rupel, 'Christmas – once a year', in Fyrth, *Women's Voices from the Spanish Civil War*, p. 219.
19. Martha Rupel, 'Christmas – once a year', in Fyrth, *Women's Voices from the Spanish Civil War*, p. 219.
20. Letter from Dorothy Morris, early 1939 (courtesy of Mark Derby).
21. Notes on Spanish Relief Work, 18 February 1939 (Committee on Spain, 1939, Box 13).

Chapter 7

1. Edith Pye, 'A tragedy so immense', in Fyrth, *Women's Voices from the Spanish Civil War*, p. 328.
2. Interview with Brigitte Twomey (Carmen Canadell's daughter), 28 April 2017.
3. Kershner, *Quaker Service in Modern War*, p. 28
4. Mendlesohn, 'Practising Peace', p. 207.
5. Mendlesohn, 'Practising Peace', p. 205.
6. Letter from Dorothy Morris to her parents, 14 February 1939 (courtesy of Mark Derby).
7. Letter from Dorothy Morris to her parents, 25 March 1939 (courtesy of Mark Derby).
8. Minutes of the AFSC, Murcia, Spain (Friends House library, FSC/R/SP/3/1/1).
9. Comment made in an interview she gave in 1998 (courtesy of Bernard Wilson).
10. Quoted by Derby in *Petals and Bullets*, p. 102.
11. Quoted by Mendlesohn in 'Practising Peace', p. 216.
12. Interview in 1998.
13. Patrick Danjou, personal communication.
14. Quoted by Holloway in 'The Flight to France and Concentration Camps'.
15. FSC letter, 14 July 1939.
16. Kershner, *Quaker Service in Modern War*, p. 28.
17. Quoted by Preston in *The Spanish Civil War*, pp. 301–2.
18. Nancy Cunard, 'A whole landscape moving', in Fyrth, *Women's Voices from the Spanish Civil War*, p. 332.
19. Francesca Wilson, 'The margins of chaos', in Fyrth, *Women's Voices from the Spanish Civil War*, p. 220.
20. Postcard from Lieutenant Albert Belloc to his parents, 8 February 1939 (Archives Départementales Pyrénées-Orientales, 1 Ph 2/17).

21. Kershner, *Quaker Service in Modern War,* p. 28.
22. Francesca Wilson, 'The margins of chaos', in Fyrth, *Women's Voices from the Spanish Civil War,* p. 225.
23. From the AFSC records relating to humanitarian work in France, 1933–1950 (RG-67.007M).
24. Kershner, *Quaker Service in Modern War,* p. 29.
25. Confidential report: Memorandum on the conditions in the concentration camps (SFA, FSC/R/SP/3).
26. AFSC archives, b14, f63, pp. 4–7.

Chapter 8

1. Letter from Agustí Bartra to American Friends Fellowship Council, 4 February 1946, quoted by Emma Cadbury, chairperson, Wider Quaker Fellowship (Danjou family collection).
2. Letter from Dorothy Morris to her parents, 19 August 1939 (courtesy of Mark Derby).
3. Letter from Dorothy Morris to her parents, 19 August 1939 (courtesy of Mark Derby).
4. Letter from Dorothy Morris to her parents, 19 August 1939 (courtesy of Mark Derby).
5. Letter from Dorothy Morris to her parents, 19 August 1939 (courtesy of Mark Derby).
6. Pons, *Barbelés à Argelès,* p. 39.
7. Resch Synnestvedt, *Over the Highest Mountains,* p. 147.
8. Pons, *Barbelés à Argelès,* p. 183.
9. Pons, *Barbelés à Argelès,* pp. 185–6.
10. Pons, *Barbelés à Argelès,* pp. 198–9.
11. Pons, *Barbelés à Argelès,* p. 199.
12. Kershner, *Quaker Service in Modern War,* p. 35.
13. Letter from Dorothy Morris to her parents, 19 August 1939 (courtesy of Mark Derby).
14. AFSC archives, b15, f72, p. 32.
15. AFSC archives, b60, f55, p. 3.
16. Martínez-Vidal and García-Ferrandis, 'Medicine in exile after the Spanish Civil War.'
17. Martínez-Vidal and García-Ferrandis, 'Medicine in exile after the Spanish Civil War.'
18. AFSC archives, b1, f8, p. 116.
19. Casals, *Joys and Sorrows,* p. 233.

20. Casals, *Joys and Sorrows*, p. 224.
21. Casals, *Joys and Sorrows*, p. 234.
22. AFSC archives, b14, f64, pp. 34–9, and letter from Pablo Casals, Prades, to Mary Elmes, 30 August 1943 (Danjou family collection).
23. Bernard Wilson, personal communication.
24. AFSC archives, b60, f55, p. 4.
25. AFSC archives, b60, f55, p. 5.
26. Letter from Dorothy Morris to her parents, 19 August 1939 (courtesy of Mark Derby).
27. AFSC archives, b15, f72, p. 32.
28. Mary Elmes, Report on the Cultural Work in the Refugee Camps in Southern France, 11 September 1939 (SFA, FSC/R/SP/4).
29. Letter from Dr Audrey Russell (AFSC archives, b15, f69, p. 38).
30. SFA, FSC/R/SP/3/4, part 2.
31. Letter from Dorothy Morris to her parents, 1 January 1940 (courtesy of Mark Derby).
32. Letter from Lois Gunden to her family, letter 36 (courtesy of her niece Mary Jean Gunden).
33. Mark Derby, personal communication.
34. AFSC archives, b9, f11, p. 23.
35. Letter from Mary Elmes to Emily Parker, 3 April 1940 (Danjou family collection).

Chapter 9

1. Wall, *The World I Lost*, p. 580.
2. Wall, *The World I Lost*, p. 520.
3. Shennan, *The Fall of France*, p. 7.
4. Georges Sadoul, *Journal de Guerre*, quoted by Shennan in *The Fall of France*, p. 7.
5. Wall, *The World I Lost*, p. 520.
6. Edith Pye, 26 June 1939, Perpignan office correspondence, 1939–1940 (SFA, FSC/SP/3/4).
7. AFSC archives, b14, f64, p. 88.
8. AFSC archives, b9, f4, p. 2.
9. AFSC archives, b28, f18, p. 23.
10. AFSC archives, b28, f18, p. 23.
11. AFSC archives, b9, f4, p. 5.
12. AFSC archives, b9, f4, p. 9.
13. AFSC archives, b9, f4, p. 14.

14. AFSC archives, b28, F18, p. 29.

15. AFSC archives, b6, f2, p. 13.

16. Bailey, *Love and War in the Pyrenees,* p. 123.

17. AFSC archives, b12, f37, p. 11.

18. AFSC archives, b12, f37, p. 15.

19. AFSC archives, b60, f55, p. 36.

20. Kershner, *Quaker Service in Modern War,* p. 5.

21. AFSC archives, b60, f55, p. 40.

22. AFSC archives, b11, f27, pp. 41–2.

23. AFSC archives, b11, f27, p. 41.

24. AFSC archives, b12, f36, p. 5.

25. AFSC archives, b60, f55, p. 45.

26. AFSC archives, b60, f55, pp. 74–5.

27. Bailey, *Love and War in the Pyrenees.*

28. AFSC archives, b11, f27, p. 23.

29. AFSC archives, b9, f4, p. 58.

Chapter 10

1. The account of Marjorie McClelland's visit is taken from a three-page report she sent to the Quaker head office in Philadelphia in April 1942 (AFSC archives, b15, f77, pp. 48–53).

2. AFSC archives, b6, f6, p. 41.

3. Bohny-Reiter, *Journal de Rivesaltes,* pp. 93–4.

4. Patrick Danjou, personal communication, April 2017.

5. AFSC archives, b11, f28, p. 49.

6. AFSC archives, b15, f77, p. 53.

7. Interview with Gilbert Susagna, 13 December 2016.

8. Account from Alfonso Cánovas quoted by Giles Tremlett in 'Barcelona pursues Italy over 1938 bombing,' *Guardian* (London), 27 January 2013 (www.theguardian.com/world/2013/jan/27/barcelona-pursues-italy-1938-bombing).

9. AFSC archives, b60, f55, p. 53.

10. AFSC archives, b60, f55, p. 53.

11. AFSC archives, b60, f55, p. 54.

12. AFSC archives, b60, f55, pp. 54–5.

13. Lois Gunden's diary, 12 November 1941 (courtesy of Mary Jean Gunden).

Chapter 11

1. AFSC archives, b1, f8, pp. 21–3.
2. AFSC archives, b1, f7, p. 59.
3. AFSC archives, b1, f7, p. 64.
4. AFSC archives, b12, f38, p. 67.
5. AFSC archives, b1, f7, p. 26.
6. AFSC archives, b1, f8, p. 43.
7. AFSC archives, b1, f7, p. 51.
8. AFSC archives, b12, f36, p. 10.
9. AFSC archives, b10, f18, p. 115.
10. AFSC archives, b34, f10, p. 41.
11. AFSC archives, b34, f10, p. 42.
12. From the *Gazette Lausanne*, 6 May 1942, quoted by Alice Resch Synnestvedt in *Over the Highest Mountains*, p. 87.
13. AFSC archives, b34, f10, p. 3.
14. AFSC archives, b6, f6, p. 25.
15. Brigitte Twomey, personal communication, 28 April 2017.
16. AFSC archives, b12, f38, p. 17.
17. AFSC archives, b27, f10, p. 30.
18. AFSC archives, b27, f10, pp. 30–31.
19. AFSC archives, b11, f27, p. 23.
20. AFSC archives, 'I have come out of the night, and you fed me' (www.afsc. org/story/i-have-come-out-night-and-you-fed-me).

Chapter 12

1. Paul Niedermann, personal communication, 14 May 2017.
2. Niedermann, *Un Enfant Juif,* p. 60.
3. Niedermann, *Un Enfant Juif,* p. 63.
4. Niedermann, *Un Enfant Juif,* p. 65.
5. Michal Ostrovsky, '"We Are Standing By": Rescue Operations of the United States Committee for the Care of European Children' (University of Oxford, Holocaust and Genocide Studies, at https://academic.oup. com/hgs/article-abstract/29/2/230/562412/We-Are-Standing-By-Rescue-Operations-of-the-United).
6. AFSC archives, b15, f77, p. 25.
7. AFSC archives, b15, f77, p. 22.
8. AFSC archives, b11, f27, p. 8.
9. AFSC archives, b15, f77, p. 24.
10. AFSC archives, b11, f27, p. 14.

11. Niedermann, *Un Enfant Juif*, p. 65.
12. AFSC archives, b15, f77, pp. 53–4.
13. AFSC archives, b11, f28, p. 48.
14. Niedermann, *Un Enfant Juif*, p. 135.
15. AFSC archives, b12, f45, p. 82.
16. AFSC archives, b34, f9, p. 77.
17. Newspaper articles from March 1941 (Chiroleu-Escudier archive).
18. Lois Gunden journal, 22 October 1941 (by courtesy of Mary Jean Gunden).
19. Lois Gunden journal, 15 February 1942.
20. AFSC archives, b12, f45, pp. 99–103.
21. AFSC archives, b12, f45, p. 100.
22. AFSC files.
23. AFSC archives, b11, f27, p. 69.
24. Rees, *The Holocaust*, p. 273.
25. Marrus and Paxton, *Vichy France and the Jews*, p. 234.
26. Marrus and Paxton, *Vichy France and the Jews*, p. 234.
27. Marrus and Paxton, *Vichy France and the Jews*, p. 241.
28. McClelland, p. 3.
29. McClelland, p. 5.
30. McClelland, pp. 6–7.
31. McClelland, p. 10.
32. McClelland, p. 12.
33. McClelland, p. 8.
34. McClelland, p. 19.
35. Samuel, *Sauver les Enfants*, p. 92.
36. McClelland, p. 21.

Chapter 13

1. Lindsley Noble, notes and content of a wire from the US embassy in Vichy to Clarence Pickett, executive secretary, AFSC, August 1942 (personal archive of Ronald Friend).
2. Lindsley Noble, notes and content of a wire from the US embassy in Vichy to Clarence Pickett, executive secretary, AFSC, August 1942 (personal archive of Ronald Friend).
3. Lois Gunden, journal entry, 9 August 1942.
4. Lois Gunden, journal entry, 10 August 1942.
5. Resch Synnestvedt, *Over the Highest Mountains*, p. 117.
6. Samuel, *Sauver les Enfants*, p. 97.

7. Lois Gunden, journal entry, 11 August 1942.

8. AFSC archives, b15, f78, p. 35.

9. AFSC archives, b12, f45, p. 97.

10. AFSC archives, b67, f107, pp. 110–11.

11. Bernard Wilson, 'Internment camps of south west France, 1939–1944' (http://campsofshame.webplus.net/chateaudelarade.html).

12. Castanier, *Autour de la Maternité d'Elne*, p. 174.

13. Bohny-Reiter, *Journal de Rivesaltes*, p. 31.

14. Katie Kellerman, 'Marie-Rose Gineste and the bishop's letter' (http://www.raoulwallenberg.net/es/generales/marie-rose-gineste-and-the/).

15. Lindsley Noble, notes and content of a wire from the US embassy in Vichy to Clarence Pickett, executive secretary, AFSC, August 1942 (personal archive of Ronald Friend).

16. Lindsley Noble, notes and content of a wire from the US embassy in Vichy to Clarence Pickett, executive secretary, AFSC, August 1942 (personal archive of Ronald Friend).

17. Quoted by Poznanski in *Jews in France during World War II*, p. 276.

18. AFSC archives, b9, f10, p. 51.

19. AFSC archives, b8, f5, p. 51.

20. AFSC archives, b9, f5, p. 62.

21. AFSC archives, b9, f5, p. 63.

22. AFSC archives, b11, f28, p. 62.

23. AFSC archives, b11, f27, p. 123.

24. Lois Gunden, journal entry, 3 February 1942.

25. John Baskin, personal communication.

26. Gunden family letter, number 41, 20 August 1942.

27. Lois Gunden, journal entry, 16 August 1942.

28. Grynberg, *Les Camps de la Honte*, p. 322.

29. Grynberg, *Les Camps de la Honte*, p. 322.

30. AFSC archives, b2, f16, p. 124.

31. Yad Vashem testimony (www.yadvashem.org/yv/en/exhibitions/through-the-lens/escaping-deportation-from-rivesaltes.asp).

32. Lois Gunden, journal entry, 1 September 1942.

33. Lois Gunden, journal entry, 1 September 1942.

34. AFSC archives, b55, f83, p. 49.

35. Quaker report, 'Visit to Rivesaltes,' written in Marseille 29 October 1942 and destined for Philadelphia (Danjou family collection).

36. Quaker report, 'Visit to Rivesaltes,' written in Marseille 29 October 1942 and destined for Philadelphia (Danjou family collection).

37. Quaker report, 'Visit to Rivesaltes,' written in Marseille 29 October 1942 and destined for Philadelphia (Danjou family collection).

38. Lindsley Noble, notes and content of a wire from the us embassy in Vichy to Clarence Pickett, executive secretary, AFSC, August 1942 (personal archive of Ronald Friend).

39. Lindsley Noble, notes and content of a wire from the us embassy in Vichy to Clarence Pickett, executive secretary, AFSC, August 1942 (personal archive of Ronald Friend).

40. Quaker report, 'Visit to Rivesaltes,' written in Marseille 29 October 1942 and destined for Philadelphia (Danjou family collection).

41. Report on Relief Activities of Secours Quaker in France (based on conversations with Helga Holbek), Marjorie and Ross McClelland, Geneva 1943 (Danjou family collection).

42. AFSC archives, b9, f4, p. 86.

43. Resch Synnestvedt, *Over the Highest Mountains*, p. 115–16.

44. AFSC archives, b55, f83, p. 53.

45. AFSC archives, b56, f84, p. 48.

46. AFSC archives, b56, f84, p. 51.

47. AFSC archives, b56, f84, pp. 56–7.

48. AFSC archives, b56, f84, pp. 56–7.

49. AFSC archives, b56, f84, p. 58.

50. AFSC archives, b56, f84, p. 59.

51. Resch Synnestvedt, *Over the Highest Mountains*, pp. 115–17.

52. AFSC archives, b15, f77, p. 29.

53. AFSC archives, b10, f14, p. 72.

54. AFSC archives, b10, f14, p. 73.

55. AFSC archives, b6, f5, p. 55.

56. Bauer, *American Jewry and the Holocaust*, p. 260.

57. AFSC archives, b7, f14, pp. 4–12.

58. Resch Synnestvedt, *Over the Highest Mountains*, p. 143.

59. Paul Niedermann, personal communication, 14 May 2017.

60. AFSC archives, b67, f107, pp. 64–7.

61. AFSC archives, b67, f107, p. 70.

62. Doulut, *Les Juifs au Camp de Rivesaltes*, p. 111.

63. Doulut, *Les Juifs au Camp de Rivesaltes*, p. 109.

64. Wriggins, *Picking Up the Pieces*, p. 143.

Chapter 14

1. Personal communication, 6 November 2016.
2. AFSC archives, b11, f29, p. 63.
3. AFSC archive, b11, f29, p. 66
4. Documents from the Ancien Hôpital Saint-Louis state that the children arrived at 3 p.m. on 27 September from a colony at Vernet-les-Bains. This is supported by the OSE letter, which says the children were taken to Vernet, discovered to have scabies, and sent immediately to Saint-Louis. The hospital papers say they were discharged on 14 November, but they do not say to where. (Papers in Bernard Wilson's and Ronald Friend's archive.)
5. Letter from Mme Lobstein (Ronald Friend's archive).
6. Letter written by Michael Freund as a child (Ronald Friend's archive).
7. AFSC archives, b60, f55, p. 38.
8. Letter from Eva to her brother Max Wilhelm Brauer, 19 December 1944 (Ronald Friend's archive).
9. Holocaust Survivors and Victims database (https://www.ushmm.org/online/hsv/person_view.php?PersonId=5324364).
10. McClelland, p. 32.
11. McClelland, p. 33.
12. Interview, 23 February 2017.
13. Letter from Ziegmond Kaufman to his aunt, 26 February 1943 (Vad Yashem testimony, at www.yadvashem.org/gathering-fragments/stories/correspondence/kaufman).
14. Interview, 22 February 2017.
15. Chiroleu-Escudier, Chiroleu and Escudier, *La Villa Saint-Christophe*, p. 167.
16. Lois Gunden, journal entry, 26 August 1942.
17. Article by Lois Gunden, 'What is a convalescent home?' 8 December 1941 (courtesy of Mary Jean Gunden).
18. Letter from Lois Gunden to her parents, 11 August 1942 (courtesy of Mary Jean Gunden).
19. Rees, *The Holocaust*, p. 188.

Chapter 15

1. Patrick Danjou, personal communication, 7 September 2016.
2. Resch Synnestvedt, *Over the Highest Mountains*, p. 144.
3. AFSC files, prison letters. The file contains a series of letters written between January 1943 and August 1943 (courtesy of Don Davis, archivist at the AFSC, Philadelphia)

4. AFSC files, prison letters.

5. AFSC files, prison letters.

6. John Baskin, personal communication.

7. AFSC files, prison letters.

8. Letter from Elisabeth Elmes to Margaret Frawley, Philadelphia, 13 March 1943 (AFSC files, prison letters).

9. Letter from Margaret Frawley to Elisabeth Elmes (AFSC files, prison letters).

10. Letter from Elisabeth Elmes to Margaret Frawley, 4 October 1943 (AFSC files, prison letters).

11. John Baskin, interview with Mary Elmes Danjou, 1996.

12. John Baskin, interview with Mary Elmes Danjou, 1996.

13. Hany-Lefèbvre, *Six Mois à Fresnes*, p. 18.

14. Hany-Lefèbvre, *Six Mois à Fresnes*, p. 18.

15. Patrick Danjou, personal communication.

16. Duchen, *Women's Rights and Women's Lives in France*, p. 28.

17. Caroline Danjou, personal communication.

18. Letter from Roger Danjou to Quaker office in Perpignan, 6 March 1943 (Danjou family collection).

19. Henri Calet, *Les Murs de Fresnes*, pp. 49–51.

20. Hany-Lefèbvre, *Six Mois à Fresnes*, p. 38.

21. AFSC files, prison letters.

22. Letter from James Vail, foreign service secretary of Quakers in Philadelphia, to Robert Brennan, minister of Ireland to the United States, Washington, 7 May 1943.

23. Letter from Seán Nunan to James G. Vail, 16 June 1943 (AFSC archives, prison letters).

24. AFSC archives, b55, f81, p. 26/7.

25. AFSC archives, b55, f81, p. 26/7.

26. AFSC archives, b55, f81, p. 24.

27. Letter from Elisabeth Elmes to Margaret Frawley (AFSC archives, prison letters).

28. Letter from Elisabeth Elmes to Margaret Frawley (AFSC archives, prison letters).

29. John Baskin, personal communication.

30. Hany-Lefèbvre, *Six Mois à Fresnes*, p. 22.

31. Hany-Lefèbvre, *Six Mois à Fresnes*, p. 33.

32. Hany-Lefèbvre, *Six Mois à Fresnes*, p. 36.

33. Calet, *Les Murs de Fresnes*, p. 20.

34. AFSC archives, prison letters.
35. Letter from Elisabeth Elmes to Margaret Frawley, 15 July 1943 (AFSC archives, prison letters).
36. National Archives Dublin, DFA/49/16 Part 1.
37. AFSC archives, prison letters.
38. Letter from Margaret Frawley to Elisabeth Elmes, August 1943 (AFSC archives, prison letters).
39. Letter from Edith Pye to Elisabeth Elmes (AFSC archives, prison letters).
40. National Archives Dublin, DFA/49/16 Part 2
41. AFSC archives, prison letters.
42. AFSC archives, prison letters.
43. Letter from the préfet, Monsieur Henry, to the commissaire des renseignments generaux, 20 December 1942 (Chiroleu-Escudier archive).
44. Letter from the préfet, Monsieur Henry, to the commissaire des renseignments generaux, 22 December, 1942 (Chiroleu-Escudier archive).
45. Resch Synnestvedt, *Over the Highest Mountains,* p. 144.
46. Wriggins, *Picking Up the Pieces,* p. 143.
47. Patrick Danjou, personal communication.

Chapter 16

1. Account written by F. Charles Thum (Danjou family collection).
2. AFSC archives, b7, f16, p. 33.
3. AFSC archives, b9, f9, p. 15.
4. AFSC archives, b9, f10, p. 42.
5. Personal communication, Patrick Danjou.
6. Wriggins, *Picking Up the Pieces,* p. 143.
7. AFSC archives, b60, f53, p. 3.
8. AFSC archives, b60, f53, p. 3.
9. AFSC archives, b7, f18, p. 60.

Chapter 17

1. AFSC archives, b19, f121, p. 38.
2. AFSC archives, b19, f121, p. 39.
3. AFSC archives, b19, f121, p. 39.
4. AFSC archives, b19, f121, p. 39.
5. *Irish Times,* 22 June 1946, p. 10.
6. Telegram in the Danjou family archive; death notice in the *Irish Times,* 7 September 1946, p. 15.
7. *Marie-France,* 31 May 1945, quoted by Duchen in *Women's Rights and Women's Lives in France,* p. 35.

8. Duchen, *Women's Rights and Women's Lives in France*, p. 36.
9. Duchen, *Women's Rights and Women's Lives in France*, p. 102.
10. Patrick Danjou, personal communication, 14 December 2016.
11. AFSC archives, b19, f121, p. 38.
12. AFSC archives, b19, f121, p. 50.
13. Quoted by Castanier in *Autour de la Maternité d'Elne*, p. 180.
14. Caroline and Patrick Danjou, personal communication.
15. Resch, *Over the Highest Mountains*, preface, p. xi.
16. Mack Morum, personal communication.
17. Marrus and Paxton, *Vichy France and the Jews*, p. 344.
18. Letter from the Direction Interdépartementale des Anciens Combattants et Victimes de Guerre de Montpellier to Mary Elmes, 25 April 1986 (Caroline and Patrick Danjou's family archive).
19. Resch Synnestvedt, *Over the Highest Mountains*, p. 248.
20. Letter from Alice Resch to Mary Elmes, 28 September 1992 (Caroline and Patrick Danjou's family archive).
21. John Baskin, personal communication.
22. Letter courtesy of Jacinta Ryan, Ballintemple.

Chapter 18

1. Larrieu, Gual and Tubert, *Vichy*.
2. Lindsley Noble, notes from 1942 (Caroline and Patrick Danjou's family archive).
3. Chiroleu-Escudier, Chiroleu and Escudier, *La Villa Saint-Christophe*.
4. Marc J. Masurovsky, personal communication.
5. Special thanks to Adi Trudler, who reported from Yad Vashem.

BIBLIOGRAPHY

Archives
— American Friends Service Committee Archive, Philadelphia (courtesy of the archivist, Don Davis)
— Archives Départementales des Pyrénées-Orientales, Perpignan
— Bernard and Janet Wilson's private archive
— Caroline and Patrick Danjou's family archive
— Cork City and County Archives, Cork
— Dorothy Morris's letters, Mark Derby archive
— Friends House Library, London
— London School of Economics student files
— Manuscript Library, Trinity College Library, Dublin
— Mark Elmes's family archive
— National Archives, Dublin
— Prof. Ronald Friend's private archive
— Shoah Memorial, Paris
— Young family archive (courtesy of Lady Aurelia Young, Charles Young and Bernard Wilson)

Unpublished sources
— Gunden Clemens, Lois, personal journals and personal letters to family, 19 August 1941 to 31 October 1942 (Villa Saint-Christophe, Canet-Plage), transcribed and edited by Mary Jean Gunden
— League of Pity register (Cork City and County Archives)
— McClelland, Roswell, unpublished chapter in the history of the deportation of foreign Jews from France in 1942, written by Roswell McClelland, a representative of the American Friends Service Committee (United States Holocaust Memorial Museum Archives)
— Moran, Mack, 'To See What Love Can Do', a short biography of Mary Elmes
— Rochelle School, admission registers from 1914 to 1934 (Cork City and County Archives)
— Rochelle School, minutes of the School Governors (Cork City and County Archives)
— Rochelle School, undated prospectus, early twentieth century (Cork City and County Archives)

— Young, Gerry, 'Whence Green Apple Tree: Memoirs of Gerry Young, 1908–1931' (courtesy of Charles Young)

Newspaper articles
— *Cork Examiner*
— *Irish Independent*
— *Irish Times*
— *Manchester Guardian*
— *Weekly Irish Times*

Online sources
— Martínez-Vidal, Àlvar and García-Ferrandis, Xavier, 'Medicine in exile after the Spanish Civil War: A clinical trial in a French concentration camp, 1939–1940,' in 'Munitions of the Mind' (University of Kent blog), 4 April 2017.
— Mendlesohn, Farah, 'Practising Peace: Quaker Relief Work in the Spanish Civil War' (PhD thesis)

Books
— Allan, Ted, and Gordon, Sydney, *The Scalpel, the Sword: The Story of Doctor Norman Bethune* (New York: Monthly Review Press, 1973), Kindle edition.
— Bailey, Rosemary, *Love and War in the Pyrenees: A Story of Courage, Fear and Hope, 1939–1944,* London: Phoenix, 2008.
— Bauer, Yehuda, *American Jewry and the Holocaust: The American Jewish Joint Distribution Committee, 1939–1945,* Detroit: Wayne State University Press, 1981.
— Bohny-Reiter, Friedel, *Journal de Rivesaltes, 1941–1942,* Genève: Editions Zoé, 1993.
— Borgonovo, John, *The Battle for Cork: July–August 1922,* Cork: Mercier Press, 2011.
— Borgonovo, John, *The Dynamics of War and Revolution: Cork City, 1916–1918,* Cork: Mercier Press, 2013.
— Calet, Henri, *Les Murs de Fresnes, 1945,* Paris: Éditions Viviane Hamy, 1993.
— Casals, Pablo (as told to Albert E. Kahn), *Joys and Sorrows: His Own Story,* London: Eel Pie Publishing, 1981.
— Castanier, Tristan, *Autour de la Maternité d'Elne: L'Action Humanitaire de la Guerre d'Espagne à Nos Jours,* Paris: Riveneuve Éditions, 2015.

— Chiroleu-Escudier, Simonne; Chiroleu, Mireille; Escudier, Eric, *La Villa Saint-Christophe: Maison de Convalescence pour Enfants des Camps d'Internement*, Saint-Estève: Alliance Éditions, 2016.
— Dahrendorf, Ralf, *LSE: A History of the London School of Economics and Political Science, 1895–1995*, Oxford: Oxford University Press, 1995.
— Day, Susanne R., *Round About Bar-le-Duc*, London: Skeffington and Son, 1918 (available at https://archive.org/details/roundaboutbarledoodaysrich).
— Derby, Mark, *Petals and Bullets: Dorothy Morris, New Zealand Nurse in the Spanish Civil War*, Brighton: Sussex Academic Press, 2015.
— *Directory of Munster, 1886*, Cork: Francis Guy.
— Doulut, Alexandre, *Les Juifs au Camp de Rivesaltes: Internement et Déportation, 1941–1942* (Cahiers de Rivesaltes, No 1), Paris: Liénart, 2014.
— Dublin University Calendar for the Years 1929–1930, 1930–31, 1931–32, 1932–33, Dublin: Hodges, Figgis, 1929.
— Duchen, Claire, *Women's Rights and Women's Lives in France, 1944–1968*, London: Routledge, 1994.
— Fyrth, Jim (with Sally Alexander), *Women's Voices from the Spanish Civil War*, London: Lawrence and Wishart, 1991.
— Grynberg, Anne, *Les Camps de la Honte: Les Internés Juifs des Camps Français*, Paris: Editions de la Découverte, 1991.
— Hany-Lèfebvre, Noémi, *Six Mois à Fresnes*, Paris: Flammarion, 1946.
— Holloway, Kerrie, 'The Flight to France and Concentration Camps: The NJC and the Spanish Refugees' (a chapter in her dissertation 'Britain's Political Humanitarians: The National Joint Committee for Spanish Relief and the Spanish Refugees of 1939').
— Homan, Gerlof D., 'Friends and enemies: The World War II origins of MCC work in France,' *Mennonite Historical Bulletin*, April 2010.
— Kershner, Howard E., *Quaker Service in Modern War*, New York: Prentice-Hall, 1950.
— Larrieu, Jean; Gual, Ramon; Tubert, Jean, *Vichy: L'Occupation Nazie et la Résistance Catalane* (4 vols), Prades: Terra Nostra, 1994–1998.
— McAvoy, Sandra, 'Relief work and refugees: Susanne Rouvier Day (1876–1964) on war as women's business,' *Women's History Review*, 2016 (available at http://dx.doi.org/10.1080/09612025.2016.1221288).
— McDowell, R.B., and Webb, D.A., *Trinity College, Dublin: An Academic History, 1592–1952*, Cambridge: Cambridge University Press, 1982.
— Marrus, Michael R., and Paxton, Robert O., *Vichy France and the Jews*, New York: Basic Books, 1981.

— Mendlesohn, Farah, *Quaker Relief Work in the Spanish Civil War*, Lewiston (NY): Edwin Mellen Press, 2001.

— Nelson, Cary, *The Aura of the Cause: A Photo Album for North American Volunteers in the Spanish Civil War*, New York: Abraham Lincoln Brigade Archives, 1997.

— Niedermann, Paul, *Un Enfant Juif, un Homme Libre: Mémoires*, Karlsruhe: Info Verlag, 2016.

— Palfreeman, Linda, *Aristocrats, Adventurers and Ambulances: British Medical Units in the Spanish Civil War*, Brighton: Sussex Academic Press, 2014.

— Palfreeman, Linda, *¡Salud! British Volunteers in the Republican Medical Service during the Spanish Civil War, 1936–1939*, Brighton: Sussex Academic Press, 2012.

— Parkes, M. Susan (ed.), *A Danger to the Men? A History of Women in Trinity College, Dublin, 1904–2004*, Dublin: Lilliput Press, 2004.

— Pilcher, Rosa, *Trinity Hall, 1908–2008: Trinity College Dublin Residence*, Dublin: Hinds, 2013.

— Pons, Francisco, *Barbelés à Argelès et Autour d'Autres Camps*, Paris: Éditions L'Harmattan, 1993.

— Poznanski, Renée, *Jews in France during World War II*, Lebanon (NH): Brandeis University Press, in association with United States Holocaust Memorial Museum, 2001.

— Preston, Paul, *The Spanish Civil War: Reaction, Revolution and Revenge*, London: William Collins, 2016.

— Rees, Laurence, *The Holocaust: A New History*, London: Viking, 2017.

— Resch Synnestvedt, Alice, *Over the Highest Mountains: A Memoir of Unexpected Heroism in France during World War II*, Pasadena (Calif.): Intentional Productions, 2005.

— Rousso, Henry, *Le Syndrome de Vichy de 1944 à Nos Jours*, Paris: Éditions du Seuil, 1987.

— Rudd, Dorothy, *Rochelle: The History of a School in Cork, 1829–1979*, Naas: Leinster Leader, 1979.

— St Leger, Alicia, *A History of Ashton School: Rochelle School, Cork High School, Cork Grammar School*, Cork: Ashton School, 2016.

— Samuel, Vivette, *Sauver les Enfants*, Paris: Liana Levi, 1995.

— Shennan, Andrew, *The Fall of France, 1940*, London: Routledge, 2000.

— Wall, Daphne, *The World I Lost* (ebook).

— Wriggins, Howard W., *Picking Up the Pieces from Portugal to Palestine: Quaker Refugee Relief in World War II: A Memoir*, Lanham (Md): University Press of America, 2004.